Brand Storming

BRAND STORMING

Managing Brands in the Era of Complexity

Michele Fioroni and Garry Titterton

This book was originally published in 2007 as *Brand Storming: Gestire la marca nell'era della complessità* by Morlacchi Editore, Perugia, Italy

English translation published 2009 by
PALGRAVE MACMILLAN

Palgrave Macmillan in the UK is an imprint of Macmillan Publishers Limited, registered in England, company number 785998, of Houndmills, Basingstoke, Hampshire RG21 6XS.

Palgrave Macmillan in the US is a division of St Martin's Press LLC, 175 Fifth Avenue, New York, NY 10010.

Palgrave Macmillan is the global academic imprint of the above companies and has companies and representatives throughout the world.

Palgrave® and Macmillan® are registered trademarks in the United States, the United Kingdom, Europe and other countries

ISBN-13: 978–0–230–22243–4
ISBN-10: 0–230–22243–9

This book is printed on paper suitable for recycling and made from fully managed and sustained forest sources. Logging, pulping and manufacturing processes are expected to conform to the environmental regulations of the country of origin.

A catalogue record for this book is available from the British Library.

A catalog record for this book is available from the Library of Congress.

10 9 8 7 6 5 4 3 2 1
18 17 16 15 14 13 12 11 10 09

Printed and bound in Great Britain by
Cromwell Press Ltd, Trowbridge, Wiltshire

To Ester and Rodolfo Mauro – my joy, my comfort, my inspiration
(MF)

To Monique, Rebecca, Daniel, Alicia and Boris
(GT)

NOTE ON AUTHORSHIP

Parts I and V of this volume ("The Brand in Relation to Society, Belief, Culture and Change" and "Lessons in Branding: How to Learn from the Best") are the work of Michele Fioroni; Parts II, III and IV ("The Brand as a Living Organism: DNA, Human Features and Sensory Perception", "The Fundamentals of Branding: Some Rules for Keeping on the Right Track" and "The Brand as a Citizen of the World") are the result of collaboration between Michele Fioroni and Garry Titterton. The translation from Italian was done by Michele Homewood.

CONTENTS

CONTENTS

PREFACE

The market economy is linked genetically to the sale of products, and it is this which has led to marketing being both a scientific application and a theory. The essential thematic nucleus of marketing – both practically and conceptually – is represented by the brand rather than by the object or goods item itself.

For decades, the brand more than anything else has been the object of *Homo consumans*'s unbridled creativity. With a "wallpaper effect," brands have enveloped the stage of every representation of consumption, changing genetically with the needs and expectations of their public, evolving and widening their sophisticated vocabulary together with the language of their proposals, riding change and sometimes anticipating it, even becoming "prophets" of the requests of society. The brand has by now pervaded the entire field of human existence, filled every corner of the planet – even the most remote ones – and it has moved its front line well beyond the commercial latitudes and the areas of competence it inhabited traditionally. In a postmodern society, the brand must satisfy a multitude of social and psychological expectations which cannot be traced back to resolving a specific problem of daily life. We have, in fact, witnessed a revolution in the way consumers relate physically to a product – the ways in which they perceive its *objective* and *functional* characteristics: the physicality of the product has lost consistency compared with the story it is able to tell. In this new vision, even the most banal products are able to satisfy needs such as self-affirmation, health, love, belonging and spirituality, once the exclusive prerogative of the "luxury sphere."

So, faced with a market in which the multiplication of references seems to be inconsistent with the expectations of clarity and simplification of the choices expressed by society, the brand must take on a new role of social mediator, able to exist side by side with relationships between individuals, and sometimes substitute itself for such relationships. Consumers are tending increasingly to reject brands which continue to offer overextensive lines in favor of those able to offer ideas, creativity, meanings and projects. A brand must provide an answer to both collective and individual anxieties and desires, by showing the road – the guiding path – to follow, proposing itself as a "compass" in today's complex society.

Therefore, while it is necessary for a brand to keep its founding values constant, it must also *evolve* to take into account the changes taking place in the economic, social and cultural ecosystem it is part of, highlighting the constantly bi-univocal sense of its relationship with its environment. A brand's change (or evolution) in time reflects naturally on communication, but it also closely regards innovation of the product. This continual adaptation, the "sufficient condition" for the survival of the brand, presents interesting analogies with biological evolution. Only brands which are able to evolve by adapting to changes in the environment are destined to survive and develop in the marketplace.

The market economy is spreading at incredible speed to realities which are culturally very distant, and the outcomes of this "hybridization" have yet to be verified. This aspect was ignored as long as the economic process began and ended in the West, and while the East was thought of simply as a place in which to produce at low costs (and with little or no regard for workers' conditions). Today, however, it is a significant problematic complexity for big brands. Remote places have really become the new competitive scenario where many brands risk their survival. Faced with increasingly open markets, the brand, like any other cultural product, cannot be separated from the social context in which it finds itself operating.

Brand Storming takes the reader on a journey through the contemporary iconological universe in which brands have ended up taking on extra or post-economic values, values of an artistic, philosophical, cultural and social type. Through the brand and the increasingly sophisticated ways it is advertised, symbols and lifestyles, behavioral models and existential suggestions are communicated which form part of what we summarily define as "postmodernity."

The aim of our work has been to carry out a thorough investigation into the role of the brand in the new millennium. The work combines the benefits of sociological analysis and economic theory, and attempts to integrate a deductive approach with an inductive one, with the aim of offering managers a compass to guide their decisions and provide a useful tool for investigation (economic, social and marketing theory) for students and marketers.

MICHELE FIORONI & GARRY TITTERTON

PART I

THE BRAND IN RELATION TO SOCIETY, BELIEF, CULTURE AND CHANGE

CHAPTER 1

THE BRAND AS A SOCIAL PHENOMENON AND CULTURAL ICON

Nothing is any longer immune from brands. Even the fantastic world of fairy tales, represented these days by cartoons, is profoundly pervaded by them. Every representation of modernity, be it real or imaginary, takes place in a setting of brands, with brands an integral part of the narrative process.

When the ogre Shrek, the main character in the cartoon of the same name, leaves the putrid waters of his swamp to set out on his journey to the Land of Far, Far Away, his experience is not so very different from that of normal human beings, as he comes into contact with modernity via its icons and myths – brands of coffee, fast food chains, designer labels and sparkling shop windows. Even in his fantastic world, Shrek is forced to become aware of the presence of a Starbucks on every street corner, and he does so unconsciously, taking it almost for granted, just as we tend to now, without even thinking about the fact, that that brand name has become part of the urban wallpaper. And then, of course, there is Marty, the zebra in the cartoon *Madagascar*. Marty thinks that the alternative model to the life in the zoo cage he has escaped from is that of the glittering lights of Times Square, where luminous signs and billboards create a mass media representation of the crowdedness of modern competitive scenarios.

Brands have invaded every sector of our lives, their fields of action having now moved well beyond the commercial spaces and areas of competence in which they were traditionally collocated. In short, just as we think we have developed antibodies against the most sophisticated brand policies, just as literature presents us with images of a consumer who is ever more knowledgeable, critical and less willing to be taken in, so a new brand era is beginning in which brands are definitively consecrated and collocated among the earth's powerful.

Brands and their derivatives, products, have become integral parts of society and a basic element of its DNA. Any attempt to resist the power of brands by discrediting, blacklisting or boycotting them is in vain. Publications such as Naomi Klein's *No Logo*,[1] or images of groups of protestors destroying cans of Coca-Cola or smashing the windows of a McDonald's, are authentic celebrations of the power of brands, visual representations of their definitive consecration and social acceptance, albeit by negation.

The attention which, as society evolved, was often given to the powerful – to dictators, to governors – is nowadays given to an object, and that object has consequently acquired ever more human and therefore pervasive characteristics and a recognized social identity as both actor and spectator in the bi-univocal cause and effect relationship of social change.

Many people have claimed that branding has now entered a phase of inexorable decline, and more than a few have prematurely announced its funeral. We firmly believe however that we have not reached the end of the book; on the contrary, we have only just finished the preface. We are in fact entering a new phase which will see brands ready to take on a more sophisticated, complex role, a more pervasive, multi-faceted identity destined to rise even further to the role of undisputed protagonist in society.[2]

As brands have become more and more aware of their growing susceptibility to public opinion, and consequently of the fact that their behavior is increasingly visible, they have begun to take social criticism into account, metabolize it and adopt ethical paths which are essential to their survival. They have learnt the hard way that being incorrect does not pay, and that what may be economic in the short term can undermine their very existence in the long term. Being ethical in order to be competitive has become the new axiom for survival in a market where brands must pursue new aims which are increasingly linked to reinforcing individual values if they want to achieve their economic aims. As Mohanbir San Sawhney notes, modern brands must be encouraged to give greater importance to a series of factors which aim at more than just profit. It is only by giving attention to these aspects that a brand can build the foundations for generating value and thus long-lasting economic stability. This means that a company must rethink its very nature – overcome the material image of its being – in order to open the door to a more emotional, mental and spiritual vision.

The increased social value and power thus derived obliges brands to adopt new codes of behavior. Just as in politics, joining the ranks of the more powerful has significant implications in terms of public expectations, and therefore dictates a greater level of social responsibility when managing a brand.

As a result of being richer and more powerful in terms of social judgement, brands are obliged to be increasingly more sensitive toward collective problems, a responsibility which is not limited to the products which bear the brand name, but also involves taking on the complex needs expressed by today's society, needs which go well beyond the traditional functional requirements and symbolic representation of a brand.

Politics is also beginning to view brands with some wariness, aware of their increased power and the consequent influence they can exert on it in a relationship which has become more and more one of parity. Brands today are atypical leaders in our postmodern society and must behave as leaders by adopting new methods of communication. Men have always communicated through stories, and the great leaders have been, above all, great storytellers – think of Gandhi, Reagan, Churchill and, further back in time, Napoleon, St Francis, Julius Caesar. Great leaders however do not only know how to tell stories; they assimilate them and often represent those stories by becoming personifications of them. Every story has an identity and its own narrative structure which helps individuals to think about and feel what they are, where they come from and where they want to go: narration represents one of the most powerful weapons leaders have in their arsenal.

As Napoleon stated, leaders are dealers in hope. This does not mean that a brand should make false promises or sell false hopes; it means, rather, that only those able to tell believable stories, parables which provide guidelines for life, will really be able to differentiate themselves from the others.

In an era many have characterized as that of the decline of grand ideologies and a crisis in great tales, it is consumption which has become the dominant story, and brands, with their tales, perform the task of social marker, bring the collective together and act as vehicles for identity.[3] The two-way relationship between brands and society finds a further element of fortification in the consideration of the brand as a cultural phenomenon. A brand in fact represents a product's cultural system, and as such acquires meaning the moment it circulates within society. The more powerful a brand, the greater its circulation and therefore the greater the influence it exerts in the social reference context. Unlike politics, which is increasingly subject to regulation via what is known as *par condicio*, a brand's media exposure is not limited in any way, except, perhaps, under anti-trust laws. Products have thus become cultural artifacts in the fullest sense and brands cultural promoters. However, if we are really to be able to talk about *brand culture*, a brand's originating idea must somehow be promulgated within society: it is by frequent repetition over time that meaning is progressively intercrossed and conventionally recognized, regardless of whether it is accepted or shared. Legitimization of a product via a brand has increasingly taken on connotations of cultural legitimization rather than functional legitimization – being a cultural model has therefore become more important than doing something or being able to do it.

Time undoubtedly plays an important role in this cultural legitimization process. Mere existence is not enough to substantiate claim that a product is a cultural phenomenon; for this, tales about the product must be born, stories which are the fruits not only of the product's creator – the producer – but also of the real-life experiences of the product's users, the public who are directly involved to varying degrees. Only when ideas, perceptions, feelings and reactions accumulate with time can it be declared with certainty that a brand has definitively built up its own culture.

Consumers obviously play an important role in this co-authoring process of brand culture: the more interaction users have with the product, the more stories about the product they will circulate in society, thus contributing to the creation of the culture. Word of mouth, talking to friends and every other form of informal communication thus becomes an important step in the process of founding a brand's culture. In fact, it is no coincidence that in recent years new marketing strategies, such as "viral marketing," have successfully evolved, which make ample use of informal means of communication in order to assert brand culture and to do so in the shortest possible time. Forms of promotion based on word of mouth are becoming an important tool, able to catapult products and brand names from obscurity to commercial success.[4]

Those companies which have felt the need to assert the cultural model of their brands have officially entered into the new era of branding: they have understood that it is essential to get out of the fog generated by the overcrowding of competitive arenas. Above all, however, they have perceived that brands are less and less a market phenomenon and increasingly more a cultural phenomenon, in a society which desperately feels the need to grab hold of new anchors, its traditional ones having shown themselves to not represent effectively the fundamental values of individuals.

The important thing is not for a product to be consumed, but for it to be talked about. Even disapproval of a product, its boycotting on ideological grounds, or its social negation is an element which helps to strengthen the culture of a brand inasmuch as they legitimize its existence. The more stories in circulation, the more the urban legends pass by word of mouth, the more a brand increases its cultural power and takes on the symbolic office of an authentic icon of modern society.[5]

The diffusion within society, within its everyday life and conventions, of stories and images linked to a brand thus becomes an essential element in generating the cultural model of that brand. When these stories are accepted and become a part of social integration – even through disapproval, which is still a form of recognition of the phenomenon – we can affirm that a culture has been born and has become an integral part of society's DNA. Thinking of a brand as having a culture means overcoming the arid and ascetic market vision in order to promote a more sophisticated image which attributes to the brand the role not only of a receiver of social phenomena, but also of a promoter of new ones. Brands which are able to create a culture inside themselves are thus able to influence events both as protagonists and as spectators of social change.

It is in a reference context such as today's, where consumers have to cope with an extraordinary surplus of information, that less rational modes of purchasing and consumption gain hold. This is perhaps the result of a spasmodic need to seek refuge from the very elements which should simplify choices but which very often, instead, contribute to making life more complicated.

Choosing a brand has become more and more a question of choosing a social anchor, and this choice will increasingly favor brands which are consolidated by a culture and therefore *conventionalized*. The presence of a culture can therefore be even more important in the choice process than information, once the main basis. Where a brand's culture gains consistency and becomes convention, consumers have found certainties which they will abandon only with difficulty, particularly when these certainties have a spiritual basis. The fact that this culture finds expression and is shared in numerous contexts further strengthens consumer's identification with the cultural model the brand conveys.[6]

The creation of a brand culture is therefore a collective phenomenon and as such it has a significant impact on society: it not only is subject to the moods of society, but also contributes to determining new ones. In this way, a brand increasingly becomes a mutating being, continually interchanging with its surrounding environment, able to interpret each subtle alteration happening in the social reference context to such a point that it can itself determine alterations.

Throughout society's evolution, man has made ample use of material culture in order to define values and identities, and brands perform a powerful symbolic function in this sense; products, which are presented as tools for expressing status, lifestyle, political beliefs, ambitions and so on, are the functional element through which the process is achieved. This is how the prophets of the so-called new economy made Apple a symbol, a real social marker of their way of being and of viewing information technology, in keeping with their own personality – creative, rebellious liberals with an almost genetic aversion to preconceived rules and accepted beliefs. In this way, brands assume notable social value, making it possible to express what society often does not allow, by means of symbolic representation of desired and hoped-for values rather than imagined and dreamed identities. A brand becomes a collection of stories, visions and associations made up of reputation, experiences, long-lasting relationships and symbolic value.

Brands have in fact always accompanied the evolution of society by promoting and encouraging the most profound changes. In the beginning, they responded to the need for solutions, the need to distinguish one object from another one with the same function and the need to steer choices. In the era which some refer to as that of classic brands, the brand satisfied specific and precise needs by focusing on what the product did; only later did brands become expressions of social change by assimilating the multiple aspects of such change.

A brand can be thought of as a chameleon which has to change the color of its skin in order to survive the dangers of its surroundings. Like every living organism it is the protagonist of its time and an active spectator as the reference scenario evolves. However much its personal story may be a story of success, a brand is forced to change its skin when social trends and technological and demographic changes do not allow it to maintain its status quo. Just think, for example, of household cleaning products. In the period when women were considered "angels of the hearth" and confined within the household walls, with no possibility of pursuing careers in society, household cleaning products had an identity very different from that of today. They were in fact authentic little cleaning professionals, chosen by women who were equally professional in a society which had mainly relegated women to solving domestic problems, where the choice of such products was one of the few areas in which women had decisional power. In this context, a washing powder could give itself the airs of "a little washing machine" and take on a technical identity far superior to its real function, since it was through this choice that a woman could demonstrate her skills in other fields which were closed to her. Household cleaning products responded to the needs of women to assume, at least in that field, an authoritative, leading role. As women have become progressively more emancipated, such decisions have become less important for them since they have become less representative of their new roles. Women's competence has now been expanded into new areas and it is the rejection of the roles to which they were long relegated that has led women to give less symbolic importance to such choices: products are now chosen solely (and more correctly) for their functional value, leading to their being viewed increasingly as undifferentiated and therefore easily substituted by another brand.

Demographic changes also have an important impact on the genetic mutation of brands by forcing companies to interpret the future of their brands by reinterpreting their past over the long term. In order to maintain their appeal, brands must be able to reach the new consumers who over the years replace others as the brand's reference audience. What pleased past generations may not be all right today, and a brand may progressively lose its ability to attract a public which is demographically identical but vastly different from a social point of view. There are in fact profound differences between the generations active in the marketplace today, and this requires an increasing ability to manage and include the various needs of these generations and the reference mindset of each.

Various experts have noted how often re-proposing the past reveals elements of continuity with the present which can be used in planning strategies for the future.[7] In fact, notable cases of brands once thought extinct returning from the past and reappearing on the market are not rare in the history of branding. This results from what could be termed as "nostalgia marketing." Nostalgia, increasingly a distinctive feature of modern society, can in fact play a fundamental role either in the creation of new markets or in the repopulation of existing markets which are revitalized by the return of certain brands.

Nowadays, faced with a society ever more complex and fragmented, brands must aim less and less at meeting functional needs in terms of the efficacy of a product and more and more at developing the ability to cope with a multitude of requirements, many of which are unconnected with the need to solve a specific problem. The varying needs of today's consumer mean that brands cannot limit themselves to solving functional problems. It this multidimensionality that makes it less and less possible to apply universal, invariable rules to brands. We therefore need to mistrust those who propose absolute and immutable rules and patterns. Each brand has its own story and becomes author of its own future in unique ways which cannot be copied.

Brands are condemned to act and operate in a much more complex scenario, where quality is not enough to compete. This complexity derives, in particular, from the numerous roles a consumer has to perform in postmodern society. In what can be described as a 24-hour society, where individuals have progressively less free time, there has been an increase in people's inner expectations – those linked to psychological, physical and moral wellbeing.[8] This means that a company must rethink its brands, going beyond their material image in order to develop a more emotional and spiritual one.[9]

Our work occupies a central role in the restructuring of our daily timetables. The most obvious paradox can be seen in the fact that in recent years we have witnessed the arrival of technology which, both at home and at work, should have made various tasks simpler, cheaper and quicker to carry out, thus making it possible to better manage the time available for family, leisure and relaxation. Paradoxically, however, in many cases this has led to a progressively increased workload.

Technology has in fact increased work pressure, particularly since it has created the possibility of accessing an enormous amount of information in real time. One can just think how nowadays a large part of a manager's working day is spent answering dozens and dozens of emails which require "immediate attention." With this change in society has grown the need to escape, and brands must also satisfy this requirement.[10]

Colors, images and brand names on packaging have precisely the aim of helping the consumer make choices as quickly as possible, inside the point of sale. Visual merchandising plays an increasingly important role in managing purchase time by orientating customers, providing information simply and quickly and thus facilitating choices. The consumption of goods can increasingly be thought of as the consumption of signs and symbols, which anybody going round a point of sale is forced to read quickly.

In a world where time constrictions are becoming greater and greater, it is in this way that individuals affirm their spasmodic need for professional fulfillment, health, love, belonging, spirituality, free time and recognition: unexpressed, often conflicting, requirements which brands must nevertheless satisfy simultaneously.

Even the most banal products have to deal with this complex range of needs: for example a bottle of water has to be able to quench thirst and at the same time provide the correct quantity of minerals, being appropriately packaged for its intended function – be it for drinking while doing sports or during meals, or, as with premium waters, acting as a show of status.

We can also think of what is happening within the family. At one time, roles were clearly defined: the man worked and the woman (in most cases) looked after the housework. These days such role distinctions have disappeared and this has introduced new players into old roles: when a man comes home from work he now has to put on his chef's or babysitter's hat, just as at work a woman has to step into the shoes – and not just the lace-ups – of a top manager. The need to achieve aims which once seemed conflicting and incompatible (such as the need for social achievement, more free time, an intense family life and so on) now dictates the rhythms of life and that tempo is part of modern living. Brands perform the role of social mediator in this multiplication of roles, making them accessible by means of meta-language which is not connected to the product's classic function.[11]

There have been many cases of companies which have tried to develop this policy. Levi's, with its line Dockers, launched a campaign aimed at companies to encourage the adoption of a special dress code for Fridays, the last day of the working week, better known as Casual Friday. The basic principle was that all week workers were forced to wear the austere uniform which goes with the job: jacket, tie and shiny shoes. The aim was progressive homogeneity (albeit with various standards of smart dress), with no real difference between that uniform and a policeman's. Casual Friday aimed at combining the needs of the individual to taste freedom and to be able to express themself culturally, even if only for a day, in a working environment usually characterized by rules and behavioral norms. It matters little that the commercial aim of those behind Dockers was to encourage people to wear casual clothes during the week, not just at the weekend, and thus increase the frequency of use. What is important however is that Dockers took on the role of expressing the deepest sentiment of today's armies of company workers: that of being able to taste liberty, by breaking down, at least for a day, the strict barrier between work and pleasure, even if only by wearing a pair of trousers.

Finally, brands continually have to face new challenges launched by the new technology which has invaded every social reference context, without exception. Today, consumers have a new and extraordinary wealth, something represented not so much by their greater purchasing power but more by their ability to gather information about products and brands easily and quickly.

The arrival of new technology linked to the web has however reduced the potential of one of the characterizing features of brand policy: the reduction of research costs. The traditional functions performed by brands, which were linked to simplifying the choice process and reducing research costs, are now the realm of technology. Today the consumer can simply key a specific need or functional requirement into a search engine and be flooded by information which makes it quick and easy to compare brands.[12]

The result however is that we are faced today with a plethora of brands and products quite unknown in the past. The consumer's easy access to information, considered so important in helping them to choose, obliges brands to review their way of presenting themselves to the market, and, above all, reduces the impact of the type of information of which brands used to be the consumer's principal source.

This argument is even truer if we consider the fact that until recently consumers had to memorize few brand names and therefore less information, whereas today that extraordinary database, the human brain, is required to memorize an infinite amount of information as a result of the extraordinary abundance of brands present on the market. Consumers have therefore decided to externalize this brand-linked database, by accepting that only a small proportion of this information is memorized by the brain while most of it is stored online, on the web.[13]

All this forces companies to fight without ceasing, on the one hand to gain dominance among the information the consumer has decided to keep in their personal, human database, and, on the other hand, to dominate the visibility which can be gained on the web. In fact, only a few brands are so strong that they can remain in the human memory permanently, and they are those which over time have known how to build an effective brand strategy, by adapting to each change in events, while still maintaining spatial–temporal transcendence. For the others, the fight focuses on new media forms, a battlefield already crowded and where day after day it is always more difficult to find a space in which there can be visibility and therefore memorization and fame.

Information and intelligence are becoming more and more the realms of modern technology, and it is not unrealistic to imagine a society in which increasing importance will be given to the only capability of man which cannot be automated: the emotions. Therefore, more and more attention will be given not only to market shares, but, as Nordstrom and Ridderstrale suggest, to the heart and memory space a brand will be able to win.[14]

Today, consumers want to be told a myriad of stories, and brands must take on the role of narrator, able to tell stories which are always different. This means brands can expand their audience beyond consumers, bringing into question the traditional strategies of segmentation: just as the strength of a brand increasingly depends on how it is talked about globally, so the more actors are involved the greater is the brand's fame. One example of this is the famous clothes chain for young people, Abercrombie & Fitch, which teaches us how a brand can be managed in an extreme way in order to gain fame and get a multitude of stories told about it. The marketing approach of the company has always been characterized by a significant break with pre-established rules: the approach concentrates not so much on how young people should dress, but how they should not dress. In keeping with this "anti" image, Abercrombie uses extreme methods of communication, making great use of sexual pull. Its advertisements, in which models are often scantily dressed, have been criticized by consumer associations for being against the interests of public morality.[15] But, just as with Benetton in the past, the case of Abercrombie shows us how such "at-the-limits" brand management helps gain increasing fame thanks to the discussions generated about the brand, even if these are highly critical. Polemics can in fact increase the value of a brand, if managed carefully; the challenge consists in understanding the line beyond which disapproval depreciates the social value of a brand, and thus does not contribute to making it more well known.

This is in keeping with the previously mentioned idea of a brand having the connotation of a cultural phenomenon. A culture has a strength and a public impact which goes beyond its direct users, precisely because it has a wider social value. The product as cultural artifact, if it has a brand, tells stories which are not strictly connected to its function but are, if anything, linked to the fact that it has become a vehicle for culture.

Companies are gradually understanding that their products are less important than the stories they are able to tell. The construction of a brand corresponds more and more to a narrative path in which the story never ends. Modern managers are therefore required to become narrators if they want to connect the brand they manage and its public in a deeper and more solid way. This means having to think of the market in a less and less objective and economic key and in a more subjective and, if we may use the term, metaphysical one. What has been said completes the argument regarding the new role which brands must rise to, one which involves entering into the heart of their public's life plans and making consumption, which has become more and more diluted in people's lives, consistent with such projects by ascribing a sense to them or, where one already exists, strengthening it.[16]

What has been stated could appear to conflict with the general picture of tendencies, above all those connected with the evolution of technology. We believe however that it is precisely in a more technological context that an appeal to the emotions will make it possible to fill the gaps that the technological "caterpillars" have caused on a social level. Individuals have delegated more and more aspects of their lives to technology, creating a society which is undoubtedly more efficient, but less and less able to excite emotions. Soon we will be looking for comfort in everything that technology is not – in other words in emotions. Brands are therefore faced with yet another challenge, that of being an emotional refuge against the cold, the asceticism and the consequent anxieties of modernity. It is thus precisely in the technological era, where everything functions, where everything is designed to perform its task to perfection, that the ability to excite emotions will become the key to a brand's success. The purchase of a brand will be increasingly more related to its ability to offer emotions, to make people dream and make dreams come true, and less and less related to the use of the product.

Brands are ready to ride into new territories, lands which are far vaster than those in which they have been confined, relegated as they were to the concrete sphere of consumption space.

CHAPTER 2

BRAND RELIGION

Brands and religion have many things in common. Although putting them together may seem sacrilegious, in fact it is not. Empirical evidence increasingly demonstrates how faith, belief and community can become the basis of new marketing strategies.[1] In fact, examples of advertising campaigns where an approach employing ultimate reality, the superior aim of existence or even mysticism as the main theme are not rare.

A few years ago, Nike launched an advertising campaign with the slogan "Test Your Faith." It was a campaign in which a vague and hazy figure was seen running against the background of a cloudless sky. While reading a magazine or looking at a poster, people were transported into a run in which they could identify as testers of faith. The stimulus created was that of running as a mystical experience: in other words, running lost its connotation of physical exercise and the result was an almost religious attention to fitness. The text itself seemed to suggest possible transcendental features of exercise, just as individuals daily ask themselves questions about their existence in respect of the eternal, the mystic, or faith.[2] For the runner, the exercise became the ultimate aim of his spiritual process, while the receiver was catapulted into the experience of a run which took on the symbolic significance of freedom, without constrictions or ties: anybody, whether an athlete or not, can overcome their own limits. Thus, the receiver identifies themself with that run, making the emotional meaning their own, and identifies themself with the brand, seeing it as a means of living a transcendental experience.

Religion represents the relationship which is established between a person and an indeterminate superior being. Every religion bases its appeal on man's need to believe in something which gives him a purpose in life and shows him the path he should take. The need for religion is present in every culture; its externalized forms can be seen in rites which have social value and sacred texts which contain all or a part of the divine revelations. Today, faced with this need, the major religions are going through a difficult period in their ability to provide solid points of reference and to represent fundamental individual values. On the other hand, the very ahistorical nature of religions means that we cannot expect them to be up-to-date inasmuch as this could bring into question the fundamental principles of the creed. Looking at the argument from a different angle, it could be said that it is in the very nature of dogma not to be up-to-date and therefore not to easily adapt itself to modernity. It is precisely this difficulty of accepting dogma, in a society where ways of life have become more and more individual rather than collective, that leads individuals to choose, whether consciously or not, to move away from religions and look for shortcuts. People thus decided to let go of the anchor and drift in search of new points of reference which, as facts have shown, are not as solid and leave gaps at a social level which make life harder. The more complex and competitive societies become, the more individuals try to build their own "temples" outside of traditional religious institutions; from this stems the diffusion of new tendencies such as the New Age and the success in the West of religious movements born in the East.[3]

We live in an era in which abundance rules and where consumers, above all in Western countries, have functional products which can satisfy not only their basic needs but also their desires and whims. The way to get out of this complex market situation is to appeal to their spirituality.[4] Consumers consider less and less the functional aspects of a brand, while giving more and more importance to the emotional and spiritual aspects. We would like to make it clear that we are not proposing brands as the pagan gods of the postmodern era, but are simply highlighting the fact that there are common features between a brand and religion and that this means that ideas such as belief, community and rites can be used as a basis for developing brand strategies.

Every religion in fact defines among its followers a sense of belonging, of community and of sharing. It is through this sense of belonging that the creed is created and strengthened. The same could be said for brands, whose resonance can allow access to a community and develop feelings of belonging to it.[5] We are talking about communities which are almost tribal in nature, made up of people who share the same interest in a particular brand which creates a sort of parallel universe made up of its own values, languages and hierarchy. Its members are joined by the same subjectivity, passions and experiences and by means of a series of rituals they are bearers of collective actions which are lived intensely, even if they are in reality ephemeral. As Cova notes, consumers increasingly feel the need to gather together in subgroups which are distinct from society and which celebrate their own existence through commitment to a product, a brand and a consumption entity.[6] Through that brand, they manage to create not physical but ideal places, which strengthen the collective identity of the community's members, in exactly the same way as a religious movement does.

Harley enthusiasts are a classic example of individuals who suppress their desire for freedom during the week, sacrificing it at the altar of professional responsibility and conformism. They feel the need to escape from the role they are almost forced to play, a role they do not completely identify themselves with. It is through using the brand, more than the product, that at the weekend they throw off their professional clothes, put on their "vestments" of leather, fringes and steel studs, and practice the liberating cult of the road. Tired of accepting what is daily offered (or forced on) them, and in complete contempt of the materialism of society and those conventional values which they seem resigned to accept, in the rituals of the brand they satisfy their desire to have something they can believe in.[7]

Again, as Cova suggests, in the integration of products, brands satisfy the need to perform an active memory role within a society which is ever more thirsty for something sacred. Religions provide a projection of an ideal world, of what it should be like, by the sharing of principles and reference values. This ideal world is presented through the use of myths, tales, stories and beliefs which provide a life model to be imitated, a model able to present a simplified vision of life, that simplicity being the very means by which life can be assigned a deep meaning.[8]

It is through myths, stories and beliefs that a model is created and circulated, a model which makes choices simpler and life-planning more linear. Myths are a part of realty which allow human behaviors to be systemized while at the same time motivating the behavior of individuals who find their own emotional responses and personal inspiration in them.

Brand religion obliges companies to attribute a spatial–temporal transcendence to their brands by presenting the brand in a mythological key. Consider, for example, all those companies which are part of the so-called new economy, often born in small garages and founded by young, talented geniuses misunderstood by information technology. Such a garage is where the cult is born, a modern Bethlehem where the origin of the myth is sought. It is in this way that the story of pioneers such as Steve Jobs and Steve Wozniak, the founders of Apple Computer, loses its biographical connotations and takes on a hagiographic meaning. It was in a little garage in Palo Alto that the Apple cult was born, and that garage has become an integral part of the religion, an authentic founding myth and symbolic place of pilgrimage and veneration. Since 1984, the year in which the first Macintosh was launched, Apple has introduced a new way of building a brand, creating both a real creed and groups of followers and faithful who are ready to make its holy writ their own.

Consider also music and its myths. How many Elvis fans visit the mausoleum at Memphis each year to worship the "holy" icon? For rock music, Graceland represents what the Vatican may represent for a Catholic. In different ways, and obviously with different spiritual and value significance, rituals and ways of worship which are basically similar are enacted.

Let's think about how many difficulties young people meet today, and how they need to hold on to everything which can provide a basis for their increasingly confused lives: the new generations demand – and not just from the market – something which abandons the models of the past and which, in short, is able to provide them with new beliefs.

Every religion has its icons. Today we talk more and more about cultural icons, meaning exemplary symbols accepted by people because they represent their personal values, ideas, lifestyles and personal aspirations.

The story of man is by its nature iconographic. Every society has had its icons, represented by myths, people, objects and places. In this way the story of civilization is inseparable from its icons; an outstanding example is Greek civilization, which has left its marks on time in the form of the great philosophers and religious buildings, such as the Parthenon.

Individuals increasingly look for refuge in icons to express their personal values and ideals: it is for this reason that the face of a Cuban revolutionary has become representative of an imagined society or that an American president who died young and governed for only a very short period has come to be an emblem of good government. Che Guevara and John F. Kennedy are basically two brands which society has appropriated to express iconographically the projection of ideal and imaginary values. An icon has an extraordinary value which derives from its strong symbolic weight they possess – or which society decides to assign to them – and they perform a propulsive role by proposing models which force people to think, speak and act.

Brands are not immune to this unstoppable need of society to build its own icons; on the contrary, brands have in their own evolutionary code the impulse to become icons. A brand takes on an iconographic connotation the moment it is able to represent an ideal world compared with the real one, which is characterized by increasingly rigid schemes and an increasingly coercive routine, with ever fewer possibilities of choice and escape. Consumers look not for present reality in an icon, but for the opposite: what is wished for, imagined, what is not and maybe never can be.

Holt maintains that to be an icon a brand must have an inner connotation of activism, in other words, it must be able to encourage people to go further, to act and think differently, ultimately promoting a real cultural revolution. Brands which are able to carry out these tasks do not limit themselves to evoking benefits, emotions and personality, but are true myths, able to stimulate individuals to reconsider their own existence.[9]

The case of Diesel is a useful example of how a brand can take on an identity as an activist and, in an extreme representation, become almost a social agitator.[10] In its vocation, the brand contains the message of its founder, he who created the myth and became its prophet, a doctrine of aversion to preconceived models and conventions and a strong anti-establishment feeling. It is no coincidence that Renzo Rosso, despite being one of the major exponents of Italian *nouvelle vogue* and one of the most effective Made in Italy ambassadors in the world, does not dine with the powerful elite of the Italian economy. Rosso is an authentic fashion revolutionary, with an inborn propensity to stand out from the crowd and develop, in his brand, a distinctive capacity based on social difference. Diesel is presented therefore as a counterpoint to pre-established rules and institutions, disseminating new cultural models which originated on the street. Rosso has in fact understood that innovation in fashion originates less and less in the marketing "laboratories" of companies and increasingly more spontaneously on the street, and that the voices and demands of that street have to be listened through establishing a dialogue with it. Diesel presents a new society of freedom, honesty, humor and the possibility of dissent, expressing a basic contempt for the hypocrisy of society and for the politically-correct-at-any-cost. Rosso has understood better than anybody else that young people tend to buy products and services from organizations which are compatible with their system of values and that of the "tribe" they belong to. When he launched his first products thirty years ago, his intuition was so ahead of its time that he had problems being understood, not so much by consumers as by distributors, so that retailers often sent items back to Diesel, thinking that they were mistakes. Shopkeepers were a long way from his perception of the market:, they did not have the "vintage" culture of lived-in looking clothes, rips and stonewashing: Diesel items were too anti-conformist for them, not clean-cut enough. But the young were fed up with being conventional and wanted to break away from the past: the cuts in their jeans represented their need to cut their ties with former generations. They were looking for new guides, new stimuli. New generations are not in fact frightened by authority and are ready to challenge those choices and decisions which they do not believe to be reasonable, whether made by families, by institutions or by the market. They also believe that the previous generations, while they have contributed to the creation of today's wealth and progress, have nevertheless failed when it comes to values.[11] The aversion to normative and compulsory behaviors, which some see as a form of rebellion, is in fact linked to the lack of moral authority on the part of the institutions which propose such norms. All young people ask for is to be able to identify themselves with symbols in which they can find this value system – better still if these are not clean-cut and conventional.

The need to escape characterizes most of the brands which have known how to build themselves an iconographic aura – consider, for example, Harley Davidson. People who buy a Harley translate it into a symbol of the freedom and independence for which potential customers yearn in a society in which time and stress dictate the rhythms of life. It is certainly no coincidence that Renzo Rosso is a Harley enthusiast.

To build its own religion, a brand must be able to tell stories as if they were modern parables. The stories a brand proposes today are made up of comic strips and characters which, as in every metaphorical story, have to spur the imagination and encourage doing – doing not just in the sense of buying and consuming but, above all, in attributing a symbolic value of refuge and spiritual support to these two actions.

This obliges modern business organizations to go beyond the classic functional image in order to take on a new one, that of narrator able to tell stories which involve the brand and, through those tales, to gradually seek to make the brand an icon. Consumers buy this type of brand because it enables them to live out the stories the brands recount.

Consumers tend in fact increasingly to value products for what they represent symbolically and not for what they do, and this has led to an unexpressed need for the market and society in general to construct new emotional anchors, represented by images. Consumers choose those products which represent ideals they admire or, in any case, provide a projection of what they would like to be or how they wish society could be. Brands must therefore propose a direction for collective anxieties and desires as much as for individual ones, by showing a way, a "teaching path," to follow. Thus a brand becomes a compass in this social complexity, a real pole star of modernity.

The true technological challenge modern brand managers have to face is that of designing, within the brand, myths and symbols which make the products difficult to imitate and replicate. More and more, the ability to build myths and make them a characterizing feature of the brand represents the demarcation line between successful and mediocre products.

A parable is nothing other than a metaphorical tale used to teach something, the meaning of which becomes understandable by being simplified. Through a process of analogies and identification a more or less complicated idea is transmitted in a more or less simplified way, making it understandable to its numerous recipients.[12] It is a model of communication which can directly influence people's subconscious. For the use of parables to be effective, the stories and tales must become an integral part of the organizational processes and the organization's members must be able to access them, as well as enrich them, so that they too become disseminators of the holy writ.

It is not by chance that consumers of brands which have known how to create an almost mystical aura around themselves easily remember past advertising campaigns. Those campaigns have become the metaphor of contemporary frescoes in the cathedrals of consumption which allow the historical moments in the evolution of the brand's religion to be fixed in time.

Companies therefore must tell a story, and it is precisely through their tales that personalities such as Steve Jobs, Renzo Rosso and Howard Schultz have become the prophets of new religions, which they not only gave life to, but whose creed they also continually help to strengthen by means of stories and tales which are closely linked to their very existence. These are exceptional leaders who are speeding up the process of the search for real meaning in a market which is increasingly centered on lifestyle, the health of the soul, and spirituality.

When Apple Computer presents one of its new products ready to be launched on the market, masses of Apple faithful crowd the place where the presentation is to be held, even sleeping there the night before, waiting to hear the new parable which the prophet Jobs is ready to tell them. In this way the group convention where the new product is presented loses its pragmatic connotation and takes on a much more mystical one, as it becomes a religious place and occasion, where the brand's religion is celebrated with rituals which are by now consolidated.

The launch of Apple's new product, the iPhone, saw people queue for twenty-four hours outside the New York store just to be sure of getting hold of the "sacred object." This is a classic example of how to use the mystical weight of a brand as a guarantee for an unusual version of the product: focusing attention on a single story rather than on the unique workings of a product also determines the success of products and categories which are new for the brand.

Building up stories around a brand and enhancing them with myths and beliefs therefore becomes an essential step in creating real believers in the brand – something which is more than a faithful customer base. If a faithful customer can really be thought of as a brand's powerful medium, a believer multiplies a brand's communicative capacity even more, becoming an unequalled instrument of communication. A believer takes on the task of leading others to the brand religion and does so using all the media available. Believers are powerful converters, being disciples and disseminators of the creed founded by the brand. The gatherings of Harley enthusiasts become religious places for those who take part, places where the rite of the brand and its legend is celebrated. The Harley legend is one made up of icons which mark the historical stages of its evolution; thus Jack Nicholson is the easy rider, the ideal ambassador of the brand who has become one with its iconographic representation. The rituals the Harley people take part in allow them to fill the voids of modernity, consolidating the ever more disorientated existences of those increasingly in search of something to believe in. In this way, the Harley brand presents itself as a modern icon which allows escape from modernity, carrying out the role of social adhesive where traditional institutions are increasingly unable to do so.

Now, if rites must become an integral part of a brand's system of offer, attention has to be given to the fact that, as Cova notes, consumers purchase a brand because of the rite it allows them to carry out, and not the other way round.[13] The companies which patiently manage to generate interest in the rituals which purchase of the brand allows the consumer to perform then lose their product seller connotation and take on a deeper one, that of brand evangelizer. They are the firms which are able to construct a new brand space, a ritual space where consumers slowly subscribe to the brand's symbolic significance and make it their own.[14]

The ability to stage rites around a brand is the foundation for building that mystic–religious aura which allows brands to compete in a non-conventional way in the present competitive context. In a system of offer where numerous brands which have fewer and fewer differentiating features compete with each other, the rituality which can surround a product can mean that that product stands out on a battlefield where it is increasingly difficult to do so.

As we have already said, to be credible a brand must have a spatial–temporal transcendence; this necessitates a life made up of stories, anecdotes, myths and tales. A brand is the fruit of its past, where events, facts, situations, and steps are built which become present-day, modern parables. It is therefore in its deep authenticity that a brand finds the sense of its existence and through which, like a religion, it projects a vision of an ideal world. But no brand would be anything without its faithful, its devoted followers, the real apostles of its deepest essence. We have stated that today the main market aim of modern business organizations is to help the consumer to survive psychologically. In the most confused moments of man, religions have always presented themselves as guides for the people by showing the way when the haziness of existence made seeing difficult. Every brand, like a religion, must have its own consistency, performing new roles in order to give stability over and above its functional capabilities. A brand must represent a fixed point, a certainty, above all in a context where excess supply makes the process of purchase and consumption more and more difficult for consumers faced with an endless range of alternatives to choose from. The brands destined to win in postmodernity are those who know how to affirm their own dogma. As Cova maintains, every rite has its own brief moments which repeat and repeat, its models scanned by history.[15]

CHAPTER 3

BETWEEN PAST AND PRESENT: NOSTALGIA BRANDING

Nostalgia can be defined as a psychological, cultural and social phenomenon which leads to re-evaluating, often overevaluing, the past and everything connected with it.[1] In order to find a basis for their existential searching, individuals imagine a past which was more beautiful and purer than it really was. A new concept of authenticity is now being imposed on the market, which considers the true, the authentic, to be the result of an idealized reconstruction of the past.

The postmodern consumer looks for protection in the past as if it were a sort of emotional liferaft which can save them from drowning in rough waters. Consider what has happened in the washing-detergent sector: for years products with a wide variety of fragrances were launched – mango, papaya, Alpine freshness, musk; in short, the market segmentation seemed to have progressively centered on the ability of companies to launch products which were ever more bizarre and which by widening the range brought about greater visibility of the brand on the shelves. When Chante Clair launched a line of washing products with the scent of Marseilles soap, it seemed that consumers did not want anything else. All the other manufacturers were forced to adapt by launching new detergents with the same characteristics: all the other products which had responded to the needs of market segmentation were no longer of interest. In the Marseilles soap fragrance, consumers rediscovered scents linked to memories, rites and places of the past. The fact that it is not really Marseilles soap, which has almost disappeared from the market, but just a label to apply to any type of product, is of little importance. As Dutertre notes, "consumers buy them to satisfy their nostalgia at the lowest cost possible: pure unreality."[2] The consumer has found in the scent of Marseilles soap a sort of emotional transfer which has projected them into a historical and social context which is more reassuring. Now, for a detergent to be considered authentic Marseilles soap, tight controls

24

have to be respected. Modern liquid and powder detergents, because of their chemical-physical formulation, do not respect them, but what is important about Marseilles soap is the (re)discovered authenticity in the inner life of consumption experience.

From the world of detergents, we can find another example of a product born out of the balanced combination of past and future, tradition and innovation. Dixan "Cenere Attiva" is a washing detergent launched by Henkel on the Italian market.[3] In a modern key this product presents the old way of washing clothes with a mixture of water and ashes, the lye which also purified them. (The literal translation of the product's name is in fact "Active Ashes.") It may seem paradoxical that after decades in which detergents have stayed the same but advertising has told us repeatedly that the new detergent washed whiter than the previous one, the latest arrival, the one which washes better than all the others, is something our grandmothers used. But it is not a paradox: the telltale charm of the past strikes again!

The car market provides us with further examples of recovering the nostalgic charm of some products: consider Volkswagen's New Beetle, BMW's Mini and, last but not least, the new Fiat 500, created to make the most of the charm the old model still has in the collective imagination.

This rediscovery of aesthetic canons from the past, on the part of industrial sectors which are characterized by a growth which is prevalently centered on evolving technology, is perplexing: why, in a context where creativity is backed up by tools which would potentially allow maximum expression, is there this tendency to create aesthetic appeal by looking to the past, bringing its shapes, lines and colors up-to-date? One is justified in asking if, and to what extent, this recovery of the past depends on a situation of creative sterility or, rather, on the inability to present modernity and get it accepted, or maybe on the fact that the present social context is not able to supply sufficient inspiration; or if, on the contrary, all this is in response to a real need by consumers who are increasingly looking for their roots.

In a society which in the space of a few years has achieved technological progress which until a couple of decades ago seemed unattainable, individuals have seen the wished-for future become reality, and the projection of the future has thus lost its oneiric quality; it is in this context that the recovery of the past responds to a new need, that of making people dream. In the absence of a future, people look for solace in products which bring about reintegration with a past they do not want to break with and which they attempt to justify in every way by authentication.

Even the cinema industry seems unable today to reproduce the great sagas that had so much success in the 1970s and 1980s (with the exception, perhaps, of *The Lord of the Rings* and *Matrix*). And the industry again looks to the past for inspiration for new successes; Batman, Spiderman, Daredevil and other Marvel heroes have thereby become transgenerational icons.

To understand the importance of nostalgia as a new marketing tool, we can think of the success which Gap had a few years ago when it launched its new casual wear chain, Old Navy. The launch advertising campaign was designed with a series of black-and-white advertisements which re-proposed the style of a past era – that of the 1950s – and even the points of sale were furnished and decorated in the same way. The use of nostalgia to launch Old Navy was motivated by the need to make a brand credible in its introductory phase and to avoid its being seen as something which had suddenly appeared from nothing.[4]

In the digital economic era a sort of paradox is happening, which we like to call "industrial neoclassicism," on the basis of which values, symbols, icons and myths of previous generations are successfully re-proposed on the market by bringing aesthetic canons up-to-date and enriching them with modern functionality.

One can think also of the "agriturismo" boom in recent years in Italy. This type of holiday accommodation is quite simple: the traditional organization of rural and farm life is re-proposed in the form of a holiday. The "agriturismo" sector simply sells the peasant life of long ago, but obviously with its hardships lightened. So, at weekends or during the holidays, there is an authentic escape from the city as people immerse themselves in the old dimension of peasant life. It is no coincidence that Negroponte states somewhere that the real luxury is represented by not having to wake up in the morning and by being able to keep your pajamas on all day, in a sort of new renaissance of rural life, and that this new luxury will in future lead to the disappearance of the need for cities.

This is also an effective example of how the symbolic projection of past values is reassuring, relaxing and regenerating, compared with the daily life and context of the present. It seems bizarre, to say the least, that individuals tend to flee from the modernity which day after day they help to construct and develop, in order to immerse themselves in the past.[5]

Consider also the success in recent years that Irish pubs have had in southern and eastern Europe. Only in their inspiration do they recall the traditional meeting places which are so deeply rooted in Irish social culture. One of the most characteristic features of Irish pubs is the ease with which social relationships are begun. Over a pint of Guinness perfect strangers tell their stories, confide their secrets or simply talk about rugby and soccer. Modern Irish pubs are places in which the "Irish experience" is put on stage, but where that cultural model, made up of a simple life, where starting social relationships is easy and where diffidence toward others is minimal, is not represented except symbolically and architecturally.

Notwithstanding this, the postmodern consumer does not feel insulted or as if they were having their leg pulled, but believes in the re-proposal of models from the past or of cultures which are more anchored in tradition, since they believe that these models help them to build more reassuring links with contemporaneity. Consumers are increasingly in search of authenticity: this explains the market success of natural cosmetics, traditional remedies, craftwork, organic products and "agriturismo." The real problem stems from the fact that there is nothing really authentic in what is proposed by the market, which simply revisits the past and often enriches it with functionality linked to modernity.

The approach of nostalgia marketing is extremely flexible, part of a *multi-generational* supply logic. For baby boomers, pining for the good old days, it brings back memories of a glorious past, but in so doing it also opens the "gates of time" to young consumers who think that the products of an era which to them seems like the stone age are cool, radical and extreme.[6] Although new generations declare they do not care for categories from the past, and consequently are unable to identify with products which were once symbols and icons of that past, they are still susceptible to the charm of nostalgia. This behavior is however not so contradictory as it may seem: it is contextual debt awareness, which can be understood in terms of wellbeing to be "paid" to former generations and credit to be "collected" from them in the form of values which are needed to reconstruct a society which, for the young, represents symbolically one which appears healthier and less contaminated than today's. Thus they can bitterly criticize past generations while at the same time reviving past tastes, tendencies and values toward which they gradually come to feel an irresistible nostalgic attraction. Young people have learnt from their parents that making sacrifices for work guarantees neither stable families nor long-term employment. This "crisis within the family" is exactly what drives them to build something they can believe in, to look for social anchors which will give them concrete answers to the growing demand for the moralization of traditional institutions. These answers can sometimes be found in the symbolic projection of the past.

The idea of nostalgia is not only a consequence of the baby boomers getting older, but also a need which derives from the fact that new recruits tend to think that the recovery of myths and icons from the past is particularly cool.

Naturally in an aging society, nostalgia marketing goes side by side with the marketing of anti-age products, such as nutritional supplements, melatonin, papaya: in order for a brand to be effectively placed the most important periods for certain demographic segments must be identified, correlating the brand with its specific target. In this case, we are talking about a "direct" use of the nostalgia lever.

Some periods have, over time, taken on meaning and a symbolic weight not only for those who lived through them but also for those who have become familiar with them by transmission – for example from grandparents, parents, media: we can think of the fabulous 1960s and how these have been the object of numerous forms of representation. Evidently, we are not just talking about bringing back to life the "golden times," but rather of reinterpreting them in a modern key, being careful not to betray their authentic spirit.[7] If awareness is lost of the fact that this is, nonetheless, a past which is re-presented on the stage of modernity, there is a risk of committing the mistake of just proposing something "old." As a simple source of creative inspiration nostalgia is taking hold as a collective phenomenon, pervading every social and market context.

PART II

THE BRAND AS A LIVING ORGANISM: DNA, HUMAN FEATURES AND SENSORY PERCEPTION

CHAPTER 4

THE HUMAN NATURE OF BRANDS

The big challenge which marketing has to face today is that of making human brands which by their very nature are not so human. Man's tendency to anthropomorphize inanimate objects has acquired deep roots down through the centuries and involves very different areas of social life, from religion to politics, and even the family.[1]

Consumers, as Aaker has already shown, tend to demonstrate a willingness to assign human personality traits to brands.[2] As Fournier suggests, consumers want to be persuaded to have relationships which are not merely exchanges with objects which have no tangible vitality and mortality.[3]

All this highlights the existence of a latent propensity to develop relationships with brands which are less and less "hard" – that is, linked to what a product does – and increasingly more "soft" – that is, linked instead to emotional, relational and experiential aspects. The features a brand is required to have therefore have to take on progressively a connotation in terms of greater depth, authenticity, sensitivity, seductiveness and richness, by possessing the very features people need in order to develop relationships.

In a social context in which individuals have ever increasing difficulty in entering into relationships with each other and in which diffidence toward others is increasing, the need to humanize things around them which are not human is felt more strongly. Consider, for example, the social phenomenon of chat rooms which are inundated by individuals thirsting to tell somebody about their own lives, anxieties, emotions, fears, all in a virtual context – perhaps because they are unable to do so in real life. The tendency when chatting to project aspired identities is so great that often people present themselves in an "artificial way," as something they really are not, but which is similar to how they would like to be if social rules allowed them to always express themselves freely. This tendency can, of course, also be seen in another recent web

31

phenomenon, that of "second life" sites. If in chat rooms individuals manage to bypass the obstacles to developing relationships which they seem to meet in society, they can in the same way see in brands a powerful relational catalyst and a way of beating down these obstacles. People are more and more desperately searching for points of social contact and it matters little if these are not animated by real life and are therefore inanimate objects or virtual places.

On these needs brands must build both a new reason for being and a new purchasing motivation. It is the consumer who is desperately asking them to come alive, to tell them something, to be friends, in short to become a social anchor, a real means of escape from daily life and the alienation, stress and complexity this brings. Consumers are therefore asking brands to humanize themselves; all they are waiting for is to make a brand their own, to subscribe to it in some way so that it gradually becomes a symbol of the behavior they cannot express autonomously. At an extreme, we could state that consumers delegate certain behaviors, which they do not always want to express or are unable to express, to a brand. So, it is in brands that consumers ask to realize their dreams and put their *existences* on stage, thus both affirming what they would like to be and satisfying their private aspirations.

It is for this reason that a brand today can really be thought of as being like a living organism, with an identity and a personality which the consumers themselves have asked it to take on – perhaps in order to re-appropriate them later.

As with any living organism, a brand's personality is the expression of its style, character and attitudes, and it plays an important role in building relationships with its public. Just as a person can be attractive, so too can a brand. In fact, attractiveness as a characterizing personality trait plays an important role in developing relationships. We can think of the ways individuals tend to develop relationships among themselves. Attractiveness can be thought of in terms of both a physical dimension and a less material one. There is no doubt that aesthetics perform an essential function as a relational catalyst, making the birth of relationships easier and representing a first element of evaluation. If we think of a brand as having a personality like any other human being, we need to evaluate which of its personality traits consumers consider attractive. Apple, for example, has strong intellectual attraction, linked to its being different, but also physical and therefore aesthetic attraction, linked to the beauty of its products.[4]

Designing a brand which has personality means clearly defining its objective and symbolic functions, as if we were planning its behavior. In this sense, a brand's personality can be thought of as all the human characteristics associated with a brand name. We could also state that a brand's personality represents the behavioral modes which are defined for the (inanimate) object of an exchange relationship.

It is through the perceived personality that individuals are able to gain useful information about the brand, information which would not otherwise be communicated and which becomes the basis for building relationships – and not just those of exchange.

The fact that there can be numerous levels of interaction between individuals' personalities and that of the brand does not necessarily mean that individuals can be identified on the basis of what they buy. We are well aware that self-representation can be linked only partially to the consumption of a soft drink or the wearing of an article of clothing; it is achieved in numerous ways, above all through the development of social relationships. It is true however that brands sometimes act as a social catalyst. It could be said that they represent one of the ways people affirm themselves and that they have a precise role in developing relationships, even if they are not the main generator.

As in every human relationship, individuals tend to draw elements of reassurance and acceptance as much as those of diffidence and hostility from a brand's personality. Individuals tend to grant trust and this trust grows in time through the progressive evaluation of behaviors. Building relationships with its customers means a brand must gain their trust, and personality plays an important role in fulfilling this task. A brand must therefore portray an image of competence, professionalism and effectiveness; but this is only part of the personality: the consumer must be able to feel it – perceive it – instinctively. In short, they must feel an instinctive trust toward the brand which goes beyond the seriousness with which it may carry out its task. The consumer does not want just to be won over, they want to be seduced.

The personality required of a brand can also vary depending on its consumers and the occasions of usage. There are situations in which the relationship between consumer and brand is based on completely rational choices, devoid of emotional involvement – just as happens with people. When we choose a lawyer, we are interested primarily in whether he or she can win the case, not whether they are nice or not. Individuals can develop indifference and little interest toward each other, but this does not mean that they do not enter into relations or relationships aimed exclusively at achieving a specified goal. If this is true of human beings, there are ever fewer cases in which a brand can limit itself to supplying only an image of competence and professionalism. This part of the story alone is able less and less to develop relationships with the public and become a reason for buying.

In some cases, the relationship between brand and consumer can translate into real friendship. The brand gradually communicates until it becomes a friend. The consumer first chooses the brand with diffidence, but then starts to react toward it, expressing in some way what they think of it. Only afterwards does the consumer transform the answer into a more complex relationship which can sometimes take on a connotation of friendship.[5]

Entering into a friendship with brands changes totally the relationship we have with them: they are no longer linked to a relationship of exchange, but become more and more interconnected with sentimental ties. By definition a friend is someone who is willing to listen to you, someone you know and who knows you, who respects you, someone you can put your trust in. Often it is a friend who spurs you into action, who encourages and supports; who becomes a guide in difficult moments and someone to share a joke with in more carefree ones. It has been argued that brands are able to carry out all these roles, taking on the appearance of the friend and the traits the two parties have in common.[6]

A friend has need of only a few words to encourage us, to spur us on. He knows us, knows what feelings to work on. Similarly, three simple words, "Just Do It," are all that Nike needs to invite its public to act, to do. The important thing is not the result: what counts is doing something, taking the first step and, by going for a run, expressing your desire for freedom and evasion, overcoming your anxieties and fears about personal limits or performance, supported by a friend's encouragement.

Like a person, a brand can be reassuring, exciting, anticonformist, sexy and much more besides. The most seductive brands are like a person everyone would like to be seen with, that everyone would like to know or, at least in some way "incorporate" into the building of their own life. Brands able to build such relationships not only have a strong personality; they also know how to excel in numerous dimensions, convincing their public of their importance.[7]

The character traits of brands do not necessarily have to be related to the benefits offered. Who says, for example, that a computer brand cannot be fun and anti-conformist and that it must portray only an image of professionalism, reliability and competence? PCs pervade our daily routines; nothing is any longer immune to their presence, from the workplace to the home, but the prevalent association has been one of an instrument of work. Thus a technical idea of the product prevails which characterizes the personality of the brands associated with it, inspired by ideas of effectiveness, reliability and performance. This does not mean that it is impossible to build a personality which goes beyond the hard character of the product and takes on a softer one which is therefore calm and fun, and makes it possible, particularly for people who see using a computer as something compulsory, to build a lighter and more free and easy relationship with technology. We believe that the correlation between the benefits a brand offers and its personality should become less and less direct. The identification of a brand with a category of products does not necessarily mean adoption of the traits which identify functional capacity.

Apple teaches us how the same product, which usually has this hard – and therefore unable to excite – connotation, can take on a totally different identity based on the personality of the brand which identifies it. The Mac has been able to rescue the computer from the ghetto of routine and give it a new role which is not necessarily relegated to the working environment: the computer is also a real spare-time companion, attributed with a more modern, fun, spiritual – and therefore more up-to-date – meaning. We could say that, being the first to understand that technology's social function is linked not only to the sphere of work and productivity, Apple took the computer's tie off.

With Apple, the computer has become not simply a product but the basis for new narration processes in the lives of individuals by encouraging them to recount new stories related not only to their existences but also to their imagination. With Apple, technology has lost its "have to do" image to take on a new one of "like to do," thus significantly reducing its coercive character.

In the semiotic approach, a brand's identity is the combination of all the discourses about it by all the subjects involved in its generation. It seems evident that brands are not only the fruit of their designers, but also the direct consequence of the relationship that they manage to establish with their public, and even more than this: where brand identity is strong, the relationship tends also to involve those who are not part of its public.

In order for a brand to build an effective identity it must present itself as credible and legitimate and be able to excite affection. In other words, it must meet all those requirements which are indispensable for building relationships between individuals.[8] Consider, for example, the sports drink Powerade: the reference to power goes well with the product's function of recharging the body, reintegrating the minerals lost when doing physically strenuous sports.

Legitimacy, on the other hand, concerns the brand's capacity to develop a spatial–temporal transcendence. Every brand is the child of its history and its past, and its links with its roots allow it to remain up-to-date. There are brands which seem to have existed forever – for example Coca-Cola – simply because they have known how to develop a spatial–temporal transcendence.[9] One of the consequences of global-ization is that some brands have come to be characterizing elements of mankind; as well as a brand's history, its presence in every remote corner of the world makes it something more than a label put on a product: a real social phenomenon. The link with their own roots is another feature which brands and human nature have in common. Think of the social value of ancestors. We can say that a person is ill bred: this literally means that somebody, usually the parents, has not carried out their educational role effectively. Consider also the saying that a person "comes from a good family": this links them to the social acceptance that their ancestors have had. A brand's legitimization can, in part, be found in genetic transmission. However, the generational replication of the model must not just be copying; in order to adapt to the times and propose new values, a brand must be extremely careful not to depreciate its "genetic patrimony."

The spatial–temporal transcendence which legitimizes the brand as a leading actor in postmodern society must not however be interpreted as an incentive to maintain its status quo. Brands which in a specific his-torical and cultural context are unable to interpret the changes which are happening can lose their public's affection, and thus risk extinction. The placing of a brand's identity, even a brand which has deep roots in time, in the current framework of tendencies becomes an extremely critical factor in a modern business organization's competitive action.

It is precisely those brands which have achieved a strong spatial–temporal transcendence, those same brands which seem to have existed for ever, which consumers ask to play a primary role as mediator between modernity and past. Often the balance between these two ten-dencies is difficult to attain. Cases of brands which have tried to renew themselves and so risked damaging what they had built in decades of history are not rare. Think of when Coca-Cola launched New Coke on the market. The new identity built by proposing a new taste and new graphics, and anticipated by a powerful teaser campaign, sent American consumers into crisis. It was not just the formula of a fizzy drink which had been changed, but the soul of what represented an authentic American icon had been stolen.[10] The history of American society was the history of Coca-Cola and changing the formula meant in some way denying it. The affective response of consumers had the upper hand, expressing an emphatic rejection of New Coke. But, what other reaction was to be expected from consumers when such changes regarded a brand which is so deeply rooted in their cultural model that it is able to change the color of Santa Claus's clothes? (In the US, Santa Claus was traditionally dressed in green until Coca-Cola launched a massive advertising campaign in the 1950s in which he wore Coca-Cola's "company colors.") The management of Coke bitterly realized that adapting the brand to a changed social context had to be done in other ways and not simply by modifying the graphics and formulation. Coca-Cola had to become an interpreter of the cultural changes which were going on in society; to this end, the company now employs street teams, groups of young people who identify the emerging trends among their peers in discos, bars, shopping centers and squares.

A brand's identity can be visible as well as verbal, something which contributes to strengthening the process of the brand's assimilation to a human being. Individuals often communicate without being aware of the fact: we can gain a lot of information about a person's personality by the way they move, speak, dress and gesticulate. A brand's verbal identity represents the translation of promises, personality and positioning within a system of rules used to communicate the brand.[11] Promises of personality and positioning must be translated into a system of symbols, colors, shapes, characters and images.[12] We expect a product to be able to change in time: think, for example, of how Kodak had to revise its product following the digital revolution in the photographic sector. At the same time, we expect the associations – music, colors, style of communication, distribution channels and testimonials – to change. To sum up, everything must be able to adapt to the times. A brand must stay up-to-date and this requires updating the associations connected with it.[13]

Values, because of the deeper connotation they have, present a more stable character inasmuch as we expect them to remain intact and to continue to act as a relational adhesive and a "conceptual place" which is always current and where the consumer can find comfortable refuge.

In this sense brands have traits in common with human beings, taking on an ever more anthropomorphic nature. Just as we evaluate the evolution of a person, so must we evaluate the evolution of a brand, expecting this to change with time: an individual cannot remain a student for ever – sooner or later they will begin work and eventually retire. Moreover, it is also plausible that the associations which surround that person tend to change with time. In fact, tastes, meeting places, ways of dressing and thinking will change; new interests will be born and new priorities will be defined. Just think of how a fifty-year-old with long hair, psychedelic shirt and sneakers would not be up-to-date today. Changes at the level of associations are therefore part of the evolution of individuals and are accepted as such on a social level. What is not accepted, on the other hand, is a change in values. Values must represent the infrastructure of the evolutionary process, a thin line of continuity between past and present, and individuals consequently are required to be consistent on this front, at least to some extent.

What has been said about people is also valid for brands. Values are the main elements of consistency and cohesion which surround a brand and they become the basis for motivating people to believe in it, and therefore the reason for choosing that brand compared with others. Maintaining a certain stability in the value system means however that, at least in its deepest essence, a brand must resist change. What anchors a value to a brand becomes the reason for believing in it. Belief in a brand represents what that brand can do in the world. We can think here about those few brands which have managed to achieve a recognized stature on a global scale. In the majority of cases they are commodities and therefore it could seem paradoxical to think, for example, that a sweetened fizzy drink can do something for the world. In reality, though, what counts is not the function or the associations linked perhaps to the evolution of social customs as much as the values which that banal product, where it is identified by a name, can convey: for example social brotherhood, a theme which characterized Coca-Cola's communication for years.

There must however be complete coherence between the values and the relative ability of the brand to perform an active role in society. In fact, consumers tend to be less and less forgiving of incongruence in values, and deplore it more than certain functional limits or defects.

A brand that can propose a system of credible values becomes a moral guide for society but also a guide for a multiple series of decisions. We must however be careful when talking about what is "moral": this is the only argument consumers will not accept jokes or even irony about; the imperative is "be coherent or die." The market will push those brands which have betrayed consumers on values beyond its borders, in ways which are quicker and quicker and harder and harder to reverse.

Every brand, like a person, has its character, possesses the unique traits which configure its ways of conducting relationships, the expression and demonstration of its own inner universe. It goes without saying that each character has a temperament which can take on numerous representations: happy, melancholic, austere and closed, extrovert and simple, friendly or standoffish. What is important for us is that the success of a brand is linked to its character, just as is the development of interpersonal relations between individuals. A singular recognizable character is able to confer on the brand those distinctive and peculiar recognizable exterior characteristics which are necessary to stand out from contemporary crowded competitive scenarios. Often this character reflects that of the founder or top management as if it were a natural process of genetic transmission.

CHAPTER 5

THE BRAND'S GENETIC CLOCK[1]

Like all living organisms, brands need to develop relations with their surrounding environment. Interacting with their environment, brands adapt to change through a process of constant learning. As in the natural process of evolution of the species, only those brands which adapt easily to changes in the environment by applying acquired knowledge are able to survive and regenerate: the great brands therefore are those which, thanks to this process, are able to develop new skills to cope with the changes which characterize the evolution of society and therefore of markets.

In his book *The Living Company*, Arie de Geus describes his meeting with a biochemical zoologist from the University of Berkeley, Professor Allan Wilson.[2] Professor Wilson has developed a theory centered on the fact that inside the molecules of the genes of every species there is a "genetic clock." On the basis of this theory, the molecules of the genetic material change in accordance with the constant rhythm of the evolutionary process of organisms, with temporal modalities varying from species to species. By means of biochemical analysis of the genetic material, it has been possible to measure the evolution of each species on the basis of the number of "genetic signs" they have been subjected to in order to reach their current state. The species with the most genetic signs are those which evolve the most; using the metaphor proposed by Professor Wilson, they are those which have more ticks to their genetic clock. Analysis of the behaviors of these species reveals a quicker evolutionary process, the result of greater intergenerational learning. Wilson particularly maintains that this greater acceleration in the evolutionary process takes place in those species which have three particular aptitudes, namely: innovation, social propagation and mobility.

– *Innovation* is the ability to develop new behaviors, both at individual and collective level; it is this capacity which makes it possible for the species to exploit the environment they are in.

– *Social propagation* is the transmission of these new capabilities among the species's members by means of communication processes.
– *Mobility* is the tendency to move collectively, to gather together and move *en masse* rather than remain permanently in conditions of greater isolation.

Wilson demonstrated his theory by studying the behavior of the blue tit in Great Britain. There, milk was delivered to the doorstep every day. Up until the twentieth century, the bottles did not have tops, so the milk became a tempting drink not only for human beings but also for two species of bird of comparable size, blue tits and robins; the birds had learnt to get the milk out of the bottles and their digestive systems immediately adapted to this new diet. Subsequently, the bottles were fitted with aluminum tops and only the blue tit adapted to this new situation by learning to peck through the aluminum. By about 1950, the whole blue tit population had learnt to break the aluminum foil which sealed the bottles, thanks to the process of social propagation and mobility. The blue tit had innovated its behavior, adapting itself to a change in its environment; the robin had not. The explanation lay precisely in the blue tit's social propagation process: the blue tits spread the skill of the individual to all members of the species. In fact, blue tits gather together in groups which are characterized by a high level of mobility, while robins are more individual and territorial and tend to communicate with other members of the species in prevalently antagonistic ways.

On the basis of this study, Wilson observed how those birds which flock together seem to learn more quickly and therefore evolve more quickly, thus increasing their chances of survival.

To support Professor Wilson's theory, we interviewed Luciano Binaglia, biochemist at the University of Perugia, who supplied us with further elements to develop a model of brand analysis based on the application of the principles of evolutionary and genetic science to the life and evolution of brands.

Binaglia states that each species is subject to mutations with different effectiveness. Cells have mechanisms to protect against mutations, but where the levels of protection are less "precise," there is a moving forward. Cells which mutate toward a worsening of their quality and their ability to interact with the environment disappear; those, on the other hand, whose mutations lead to interacting with the environment survive. The same Darwinian concept of evolution of the species means that each change allows greater compatibility with the environment. Consider, for example, monkeys which have learnt to wash their food in sea water to remove beach sand from it or those animals which have learnt to break coconuts using tools which are present in nature, such as branches and stones.

Professor Binaglia maintains however that it is important to highlight the fact that in biology there is also a resistance to change. Each individual has a balance (cellular homeostasis) which it seeks to maintain and when some external pressure threatens that balance, the system itself tries to "hit" it. Nevertheless, the cell protection system is not always effective: there are external factors which can modify the genetic heritage. When that happens, there can be variations which lead to death in the balanced condition which the cell itself had initially "chosen." In this case, the cell tries to "commit suicide"; where this does not happen, and the modified gene takes on a meaning for the living being, maybe by providing a new capacity to interact with the environment, we see an evolutionary leap. However, where the modifications undergone by the cells are excessive, there may be a process which leads the cell to privilege suicide over mutation. After a certain period of time, the cell which has accumulated a number of errors must inevitably die. Binaglia maintains that in order to modify the life of a being and raise it to a higher level, that higher level must have a greater capacity to resist changes in the environment in order to have an easier life than the being had previously. This comes about via a process of multiplying the genetic codes or the mechanisms which regulate the codes.

From the research carried out by Wilson, and Binaglia's indications, we can draw useful means for interpreting the development of innovative and strong brands able to survive in the face of the evolving context in which they find themselves operating. As in the evolutionary process of species, many brands continue to be born, evolve, change their own way of being, and also die, but only those which are able to learn methods and responses which allow them to adapt themselves to change will be able to evolve. To return to de Geus's metaphor, great brands are those which are more similar to the blue tits than to the robins.

Unlike man – who is born, grows up, gets old and dies – a brand should not be subject to any life cycle: according to Fabris, brands have the possibility of making – or, better, the duty to make – themselves immortal by changing their meanings, moving in line with socio-cultural changes, continually reviewing their own attributes and missions.[3] We ourselves cannot agree with Fabris's claim which, although provocative, denies the mortality of brands. Every brand is destined to die sooner or later; compared with man, however, a brand – like a postmodern Arabian phoenix – does have the possibility and the capability of rising again. Consider, for example, those brands which were filed away as "forgotten," but were then re-proposed and brought up-to-date again by other brands able to believe in their potential as linked to buyers' nostalgia.

It is true however that a brand is a constant target of numerous attempts on its life. And this danger comes not only from competitors but also from the agents in every social sphere which the brand, maybe against its will, enters in some way during its existential process. A brand must therefore be protected, looked after and accompanied when it is growing up; it must be taught how to defend itself. To put it briefly, the real duty is not the brand's, but that of its creators and managers, who must concern themselves with keeping it in good health and preserving it in the best way possible. A brand is threatened by those who imitate it and/or copy it, by non-brands, by the unfaithful, by recession; brand-killers are everywhere, even hidden among a brand's own consumers, ready to give it the kiss of Judas, maybe on just a whim or because they have got tired of it or because they are ready for new adventures.[4]

In an ever more threatening environment, where it is more and more difficult to distinguish between friends and enemies, a brand must reinforce its dominant features, manage its own distinctiveness, and pursue excellence in performance and communication, so that it develops antibodies against the numerous new viruses which may attack it. It must develop a strong capacity to adapt to historical and social changes in order to be able to detect the enemies who often appear under a false identity, but also to protect it from itself and its reluctance to question itself. Protecting a brand means that the companies which own it must try and predict all the possible crises which might affect it, even those which are hard to imagine, and define ways of managing them in advance.

Medical science has dedicated a large part of its resources to the study of the human genome, identifying in this complex formula many of the answers to the questions which research continually poses. Brands are ahead of man in this field, partly because of the lack of relevant legislation: a brand is free to modify its DNA, and therefore its most profound essence, by reformulating its genetic code without distorting its own identity. Thus, compared with man, a brand has more alternatives available to fight the ills which afflict it; but prevention is important for brands, just as it is for humans. A brand must identify the threats and the cells which can spread an illness, or the part of its organism which can generate problems, and not just intervene on a therapeutic level once the illness is already widespread. Thus for brands too, as a famous advertisement claimed, "Prevention is better than cure."

The fact that a brand has DNA is closely correlated to its "human" nature. A brand is born to distinguish one product from another one which otherwise would have seemed identical. The founder and management play a decisive role in defining the brand's genetic code, and when management changes, alterations to the genetic code could also occur. The pedigree of a brand is often found in the consanguinity of the brand and its mentor or founder. When Apple dismissed its founder and mentor, Steve Jobs, the company did not simply cut off its own head but also radically upset its DNA: the identification of the brand with its founder's genetic code was total; without its founder's "blood," Apple had no clear identity. Soon, on the edge of collapse, the company felt the need to reinstall its missing code – its last chance of salvation: Jobs was recalled and the brand's genetic code rebuilt. It was Jobs who had given life to the species, it was Jobs who was the "originating code" of the stock. Apple could have changed, but the breed would have lost its identity.[5] Besides, as we have already stated, Jobs had not limited himself to founding a company, but had founded a creed: getting rid of Jobs meant in effect getting rid of the prophet.

In the evolution of brands, we can see the features of human evolution described by Darwin. Like man, a brand is destined to fight for survival and therefore the principles which rule nature are similar to those of the market since in both cases we are talking about inaccessible and competitive places where survival is the imperative. The fittest survives – those who can adapt first to the change in conditions. Sometimes a brand must also mutate to be able to adapt to changes in its environment and one that cannot adapt dies, just as happens with the selection of species.

We find the same principle proposed by biological science in Michael Porter's elaboration of the concept of moving from "what is" to "what may be." It is a movement at the level of perception which rejects the status quo and seeks to make brands and companies evolve toward a subsequent state through innovation and imagination. None of this can happen however without the process of learning, constant innovation and mobility which is connected to the exchange of information and knowledge.

Brands are entities with a long-lasting personality and based on a special combination of physical, functional and psychological values. It is this special combination of values which leads to a brand having a set of attributes which differentiate its offering from that of others in the competitive scenario. Consumers have to deal with a vast quantity of information about a brand, information which is stored in their minds and becomes the basis for continually reviewing, adjusting and reformulating their judgement every time they come into contact with the brand. A brand, therefore, like every living organism, is not a static subject but must evolve, without however underestimating the danger that too many wrong variations can lead to suicide. The genetic clock is running and a brand whose clock ticks too slowly dies. At this point, we should recall the premise put forward by Professor Wilson regarding the basic characteristics of the species which evolve most quickly: innovation, social promulgation and mobility.

A brand is born from an idea. Ideas come to people who are curious and imaginative. These people demonstrate behavior which is similar to, though more complex than, that of the blue tits: astute observation, vivid imagination and the ability to recognize the information patterns which lead to embarking on positive action. All this can be described as a "question of mentality."

Every mentality represents a structure of knowledge, whose primary attributes are differentiation and integration:

– Differentiation is the number of elements which make up a person's or organization's knowledge.
– Integration is the organization's or person's ability to synthesize the various elements.

Mentality is crucial for the success and development of brands, and it can be defined beginning with the studies carried out by cognitive psychology on how people attribute a sense to the world and how they interact with it. Human beings are limited in their capacity to absorb information processes – particularly if we consider how they are increasingly exposed to real waves of information in every moment of their lives.

The current mentality of a person or organization acts as a guide in collecting and interpreting new information, thus reducing the risk of overlap. Where mentality and new information are in harmony the current mentality is reinforced, producing change; where there is discordance the current mentality maintains its status quo. Our mentality in fact helps us to avoid information paralysis, but at the same time it can make us blind when we are faced with alternative visions of reality. The least-conscious part of our mind emerges in relation to its rigidity in maintaining the status quo. This is extremely paralyzing in a dynamic context such as that of modern markets where brands face challenges every day.

Seeing reality from a different angle leads to developing new ways of behaving. The key to a brand's success and evolution resides today more than ever in its capacity to adopt a different point of view in respect of the opportunities offered by the market. A 1995 report by Coca-Cola did not analyze the soft drink market but posed the question of which market was the least developed. The answer was astonishing: the human body. People can go without most things for an entire day and even for more than a day. But every day each of the nearly 6 billion human beings on the planet consumes 64 ounces of liquid to live. Coca-Cola saw its existing market in only two of these ounces. There is also the success of Starbucks, based on developing a model of consumption – the coffee bar – which had always been in front of everybody's eyes but which nobody had managed to transform into a planetary experience, as Schultz has.

The market has also given us an example of how looking at the same object from a different angle can give life to an extraordinarily successful brand. Think of how Crocs have turned an item of work clothing – the clogs worn by medical and paramedical staff – into a custom phenomenon, transforming doctors and nurses into real trend-setters. Just adding strong colors and decorating them with jewels and little pendants, made a *déjà vu* object into an extraordinary market success.[6]

The hands of the genetic clock move faster in people and organizations with an open mentality, who do not passively accept the barriers imposed by the market and society. Moreover, as happens when birds assemble together, the information gathered by observing reality is diffused through human contact, thus creating a collective mentality. This means that organizations, despite not having a brain, must equip themselves with collective intelligence which transcends the single individual. Let's take as an example Procter & Gamble, which is an effective representation of how an organization can develop a collective mentality centered on market leadership. The brands the organization owns and continually launches are born to be the best in the category. It is no coincidence that a significant part of Procter's research is aimed at the consumer in order to trace, delineate and continually update the meanings and values which are important for their brands' existence, and subsequently identify how consumers can absorb a brand's meanings and values.

Mentality evolves through a process of interaction with the surrounding environment. Our current mentalities are based on present knowledge. Therefore, it is necessary to avoid being trapped in the "knowledge of what we know" syndrome and look for new stimuli in order to discover new knowledge. This is the principle at the basis of that process better known as *innovation*. Managing to acquire different interpretations of reality makes it possible to have a less banal, more articulated, more interesting view of the surrounding environment.

CHAPTER 6

GENETIC FAMILIARITY: THE BRAND IN SEARCH OF ITS ROOTS

According to a simplified definition, a brand represents the relationship which is established between the consumer and the company. This idea implies that brand planning must involve *tout court* the entire organization of the company and not be the exclusive prerogative of the marketing department, as often seems to happen in the workings of a large number of firms.[1] In fact, in many companies the management still continues to believe that defining brand strategy is something to be done in the secret rooms of the marketing department. This is an extremely shortsighted view which decreases the brand's competitive capacity.

Relegating brands to the sole functional area of marketing is the consequence of a management approach which is now out-of-date, an approach which sees the brand as a private matter between marketing and sales. According to this view, the marketing department had to create the brand and the sales office had the task of distributing the products.[2] It is no coincidence in fact that today the objectives set for salesmen are still expressed in terms of sales volume and not in terms of brand performance. Selling a brand imposes behavior which is much more complex than that needed to sell a product. In fact, if to distribute a product a salesman must be able to convince his interlocutor of the benefits offered and that these are congruous with the price, then selling a brand requires a holistic approach which makes it possible to go beyond the functional and economic aspects of the brand in order to exalt those which are more immaterial, emotive and sensorial.

Today, more than ever, the success of a brand depends on its being shared across the entire organization it emanates from. The alignment between internal and external needs and perceptions must become the basis for developing any brand strategy. This means that the entire organization must conform to the brand, thus creating a perfect overlap between the internal values and the values the brand will convey in the outside world. A brand's values must express the values of the organization and therefore of the individuals who make up that organization, at every level of the hierarchy. This need is felt even more strongly in what Nordstrom and Ridderstrale identify as "the surplus society," in which not only the products but also the firms and the people who are part of them seem to be increasingly more similar: they have similar educational backgrounds, they do similar jobs and they have similar ideas.[3] From this general homologation derives another, which leads to the production of objects of similar quality and price: according to the authors, this is the main reason for the increasing incapacity of modern brands to differentiate themselves from others. It goes without saying that if all companies draw on the same organizational and management models, maybe implementing the latest fashion proposed by management science or recruiting future managers from the same business schools, there will tend to be an army of clones characterized only by different names.

There is more. In recent years, companies have invested heavily in product development and in the evolution of management systems with routes which can overlap, thus obtaining results which are less effective than those they could have achieved by investing part of those resources in both developing their brand and positioning it both in the market and within the organization.[4] Of course, by this we do not mean that companies should not continue to invest in research and development or refine their organizational and managerial models; but the effectiveness of these efforts can be invalidated if not supported by careful brand-positioning management.

In his latest, provocative, work, Nordstrom puts forward a comparison between modern companies and karaoke. People who go to a karaoke bar imitate great singers, but, the author claims, just imitating someone does not lead to success. What is needed is to escape from the monotony of songs which have been sung before, and to be able to write and sing new ones. The world, he says, is full of "karaoke companies," precisely because of the proliferation of distracting ideas like benchmarking and best practice, which have led companies to "play the *same music*," merely limiting themselves at the most to rearranging it or interpreting it in a different way. Looking at what others do makes organizations shortsighted about the need for continual innovation: they put aside the idea of "What can we do?" which is the generating principle of growth in the markets. This approach will make it more and more difficult for companies to differentiate themselves from others if the others immediately copy: the advantage of the fast mover will tend to get smaller and smaller, forcing the innovator to adopt a policy of continual growth, which becomes a real "company obsession." Nordstrom claims, moreover, that today the critical productive resources are not infrastructures, buildings or machinery, but the skills of human beings. Organizations are increasingly poorer in talented people, that is the irreplaceable resources which really hold the key to competitiveness – or, to use Nordstrom's metaphor again, the capacity to write songs rather than sing those of others. Today talent represents a new form of competence and, as Pink states, talented people need organizations less than organizations need talented people.[5] And, what is more, talented people want to work in an organization where they can sense aspiration toward a transcendental goal.

So companies find themselves having to fight on two fronts: first, the traditional one for customers and, second, for the talented individuals they need to attract to and keep in their organizations. Therefore, they must be able to capitalize on people's skills and learn the art of creation from their customers.

If many companies have understood that getting and keeping talented people makes it possible to generate brands which are robust, consistent and have a strong distinctive capacity, few have understood how their organizational models must be structured to enable those talented people to grow and develop their abilities. We are faced with the same problems as those soccer clubs who bid against one another for the promising youngster of the moment, only for the successful club to then leave him sitting on the bench all season, losing form and morale.

Hierarchical organizational models in fact sacrifice company talents by behavior which verges on paternalism, perhaps limiting themselves to creating new opportunities for talents via old practices like job rotation or planned career paths. In reality the concept of talent implies that of *difference*: talented people are simply *different*, often less or non-conventional, and they suffer in rigid frameworks and traditional organizational models where they are unable to fully express their own personal qualities. This not only generates problems in finding talent within the organization by creating organizational barriers which stop talent revealing itself, but also leads to difficulties in drawing in talented people from the outside market through not developing the attractive qualities they are looking for. Talent management therefore requires new organizational models which allow the talented to express themselves by moving outside preconceived frameworks. Some companies have understood these problems better than others and have adopted less-conservative organizational models in which talented people have more chance of negotiating opportunities for development and emotional gratification.[6]

It is in fact no coincidence that such companies have used branding techniques to attract talented people, developing their ability to identify the most dangerous competitors in terms of being able to attract talent and having the most important attributes for building that attractiveness.

Faced with a surplus, the customer has an infinite range of choice, and this means thinking of individuals less and less in terms of rational principles and more and more in terms of their capacity to respond to emotional stimuli. This makes it necessary for firms to take on personnel who are able, at the same time, to both get excited and to excite; in short, to paraphrase the famous *Star Wars* trilogy, may the force – the true generating principle of a brand – be with you. If in fact technological innovation can in some way be imitated, then the ability to excite represents a character trait of brands that is the fruit of a process of development which is similar to that of human beings and therefore requires much time for its formation.

Understanding what the consumer wants in a particular moment, by commissioning research which is very often useless when there is no clear internal view of the brand, is an activity which cannot be given up; we believe however that the analysis should be extended not only to the company's external context but also to its internal context. A brand must in fact answer a series of questions, beginning above all with those regarding its *sense of its own existence.*

Thinking of a brand as a living organism, we can find similarities to human existence which can help us define the link between brand and company in a simplified way. When a parent is bringing up a child, they usually tend to plan that child's life – at least up until a certain stage. Planning a child's life means that the parent has to question their own, has to evaluate their own model of life and whether this can be a valid reference model for the child.

A company must behave in a similar way with its favorite child, the brand. Asking itself questions about what it wants for its children is therefore not simply rhetoric on the part of the company. The company must, above all, ask itself complex questions linked to its ambitions, the stories it wants to tell, what it thinks can act as an example and guide for the world. Questioning itself obliges the company, like a parent, to undertake the difficult task of judging, even critically, its own past and transferring it to the present in order to decide which elements it should break with and which maintain in its relationship with the future. It is in fact not rare to find parents who decide to encourage their child to choose a different path from the one they have taken, precisely to avoid the errors they made or perhaps in the hope that their children may have a more active, more gratifying, more decisive role in society.

In developing brand strategy, procreation becomes only one phase in the process – certainly an important one, but not the most critical. What counts is to mould the values of the brand, its ways of social interacting and its identity, and this means evaluating not so much how others might judge it as the representation that the organization will have of itself. It is clear that a brand, like a child, is the result of the identity of the company which owns it; but the identity must be "questioned" by means of a process of "company psychoanalysis," in order to build up a clear view of itself which may reflect on the brand's identity.

The relationship between parent and child includes, among other things, teaching, recounting life experiences and moral indicators; this is how it must also be for a company and its brand. For this, it is not enough to use a series of educational techniques drawn from organizational disciplines; what is really needed is a path which makes it possible to really build up a value system which is shared between parent, child and all the members of the extended family.

Many companies believe this objective can be achieved merely by adopting formal tools such as, for example, a written mission statement, the effectiveness of which is rather arguable. As Edwards and Day maintain, a company mission cannot be limited to the "flaccid" formalizing of a written formula full of rhetoric and common sayings linked to marketing disciplines, but must represent a real belief.[7] The main distinction between a mission declaration and the promulgation of a belief lies actually in the fact that a belief is not a simple formal indication destined to be forgotten day after day, but becomes a real inspiration, the main generator and element which joins together the activities of the individuals. Creating a shared company identity therefore means going beyond the simple literal element put up at the entrance of the company's headquarters or as part of the heading of the company's home page – all of which would seem to have an almost entirely decorative function at the most; in other words, it means creating something which cannot be read or recited but has to be felt inside, written in the hearts and minds of the members of the organization.[8]

Brand leaders are in fact characterized by a strong potential for passion, and the companies they manage do not have employees but real volunteers who decide to devote their lives to making their capacity to differentiate themselves from other brands prevail in the markets. To acquire this feeling, individuals do not want to and must not feel that they are the same as each other; they want to have something they can believe in deeply, something they can sacrifice part of their lives to. For this objective to prevail in an organization, the bosses must concentrate not simply on how to make money, but also on how to make money the means for arriving at something greater.[9] The brands which are able to generate these sentiments know how to transfer this real internal passion to the outside, by also using informal mechanisms such as word of mouth. It is this passion which makes great brands vibrate, lifting them well above the objective dimension and creating a sense of community, of social appropriation and sharing around them.

The goals which drive the members of an organization are linked less and less to economic ideas (which can be arid and ascetic, however necessary) and more and more to higher values such as the ability to influence the course of events in some way and to contribute to the wellbeing of humanity. It is necessary to inspire the action of individuals with something that can make them feel part of a unique process of social change – actors and not just spectators who are able therefore to contribute in some way to improving human wellbeing. This objective can be achieved via the brand, and therefore the men and women of the organization will transfer all their natural passion to the brand.

Apple is one of the most effective examples of this. When Apple launched its famous advertising campaign, "Think Different," it did not limit itself to simply challenging consumers to choose a product which was different from the technological reference standards; with that campaign Apple mounted a challenge to the whole world, pushing itself beyond the preconceived order of things, against all the prevailing rules, claiming its own aspirations and desire for expression. Before the challenge was launched on the market, the challenge of diversity was launched within the company itself. Being an Apple employee meant being a dreamer, feeling different from the surrounding world in some way and committed to promoting difference. The image of the headquarters with a pirate flag hoisted over the roof is one of the most exciting iconic representations in the history of marketing. The pirate emblem symbolized the company's diversity, based on a different view of the world and the role information technology should play in human development. To be pirates meant challenging the order the great colossi wanted to impose and affirming a new cultural paradigm, overcoming the homologating view of information technology as a rationalizing and economizing instrument, in order to look for another which assigned it a much greater role in the progress and development of man's wellbeing.[10] Apple's challenge was based on social diversity by tackling themes such as existential dissatisfaction, social criticism and inner alienation in order to decree the end of a world considered "wrong." By means of a product, Cupertino's company eludes the conventional canons of marketing promises, raises the aim and proposes new models of behavior and society by overcoming a world branded by the obligation of work, its restricting hours and routine. Working for Apple reflected the nature of this challenge: it could not be heavy and it had to become something exciting, enjoyable and gratifying. It is no coincidence in fact that in one of the ads which followed the launch of the first Macintosh, employees were shown playing squash during office hours.

The workers at Apple, from top management to the switchboard operator, did not feel they were just employees, but rather that in their veins flowed the blood of pirates, always ready for boarding, ready to affirm the vision of the world which the company's founder had created and which they were prepared to devote their existence to realizing. The team which launched the first Mac was made up of people who were persuaded not that they were going to change the world of information technology forever, but that they were going to change the *whole* world. When Steve Jobs contacted John Sculley to try to convince him to leave Pepsi Cola (where at the time he was vice-president) to go and work for Apple, he did not talk about earnings, strategies and business models, but simply asked him if he wanted to continue selling sugared water all his life or change the world. The visionary charm of Jobs hit the mark again.

It seems evident therefore that the success of a brand depends more and more on its vision being shared by members of the organization, and that for them to become real ambassadors of the brand they must be not only informed but also emotionally involved and effective participants. Faced with movements like that against globalization which are more and more organized and intent on questioning the very existence of a brand, a brand itself must today become a movement and put its most convinced activists – its employees and consumers – into the field.[11] The entire organization must support the promotion of the brand, not least to avoid investments made in external promotion losing their effectiveness. The brand must therefore be able to pervade every conversation, every place, every gesture inside the company, with the aim of making the identity of the company and that of the brand one, thus ensuring that its strategic management is solid, effective and long-lasting.[12]

The brands which have a strong personality have been able to excel in some of their dimensions and have known how to convince the public of their importance. They are however also brands that have known how to build a clear internal representation of their meaning. This meaning also includes their limits, which are the same as those of human beings and which condition their chances of movement. They have been able to demonstrate intellectual honesty by not claiming credentials which would have taken them beyond those limits into fields of action which could be seen as incongruous with and therefore as undermining the creed.

Coherence therefore is the source of legitimization. When McDonald's tries to promote the nutritional values of its menus, it loses coherence, since it is not socially justified in doing so. The associations which consumers develop toward the McDonald's brand are mainly connected with taste and entertainment.

Empirical evidence confirms what we have said: where company vision is strong and shared by its members, this vision reflects on the brand, strengthening the perception on the part of consumers. These are the brands which are capable of building a solid and consistent identity and an easily identifiable personality, able to emerge from the slimy swamps of modern competitive scenarios.

CHAPTER 7

BRAND NAME: "THE IMPORTANCE OF BEING EARNEST"

Naming a brand, just like naming a human being, means christening it in some way. When a name is chosen for a child, there can be many reasons behind that choice other than the desire to confer an identity, a character or a personality by means of a particular name: for example, there may be a family ancestor with the same name, or the wish to identify with a historical character or, in any case, with myths from the past. Giving a brand a name almost takes on the function of planning and prognosticating the future and implies, in some way, identification with a destiny.[1]

The name is a brand's primary indicator and represents its first point of contact with the outside world, a primary factor in its being remembered and becoming famous. However, it is important not to exaggerate the importance of the name by pretending it can do more than it is effectively capable of. To go back to the idea of the brand being a modern narrator, we need to underline that the name does not have the capacity to sustain sensible discourse inasmuch as, by itself, it is unable to tell the whole story which the brand, on the other hand, with its multiple dimensions, can propose. The name of a movie can be part of the poster, which certainly serves to attract and stimulate and can encourage people to see the film, but it does not reveal the whole plot. Therefore, its function is to anticipate the contents by synthesizing only in part the tales related to it, and not by uttering the whole narration.

The above is not meant to diminish the importance of the role the name performs; we well know in fact that the associations linked to the name of a brand can be more important than those linked to the product.[2] A brand name has within it the capacity to propose clear and descriptive meanings, as well as to appeal to the consumer's imagination. Consumers evaluate a product which is identified with a brand in two ways: the first is linked to the product's attributes and is, therefore of a tangible nature; the second is related to the name, by nature intangible and thus subject to multiple meanings. In other words, evaluating a brand is linked to a functional dimension and a symbolic one, and this dualism is at the basis of the justification of many types of purchase and consumption behavior. Leveraging this dichotomy therefore means influencing all the consumer's choices.[3] A brand, by its very nature, has both dimensions – the functional and the symbolic– and the choice of name is important in determining which of the two prevails or in achieving an effective balance between them. The functional component delineates evaluations in a practical and rational manner and represents the product's concrete values. Consumers thus evaluate the concrete advantages related to performance, what the product can do, how easy it is to use, its physical availability and the price–quality ratio. The symbolic component, on the other hand, is related to a more emotional evaluation of the brand which marks the passage from objectivity to subjectivity by introducing into the area of choice further elements such as taste, pride, the need to strengthen a sense of belonging to worlds, universes and communities and, above all, the need to express oneself through consumption decisions. A dichotomous vision of the brand is therefore affirmed, according to which the product must represent the functional benefits while the name must create the symbolic ones.[4]

In a market context where products are seen to have increasingly shorter life cycles and consumers less and less time, or desire, to identify differentiating elements from a functional point of view, differentiation based on knowing what to do is not only difficult to achieve but also not very effective. Faced with fewer and fewer differentiated offerings, consumers tend to favor the image of a product because it can simplify choice and evaluation between similar alternatives.[5] The preference consumers give today to the symbolic component of a product means the choice of name has progressively become more relevant strategically, since it represents an important part of a brand's identity – the verbal part. The real paradox is thus represented by the fact that consumers see greater differentiating elements in the name than they see in the benefits offered by the product. So the name takes on an identity which is less and less verbal and more and more symbolic, and through its promulgation can project its own self and its own imaginary world. It is precisely thanks to this component that the name performs a paradoxical "function" of symbolism, making it possible to *emphasize* a brand's identity and personality.

It seems obvious therefore that choosing a name is not only one of the most creative phases in the process of generating a brand, but also one of the most strategically critical, since the more the name manages to have a distinctive capacity the more it will be able to make the difference on the shelves by conditioning the consumer's choice. An effective name can act as a compass, guiding the brand to safe harbors, away from the increasingly stormy waters of today's consumer markets. Let's think, for example, of a John Smith who decides to embark on a career in the world of show business. His name would condemn him to the ghetto of indifference and anonymity from the start. Anybody who has a banal name and wants to break into the show business world nearly always uses a stage name, so as that their appearances will be more effective in making that name remembered. Would Louise Veronica Ciccone have had the same success if she had not been called Madonna? We could say that the name Madonna is also banal, but in the context in which it was presented it is not. Its *religious* character makes it extraordinarily innovative in the world of rock music since it is completely incongruous with it – at least apparently. Madonna's career has been marked by numerous, happy intuitions which still today, after more than twenty years, make her a real icon on a planetary scale; but the first intuition, that which generated the myth, was the choice of name.

One of the most important steps in choosing a name is, in the majority of cases, attributing meaning. It would seem therefore that the use of names and initials which do not have meaning is to be avoided, since their inability to supply meaning makes them difficult to memorize.[6] Aaker, however, leads us to reflect on the opposite principle via the "empty vase" or "blank canvas" paradigm.[7] In fact, the author maintains that sometimes being ambiguous, generic and without meaning in the choice of a name means it is possible to make that name an "open work," able to develop different associations and meanings which can be coherent with the brand's strategy. An "open work," in fact, lends itself to possible changes in theme and plot which lead to the story being reviewed, thus generating continual *coups de théatre*. The lack of meaning allows the brand to have greater flexibility, thus making it able to adapt itself more easily to the ever changing seasons and be always up-to-date. If it is true in fact that the force of a name consists in telling without affirming, non-telling also represents a form of communication. It implies projecting the consumer into a sort of large hypertext, allowing them to change meanings inside a system of values and changing signs. As Laura Minestroni suggests, a generic name which is poor in meaning provides a soil in which signs, values and discourses, established at the level of communication and marketing, can take root and bud.[8]

While it is impossible to postulate rules and principles which are valid on all occasions, we would like to pause a while to identify some general guidelines to follow when choosing a name. Although descriptive power constitutes a leading criterion in identifying a name, one must not fall into the temptation of being descriptive at all costs. Anything in the name which can identify the attributes of the brand or the product can sometimes undermine the effectiveness of the whole brand strategy. The descriptive capacity of a name certainly simplifies perception of the brand and its precise collocation in the reference product category. However, a name which is too descriptive nullifies the brand's capacity to differentiate itself within that category, since other brands will be using the same adjectives and the same descriptive capacity of their names. Moreover, a name with a purely descriptive attitude limits the brand's communicative capacity to a determined temporal context and does not allow it to make the most of opportunities nor to defend itself from the threats which may arise as scenarios evolve with time. Those same elements described via the name can in fact have relevance in one particular determined historical context, only to lose that relevance later, something which may negatively condition the future perceptions of consumers and the associations connected with the brand.[9]

Consider, for example, the famous fast food chain, Kentucky Fried Chicken. Since it was founded in 1952 by Colonel Harland Sanders, it has been famous for offering fried chicken prepared to an old recipe which has been kept secret from the moment it was created. Born in a time when taste was the discriminating feature of consumer choice, the chain became an authentic temple for all those who wanted to eat something really tasty and savory. As society evolved, and eating habits changed to reflect the growing emphasis on a more careful and healthy diet, the chain found itself having to face a sort of identity crisis. Particularly in the United States, a country where there has been a real obesity epidemic (six out of ten Americans are obese), fast food chains have been put on the index: the diffusion of fatty food at cheap prices, together with an increasingly sedentary lifestyle, has been seen as one of the principal causes of widespread obesity even among young children. Thus, physical wellbeing has become the main guideline in the development of the food sector and supermarket shelves have been filled with low-fat and low-cholesterol products. Taste has in this way been partly sacrificed at the altar of wellbeing and social responsibility, and the connotation of "fried" has taken on a value which is almost criminal and contrary to social trends, a symbol of bad eating habits, depriving it of its association with a moment of psychological wellbeing. We need to make it clear that the chain would not have been credible if it had proposed healthy menus or campaigns which focused on the nutritional principles of its products. Its identity would have been upset and, above all, it would not have been legitimized by the consumer who would have branded it as not coherent. However, the word "fried" contained in the name, which originally represented the offer's plus factor, had taken on a negative connotation. Even the word "chicken" had become limiting in a context where competitors were bringing their menus up-to-date by adapting them to new dietary habits and the evolution in taste. McDonald's introduction of salads and ethnic products is an example in this respect: when a consumer thinks of McDonald's, they do not associate it exclusively with hamburgers, but with a multitude of products such as sandwiches, salads and apple pie. In this case, a generic brand name made it possible to not limit the evolution of its offering, but still generate associations in the consumer's mind which are always coherent. In contrast to McDonald's, a descriptive name which contained the word "fried" was not only no longer up-to-date but generated negative associations. Kentucky had therefore to reposition itself, to reconsider both its name and its logo: today the organization has assumed the name "KFC," freeing itself of the dangerous associations which the words "chicken" and "fried" could generate. The company understood that the component of the name which had decreed part of the company's success would have loaded it with negative associations and meanings: changing name did not mean denying its own history.

It must also be underlined how an effective name can supply symbolic associations linked to the functionality of the product, even if it is not descriptive. Consider, for example, Speakeasy for Voice Over IP, whose name communicates a clear benefit for VOIP technology,[10] or products such as Purevision (Pioneer), which while not being descriptive communicates its consumer benefits extremely clearly. If we compare Purevision with Philips Ambilight, we can say that the Purevision is more evocative: it takes the consumer inside the vision experience. Often onomatopoeia, with the sonority and musicality associated with it, can represent a useful alternative for emphasizing the functional ability of a brand and highlighting some of its characteristic traits. Consider, for example, McCain Frips, where the sonority of the name manages to convey the product's combined traits: Frips are thin and crispy to bite, just like potato chips, but also hot and tasty, with the full potato flavor of French Fries.[11]

In some product categories, names like General Electric or Société Générale attribute a standardized connotation to the brands, projecting an aura of being average, a product able to perform its functions honestly, with average results, without the presumptions or costs, if we can put it like that, of excellence and therefore of "better" products. The generalized vocation of these brands can compromise perception of them as high-performing ones, and consequently reduce their chances of winning the competition with the "specialist." In contrast, brands like Gaggenau, Bosch, Liebher have specialist names which are able to present the brand and the product as authentic professionals in the sector, contributing to the construction of an image of high reliability and effectiveness. These are generic but not generalized names, where functionality is not cited but where the attribution of linguistic hardness (in these cases, we could say, typically German) brings an aura of reliability and professionalism to the product.

The fact is that excesses never pay when choosing a name. Being too descriptive or too generalized can limit the brand's power toward its possible receivers by conditioning their associations with it.

Another crucial element in the process of designing a name is linked to its length. In fact, we live in an era of synthesis and speed and even in interpersonal communications people use more and more linguistic shortcuts – think, for example, how teenagers communicate via chat lines and text messages: UR GR8, BRB, LOL, TB and so on. The consumer's memory threshold is becoming increasingly lower, while the mass of messages received is increasing, and communication has had to adapt by privileging greater synthesis in its processes. A television spot does not last longer than thirty seconds – the average duration is fifteen seconds. Therefore, the name conveyed by the message must succeed in exploiting ever shorter communication times to the full. Moreover, the exposition of the name must be "dosed" with extreme wisdom, since in a short time excessive repetition of the name could reduce the space devoted to all the supporting and emotional information that the spot should convey. It is no coincidence that publicists advise not repeating it more than three times.[12] So, in the era of synthesis, the tendency to choose shorter and shorter names prevails, names which, at the same time, can attribute strong meaning to the brand and are more easily remembered. We can state therefore that the real challenge of brand naming today is that of being able to bring out a brand's character, personality and image, without sacrificing its functionality, and by using only a few letters.

Oscar Wilde closed a letter to a friend saying he was sorry to have written such a long letter but that he had not had the time to write a shorter one. This means that the superfluous can be eliminated by focusing on the content. This principle has been elegantly expressed by Zen Buddhists: "For knowledge add something every day. For wisdom take something away."

It is necessary to carry out careful linguistic analysis when choosing a name, so as to check that the name is not only pronounceable but also can be pronounced correctly without being "crippled" somehow. This problem is felt even more greatly by those brands which have a strong vocation to be internationalized. It is no coincidence in fact that when Renzo Rosso chose the brand name Diesel for his products, the guiding criteria were purely linguistic, linked to the fact that the word is pronounced the same in every language.

It is also necessary to check that the name does not have negative connotations in linguistic contexts which are different from the original; the possibility that the brand could be loaded down with "unpleasant" characterizations (or at least ones which are different from the organization's intentions) must be considered in respect of each of the different markets in which it competes. The ease with which the name can be memorized and pronounced in countries other that that of origin must be verified in advance, in order to ensure that in a different geographical context misunderstandings or negative associations cannot be generated. Cases in which the same word, in different languages, can distort a brand's meaning and attribute negative values to it are not rare. Moreover, it is essential that changes in sense do not occur in translation – just think, for example, of the literal translation of "chat room" in French: from a virtual room in which one can chat it would become "the cat's room."

For brands which have a vocation to be internationalized, the name must be "one size fits all," able to adapt well to every market without taking on negative values, or conflicting with public morals, the political framework or, above all, religious beliefs. There are many examples (which are well documented) of brands which have faced more than vicissitude precisely because of the cultural implications that their name has generated. One of the most bizarre cases in the history of international marketing is that of the washing machine detergent Ariel: in Egypt, the brand name did not go down at all well because it brought to mind the name of General Ariel Sharon (later prime minister of Israel), the commander of the Israeli army during the sudden Sinai offensive in 1956. There was also the case of Der General in Germany. When it was launched on the German market, cleanliness was considered a supreme value and dirt was a national phobia, to the point where the word *Waschkraft*, literally the "washing force," had become an integral part of German lexis. Nearly all the detergents tried to give the impression of a "technical" product instead of simple white soap powder, thus giving themselves the airs of "little washing-machines." And indeed, in such a context, it seemed logical to launch a product with a military identity on the home market, while in the television spot this feature was further accentuated by the housewife's wearing collar badges which denoted the rank of general. One might be inclined to think that this idea would not have been a very happy one in a country which had emerged only a few years previously from the immense tragedy of the Second World War, and in this historical context, Der General was not at all effective, while the detergent Mr Clean had an extraordinary success since it was equally effective in the fight against dirt, but at the right dosage.

The problem that brands find themselves having to face in the progressive internationalization of markets is rather similar to that which the cinema industry, and particularly the American one, has always had to deal with when translating film titles. The difficulty is not limited only to distortion of meaning but also to the relevance of the theme the title can bring out.

Consider Oscar Wilde's famous drama, *The Importance Of Being Earnest*. In the original, there is a play on the identical pronunciation of the words earnest and Ernest. The comedy revolves around the phantom and non-existent character called Ernest, but its meaning derives from its moral, which is linked to earnestness and honesty. When the play was translated into Italian, the title became *L'importanza di chiamarsi Ernesto*, which is not only scarcely effective, but actually loses meaning, thus limiting its associations to the work.[13]

An effective name must be easy to remember: in this sense, the choice of unusual names which stimulate curiosity have positive effects on their capacity to be memorized by the consumer and on the level of attention they can generate. In this sense, it can sometimes be effective to use names which are apparently incongruous with the product they are being associated with. If a name like Speakeasy is rather obvious for a product connected with VOIP technology services, Orange stimulates curiosity by opening further scenarios for the brand other than those of a simple basic telephone service. The need to use a name which goes beyond the effectiveness of the product is particularly strong for technological products, since it makes it possible to attribute a meaning – and therefore a functionality – to them which is simpler, more accessible and understandable. So, the effectiveness of a name can be correlated to its ability to excite emotions, and create positive vibrations and moods.[14] Names with these characteristics make technological products seem more accessible. Consider, for example, Yahoo!, Excite and Apple. Associating the name of a banal object, like an apple, to a computer simplifies its idea, makes it more accessible, and therefore makes it possible to develop greater affection toward the brand. (It does not really matter if the reason for the choice is still technological in nature: Newton, according to the famous anecdote, was sitting under an apple tree when he had the insight of the law of gravity.)

A name which allows "access to a world" has a strong associative connotation since it makes it possible to recount something about the brand through images: something linked to the world it is projected in. The purchase and consumption of a product has become more and more linked to the non-verbal meaning of communication and the product's ability to enrich self-projection by means of this communication. A good name evokes a feeling of trust, confidence, durability, speed, and an entire whole of correlated advantageous associations. Brand names are in fact often poetic, metaphorical and allegorical, and are able to recall imagined or far-off worlds like times gone by, perhaps by re-proposing their nostalgic charm. As Blackett reminds us, a more abstract name can be a powerful tool for differentiating a brand, while a semi-descriptive name which makes it possible for the consumer to understand easily the benefits of the product makes the positioning of the brand simpler, something which can also provide a useful platform for the development of the brand's personality and consequently the differentiation of the brand at an emotional level. Finding the right balance is therefore essential: a brand name needs to be distinctive and memorizable, and this is often best achieved by a more abstract name; at the same time, however, a brand name which conveys sufficient information for the consumer to understand the benefits of the product also has its advantages. The best way to achieve this balance is by reference to the target consumer.[15]

CHAPTER 8

BRAND SEX: A CONFUSED IDENTITY HEADING TOWARD ANDROGYNY

A brand's values are strictly correlated to the consumer, reflecting the perception they have developed of themselves. It is almost obvious therefore that these values can take on different connotations depending on the consumer's gender. In a society where the division of jobs and roles was clearly defined and marked by the relegation of women to only domestic activities, products took on a definite sexual identity.

It was the user who defined the sex of a brand, even when this took on gender traits linked to the opposite sex. A house-cleaning product (for example Mr Clean) was aimed at a female public, since it was the women who were entrusted with choosing products related to running and cleaning the domestic environment. These choices, as we have already pointed out, became particularly important for a woman because they represented one of the few social spheres in which she was called on to express her professionalism. Household products had a prevalently female identity and connotations of virility, as in the case of Mr Clean, still evoked the female virtue of cleanliness, with all its proverbial proximity to godliness. The brand's masculine trait was linked to its technical–functional characteristics, but only in order to recall and exalt its effectiveness; the value of this effectiveness, however, had a female connotation.

Products take on sexual connotations depending on the consumer or the sex of the person who chooses them. Thus McDonald's has acquired a feminine connotation because it presents itself as the family fast-food restaurant: a place to eat a quick meal while having fun with the children. This therefore involves the female leadership in choices regarding feeding the family and gratifying the children. In contrast, Burger King takes on a prevalently male connotation by proposing bigger buns and thus recalling a concept of appetite which is typically male. Burger

King's masculinity is exalted further by the fact that the meat in the buns is grilled and not cooked on a hotplate, evoking that real mania of the US male, the barbecue.

We could also affirm that masculinity is connected to those aspects of brands which are to do with functionality, while femininity is linked to the emotions. Progressively, masculinity has taken on traits of severity, of almost military discipline, of that rigor which it is thought cannot be put aside if a target is to be achieved.[1] It is for this reason that, in a society which is ever more in need of emotions, the female side of a brand has become the more requested component. Typically male products, like cars, the decisional leadership for which was assigned to men, have progressively lost their connotation of virility. The names of cars are increasingly more female and more attention is given to detail and functionality in a purely gender key. The new imperative has become that of setting the woman's imagination on fire rather than satisfying the lucid and chauvinist side of the man.[2]

The real challenge brands have to face today is precisely the need to tone down gender connotations in a social context in which the division of roles and jobs has undergone radical change and where sexual identities are often more and more confused.

The disruption of a "game of roles" which had persisted for centuries is bringing about a process which Fabris defines as the progressive "feminization of society."[3] We have in fact witnessed a growing sharing of female values by the male part of the population and "social legitimization" of such attitudes. Women's reference values have become values which society needs; the male model, based mainly on strength, rationality and aggressiveness is not as reassuring as the female model of sweetness, sensitivity and lightness. Men have therefore started to question themselves and in so doing have discovered themselves in a dimension different from that of the physical and of working efficiency. The model at the basis of masculine identity has in fact progressively changed profoundly over the years and there is ever greater proof that what has emerged is the difficulty of defining a new one. Postmodern man's crisis of identity puts him in a situation of vulnerability which leads him to adopt attitudes and behaviors traditionally labeled as feminine.

In the face of this process of the feminization of society, we are however witnessing a process of the "androgynization" of women, who now often take on the character traits of men – which, as we have said, are based on strength, rationality and aggressiveness – above all in order to justify their presence at every hierarchical level in working and institutional fields.

It seems evident however that these two tendencies create disorientation on a social level: the disruption of roles which had persisted for centuries often leads to problems of adaptation, to real "identity crises" and to acceptance of difficulties in general, and these difficulties are particularly amplified in the family context, where continual "role conflicts" are generated. It is precisely this type of difficulty which is partly to blame for the increasing number of marriage or live-in-relationship breakdowns.[4]

This highlights the fact that a brand cannot think of having a connotation which is univocally orientated toward one particular sex, but must take on multiple facets aimed at reaching both the feminine side of men as much as the masculine side of women. However, it must be underlined that if on the one hand society is assuming a form which is more and more "female," and brands are hence obliged to increasingly feminize their own essence, on the other hand this process of change mainly affects societies which are more evolved, not only on an economic and consumption level but also on a social and cultural level. In short, while all this is valid for those brands which are sold in Western markets, it is not possible to claim that it is equally valid for brands which find themselves having to compete in markets where the condition of women is still very backward and where the process of women's emancipation is only just dawning. Think how the use of cosmetics was considered illegal in China until 1984.

The owners of "global" brands would object that it is necessary to have products which are suitable for all markets and therefore all cultures. We believe that, from this point of view, these brands can take on the function of a catalyst of social change. What protestors define as "Americanization" of the world could also be seen as an important social value if related to the condition of women. Exporting the model of consumption could be accompanied by the export of social models, and brands could become actors and promoters of change by promulgating the model of a society in which women have a role which is on equal terms with that of men.

Some traits of femininity are related to the relational context in which a woman moves and is perceived. A woman is sweet, sensitive, understanding, willing to listen, warm, amiable, smiling and not vulgar; she speaks softly and loves children. These are some of the traits associated with a woman when she socially interacts. However, these characteristics must not only be questioned in line with the new, more masculine identity which is the consequence of the new roles which women have taken on, but must also be considered in relation to a woman's view of her femininity when she is not in a relational context. Anna Fels in fact maintains that some women's qualities are not socially visible since they are related to their expression in isolation.[5] It is no coincidence that Nike Women designed a large part of its communication around the isolation of woman and her assuming the role of athlete, a role which is totally unconnected with her feminine individuality and precisely because of this, we could say, extremely representative of the real essence of woman. In isolation, a woman loses a large part of her femininity, at least as it is understood at a social and relational level, and takes on an identity which we could say is more masculine.

At the same time, women have difficulty taking on a new identity in a social and relational context. While society, which increasingly needs emotions, delicacy and sensitivity, requests those traits which traditionally represent femininity, those same characteristics are not enough for a woman to affirm herself in more competitive contexts, such as the work and political sphere. Women are therefore forced to build a new identity which adds increasingly masculine traits to the socially shared identity. Compared with the spontaneous expression of a woman's identity when she is in isolation, this process is socially driven and not completely spontaneous.

This idea is well expressed in a scene in the film *What Women Want*, starring Mel Gibson and Helen Hunt. Nick (Mel Gibson), a chauvinistic and exploitive publicity agent, gains an extraordinary power after an accident: he can hear women think, he interprets the contents and form of their thoughts, and he lets himself get emotionally involved. What follows is Nick's presentation of the advertising campaign he has created for Nike Women:

> You don't stand in front of a mirror before a run ... and wonder what the road will think of your outfit. You don't have to listen to its jokes and pretend they're funny. It would not be easier to run if you dressed sexier. The road doesn't notice if you're wearing lipstick. It does not care how old you are. You do not feel uncomfortable ... because you make more money than the road. And you can call on the road whenever you feel like it, whether it's been a day ... or even

a couple of hours since your last date. The only thing the road cares about … is that you pay it a visit once in a while.

The street becomes an inner place where you can find something that you can't find in relational contexts. Isolation means a woman can really be a woman, and on the street a woman finds a place which is safe from looks, relationships and stereotypical judgements. Nobody judges her, she doesn't have a boss to obey, a family who can never get enough attention, she doesn't have to invent tricks to survive in that place, and she can finally take on the real identity of a woman. When Nike launched the Nike Women's line, it concerned itself not so much with understanding how to sell its own brand name to a female public, but how to create a real dialogue with that public. The implication of this reflection had a cultural value which was enormously important for the company, which had made testosterone one of the predominant traits of its identity.[6] The prevalence of a masculine cultural model had already slowed down greater focus on the female market in the past: fear that a successful female line could cannibalize a business which was aimed at men, and therefore that the company could lose a little of its testosterone and depreciate the brand's virile identity, had been the principal factor for resisting the launch of Nike Women. For more than thirty years, the brand had successfully concentrated on the concept of performance, and crossing the borders toward a model where emotions had the upper hand over functionality was seen as dangerous. In short, by turning toward the female market, the brand feared losing its sexual connotation, to the prejudice of its consistency. Nothing could have been more wrong at a strategic level and the success achieved by Nike Women forced some competitors to review their own positions. Think, for example, of when Adidas called on the famous designer, Stella McCartney, to produce the new women's collection with the aim of making it more fashionable. Nike's real strength was that of freeing the athletics products market of the sole idea of performance, linking it more and more to that of "fashion" and the needs of women.[7]

This led the company to reformulate the brand's entire frame of reference, above all regarding clothing, a category where the boundaries between fitness and active wear have now become blurred. In this context, Nike's competitors are no longer called only Adidas, Puma and Reebok, but also Gap, Old Navy and Abercrombie & Fitch – and they are certainly not "direct" competitors. In fact, widening the Nike

Women lines and extending the brand toward a greater number of categories, like bags and other accessories , has certainly made it possible to increase the brand's audience, exposing it however to stronger competitive gusts. It is in fact no coincidence that only 25 per cent of the potential market that Nike Women today aims at is represented by shoes; 70 per cent is represented by clothes and the remaining crumbs are left to equipment and accessories.

The importance of this market led Nike to rethink the very format of Nike Town, whose identity lacked a sufficiently "feminine" character. Although there was an entire floor dedicated to women, the global experience of the shop focused little on female values. In Nike Town, the athletes who are the symbol of Nike share their victories, but they also reveal their personal defeats without shame, since in the "city of Nike" self-consideration, personal faith, athletic feats and team spirit become values which are shared by its "citizens." But the whole process of communication was centered (in as much as it is about victories and defeats) on the typically masculine idea of competitiveness. Women do not find Nike Town outlets attractive or exciting destinations – at least that is what numerous research studies carried out by the company have highlighted. To satisfy the need to create a sales environment around the brand where women can find an effective symbolic representation of their values, the Nike Goddess project was launched, a shop format which also had among its main aims the task of making the company management understand how to sell to women. Today we can state that the concept at the basis of Nike Goddess is a long way from the "traditional" Nike Town centers.

The affirmation of the image of a woman who is increasingly asexual and promiscuous, but at the same time seductive, determines, however, an inner contrast which derives from multiple personalities, both feminine and masculine, living together within a single identity. This is the consequence of a change which has not yet been completed and a phase in which women have difficulty finding the balance between working life and private life.

This conflict tends to be accentuated when a woman becomes a mother and the female side, brought to the fore by maternity, takes on more importance. Reconciling the role of mother with the tasks imposed by an environment which is increasingly harder and more competitive is an extremely arduous challenge for a woman. The opposition between her feminine and masculine sides becomes ever more radical. In this context, a brand has an extraordinary opportunity to

70

present itself as the element which can "make the equation work," by allowing a sort of compensation between recognition in the field of work and recognition in the family sphere.

For example, by purchasing a brand of baby products, a mother tries to lessen the sense of guilt she feels about having less time to devote to bringing up her child as a result of her having to juggle the multiple roles of a modern woman. Woman's changing status in society has involved her giving up, at least in part, what is by far the most characterizing element of femininity: not only the biological role of maternity, but that of devoting herself to the care of her children. This process is not without pain and can generate a deep sense of guilt in contemporary woman. It is in this situation that a brand acquires a therapeutic value, lessening these feelings and promoting a new idea of the concepts of maternity and family, projecting the woman into a world in which what may appear to be opposing needs find effective compensation. Strengthening the woman's sense of belonging to the competitive world "by softening" the sense of guilt and the feeling of inadequacy compared with her "ancestral functions" are the multiple and opposing needs which modern brands find themselves having to satisfy today.[8]

It seems evident that, by consuming brands, modern women affirm not only their own femininity but also their masculinity, that is on the one hand the aspect linked to their most intimate dimension, unfettered by social clichés, and on the other the aspect related to their own ambitions.

Modern woman is faced by an agonizing dilemma which doesn't seem to have an effective solution – but this is a consequence which affects every individual and every institution when social change is in progress. The problem is that of understanding what is the maximum amount of stress a woman is willing to tolerate in order to succeed in combining the ambitions connected to her traditional role and those related to her "new" social roles.

We have already stated that the role of a brand is less and less functional and more emotional, and its capacity to excite emotions responds to a precise need on the part of the consumer for psychological and social survival. It is precisely the need for psychological survival in a world which is ever uglier which leads individuals to attribute growing importance to beauty. Beauty has always been associated with women and the representation, be it outer or inner, of women. The need for beauty finds only one answer at a social level, and consequently at the brand level: take on a more feminine connotation. The challenge facing brands is increasingly that of being seductive and the ability to seduce is linked largely to female beauty.

A brand must therefore be sexier and sexier, not in a merely sexist way of thinking, but considering sexy what is beautiful.[9] This does not simply mean proposing images and products which are more and more sensual, sometimes even over-sensual, where beauty is repeatedly associated with Eros. Being sexy really means being attractive.[10] If we look today at successful products (think, for example of iPod, among others), their real strength from which their primary attractiveness derives can be traced not so much to their technological as to their aesthetic performance. The iPod has become something to wear, almost a pleasant and natural extension of the body, above all because it is beautiful. Aesthetic enhancement has always been attributed to women; while there was once a connotation almost of contempt through the association with the superfluous and useless, it is viewed now as a factor in promoting social progress.

The decline in traditionally male values (among which there is without doubt the conceptual contempt of aesthetics in the name of a misunderstood "practicality"), and the acceptance of new ones (these being pragmatically androgynous since they seek to unite the best of the male experience with the best of the female), has radically changed the way of branding. A brand must mirror this mutation, which, in its visual and verbal expression, seems to have taken on an almost genetic connotation.[11] The very places where a brand is generated and produced must reflect this aesthetic change. Only companies which manage to be sexy inside will be able to generate sexy brands.

Lingering over aesthetics could seem contradictory in a historical context in which technological revolution is literally the order of the day. Yet great revolutions always have social implications, and therefore the developments which derive from them do not always have a perfectly linear character. As the technological perfection of products gradually goes beyond the average needs expressed by the market, the intrinsic value of goods in terms of functionality is homogenized; consumer attention toward such functional aspects is reduced since they are now taken for granted, and attention toward the aesthetic dimension, and therefore a greater "femininity" in the offer system, increases. Often men, whose model has been put into crisis, find a psychological means of escape and above all a coherent justification in accepting the progressive social acquisition of female traits.

The above has further implications for the revision of traditional marketing processes. Segmentation based on targeting the sexes becomes less and less important, since brands are assuming an increasingly androgynous identity, satisfying both male and female desires in the same person. It seems that society has decided, by accepting androgynous values, to join together the best of the male experience with that of the female, and brands, like the products associated with them, must in some way reflect this genetic mutation.

CHAPTER 9

THE BRAND BETWEEN EMOTIONS AND EXPERIENCES

The current social frame of reference is characterized by the pervasive presence of technology which, if on the one hand it allows man to extend his senses toward directions which used to seem unimaginable, on the other has generated a sort of dehumanization of society. The affirmation of ever more virtual environments and the progressive overcoming of physical constraints in every sphere has in fact marked a progressive slowing down in the development of individual aptitudes, and so individuals are increasingly in search of new experiences which can reaffirm their human nature. In this increasingly technological context, where the password seems to have become "speed," individuals find fewer and fewer possibilities and more and more difficulties in developing personal interaction. Thus the need is felt to get more "physical" relationships back by means of those two components which cannot be reproduced in a virtual environment: experiences and senses. The use of experience as a basis for developing new marketing strategies today represents an effective way of retrieving "psychological satisfaction" in purchasing and consumption models, by making it possible to build new worlds, cities and neighborhoods; in short, ideal places which are not virtual, to substitute those proposed by contemporary life.[1]

Experience makes it possible to satisfy, by way of a brand, needs which are less and less linked to the supply of goods and services and increasingly more linked to the life of individuals. Moreover, it makes it possible to enhance existence, by mobilizing the senses, unburdening daily life of its material connotation, evoking "symbolic universes" full of meaning, contents and – above all – values. Experiences can spark emotions, reflections and sensations able to remain in our mind as a sort of "emotional souvenir."

We can confidently claim that the economic organizations destined to come out as winners from the modern competitive scenarios will be those that understand what the consumer wants today: not more products and services, but experiences able to make them feel good by involving the senses and giving them excitement.

Berry, Carbone and Haeckel define experience as anything that can be "perceived" or "felt." Experience does not however lend itself to a univocal definition but is the sum of a series of definitions which contribute to determining what these authors call "customer's total experience." Experience takes on a connotation in terms of functionality, related to the consumer's cognitive approach, and of emotionality, related to an "affective-sensitive" approach, which includes smells, sounds, signs, tastes and touch.[2]

Cova meanwhile defines experience as

personal experience, often emotionally loaded, which is based on the interaction with stimuli formed by products or services made available to the system of consumption; this experience can lead to a transformation of the individual in the case of so-called extraordinary experiences.[3]

In many areas of consumption, each of us is willing to purchase an experience rather than a product, an atmosphere rather than a price, a place, a way of feeling good, rather than a brand.[4]

Schmitt affirms that the traditional positioning of brands, based above all on functional characteristics and benefits, weakens the relationship between company and consumers by creating a sterile relationship, based on the product's hard attributes. According to the same author, defining a brand's market according to the benefits the brand can bring or the functions it can offer creates a short-sighted view of the category in which the company has to compete.[5]

Pine and Gilmore maintain that the economy is entering a new era, that of producing experiences. The era of experience is different from that of services from the points of view both of quantity and of quality. From a quantitative angle, while a service tries to standardize the offering within the target segments, experience tends to personalize the offering; from a qualitative point of view, while a service aims at resolving the customer's problem, experience is interested in all the problems which the *guest*, no longer the customer, may have at the moment in which they interact with the company. To put this another way, while service management is characterized by being prevalently problem-solving, experience aims at dazzling the senses, touching the heart and challenging the intellect.[6]

Moreover, say Pine and Gilmore, there is a difference in time limit: experience and service are distinguishable by the fact that the delivery of a service ends with consumption, while experience remains in the memory, taking on a connotation of being *memorable*.

The wide temporal horizon of experience is clearly identified by Arnould, Price and Zinkhan in a model which defines four moments which follow each other according to a precise chronological order, and contribute to defining the very contents of an experience, namely: anticipating consumption, choice outcome, real use and enjoyment, and memory.[7]

- The experience of *anticipating consumption* is characterized by research, planning and all those aspects which, in an almost oneiric dimension, contribute to defining the consumer's expectation level and at the same time become part of the experience too.
- The experience of purchasing represents the *choice outcome* and is influenced by the relationship with the service and the interaction with the environmental context.
- The experience of consuming is related to the *real use and enjoyment* of a product, place or service.
- The experience seen as a *memory* leads to reliving the past and reveals itself in tales.

Pine and Gilmore provide us with a model by means of which a brand is constructed around the different intensities in the use of two variables:

- The *degree of involvement* of the relational environment in which the consumer finds themself interacting with products and services.
- The *degree of participation*, or the intensity of their interaction.

As far as the relational environment is concerned, a consumer can be in the extreme situation where they enter and become a protagonist in the experience – a situation also defined as "immersion"; examples are a Disney theme park or PlayStation video games console. At the other extreme, it is the fact that the experience goes to the consumer which defines the modalities of interaction and use – a situation defined as "absorption," as in the case of a pay-TV customer who schedules television programs in their living-room.[8] The two situations, immersion and absorption, present a consumer who takes on different roles: protagonist in the first case, director in the second.

As far as the degree of consumer participation is concerned, the matrix identifies two extreme situations: passive participation and active participation. Participation is passive when consumers witness an event but do not directly influence it, as in the case of a classical music concert or a football match. On the other hand, participation is active when there is direct involvement on the part of the consumer, as in the case of treatments carried out at a beauty salon.[9]

Environment, relationship and degree of participation define four situations which draw the border lines of the kingdom of experience, and correspond to "existential" areas of an individual, namely *entertainment, learning, aesthetic and escape.*[10]

– *Entertainment*, with a high degree of absorption and passive participation, is characterized by its recreational and games-related component: entertaining essentially means making people have fun.
– *Learning*, with a low degree of absorption and active participation, is characterized by its educative function, through which it aims to inform and increase knowledge, both from an intellectual and a physical point of view, as in the case of activities carried out by a personal trainer at a fitness center or the creation of forums or communities where experiences are created and shared.
– *Aesthetic* has a high degree of immersion and passive participation.
– *Escape* has a low level of immersion and active participation.

In a social context such as that analyzed in previous chapters, where the effectiveness of products and services is taken for granted by the market, and the efficiency linked to productivity represents the basic requirement of the principal economic organizations, experience assumes an escape function in respect of reality, aimed at recovering senses, feelings and intellect. By making it possible to build one's emotions in an active way, experience can also perform a role of extreme importance by helping individuals, albeit in an artful way, to survive "psychologically" and "emotionally," thus performing an anxiety- and stress-relieving role.[11]

As Gallucci suggests, we are today witnessing a rediscovery of the importance of the emotions in a real attempt to make up for the shortage of means with which to rationally interpret the events which fill the everyday lives of individuals.[12] This need is further increased in the face of the extraordinary information surplus which today characterizes the system of offer.

In fact, if on the one hand, the availability of an ever increasing amount of information makes it possible to choose with increased rationality and awareness, on the other hand, there is no correspondingly high level of care with respect to the quality of that information and, consequently, real simplification in the decision process is not achieved. The increased information base thus becomes a further factor of complexity which makes every small choice an important one. Emotions can, in this sense, represent a factor of simplification able to facilitate the relationship between sender and receiver in the communication process, and provide the purchasing decision with new stimuli and new directions, not only orientating it toward the limited act of consumption which follows, but also supplying new directions for interpreting daily life.

Consumers are looking less and less for functional benefits in a product, because they take them for granted; they are looking more and more for guidelines for their own existence and something which helps them in a society which is ever more complex and selective.

Much though technology has changed the face of our existence, we cannot imagine a life in which every action is carried out exclusively under the guidance of reason. The real paradox of postmodern society is represented by the fact that, in this extraordinary technological context, it is more difficult to make a decision since the points of reference in the surplus of both products and information on offer are less and less distinct, if not actually absent. In this context, purchase and consumption risk being perceived as coercive activities. Too much information and little clarity: the current system of offer seems to represent more and more the chaos of urbanization and the uneasiness of modernity, contributing to the further disorientation of a consumer who is constantly looking for those emotions which modern life increasingly withholds.

Once, buying a car required comparing a few models, gathering information by visiting (at the most) two or three dealers, but today it is possible to choose by connecting to the web from the computer at home. However, we then discover that the alternatives to evaluate are far more numerous and that for each of them the features to be compared have multiplied. Is buying a car simpler today, with modern technology, than it was yesterday, in that simpler and less-evolved past?

The increasing interest of marketing in *real emotion* can be explained by a context characterized by information overload and consequent "multimedia chaos" (too many signals from too many media), as well as the need to check the drift of extemporary pleasure, which is due entirely to the consumer society.[13] It is taken more and more for granted that a product will carry out its "trade" and increasingly a product is required to have new aptitudes disembodied from its functional ones and linked, instead, to its capacity to provide pleasure and emotions. The consumer, who is increasingly surrounded by technology, requires simplicity, and this need can be created by recourse to the emotions. It is no coincidence in fact that, as Furedi maintains, our culture is taking "the emotional gusts" it is exposed to very seriously, "so seriously that almost any difficulty or adversity is seen as a threat to emotional wellbeing."[14]

Modern consumers are in fact exposed to these emotional flows and demonstrate a growing vulnerability at both individual and collective levels. Today's society is a society of speed, stress and uncertainty: the consequence is a sort of emotive–social deficit on a widespread scale. Cities seem more and more to be invaded by individuals fighting against a single enemy: time. Indeed confronting time is not simply a need today but has become a real matter of custom.

Modern consumer society, using the time factor as a discriminator, has been defined as a 24-hour society or a real-time society. In this context, every choice is influenced by the time factor; everything must be done in the shortest time possible. Marketing has adapted to this need by proposing products and solutions which respond to this need, such as for example shirts which do not need ironing, meals which are ready in a few minutes, or duvets which make it possible to make the bed simply by pulling up the cover. Not only this: colors, images and brand names printed on packaging have precisely the aim of helping the consumer choose in the shortest time possible while inside the point of sale; visual merchandising performs an ever more important role in time management, orientating the customer and facilitating choice by informing in a simple and fast way. The consumption of goods can be increasingly thought of as the consumption of signs and symbols which anybody going around a point of sale is forced to read quickly.[15]

All this simplifies choice in terms of a time-saving logic, but it does not respond to the consumer's real need, which is that of combating the stress, anxieties, fears and uncertainty which they bear more and more. Moreover, the consumer does not want to win their war against time: they would simply like not to have to fight it. The need for emotional reassurance is felt with ever greater insistence and the consumer does not want choice to be simplified, but rather a simplified life.

The real challenge facing marketing today is defined by Gallucci as one "of new happiness": in this new scenario, brands promote moods such as harmony, beauty, serenity and, of course, simplicity.[16]

This challenge has already been partly accepted – just think how much greater is the care taken of the aesthetics of brands and products and how this has become an essential phase in the brand creation process.

In a society in which it seemed that a sort of habit of ugliness was emerging, and in which beauty, seen as something ephemeral and transitory, was sacrificed at the altar of functionality, there sprang up a difficulty for individuals to understand content without the perception of form. This tendency made every strategy aimed at highlighting a brand's differentiating elements ineffective, since it was more and more difficult to understand the essence of them. Dostoevsky wrote that beauty would save the world: transferring this famous claim to the context of our analysis, we can affirm even further that beauty will give a new sense to the action of marketing, making it possible to form its contents and rendering them more understandable. It is in fact through form that substance acquires a concrete dimension. Aesthetics, in its dimension most linked to the beautiful, thus takes on an increasingly central role in planning brands, products and sales areas.[17]

Aesthetics sets itself the aim of attracting the consumer and "activating them" in some way. The aesthetic aspect of a brand loses its technological connotation of uselessness and takes on a new one of emotional gratification in using the product. As we have already noted, it is no longer enough for a product to work well – it must also be beautiful. Among the phenomena which best express the new frontiers of consumption, orientation toward the beautiful is certainly among the most important.[18]

The consumer no longer thinks of the beautiful as something to be relegated to museums: as Fabris affirms, the beautiful unravels in every dimension of daily life without interruption; the very routine of daily life cries out for the possibility of becoming an attractive stage for the beautiful and of giving individuals new experiences rich in meaning.[19] Aesthetic planning is becoming a necessary condition for competitive positioning not only of brands and products, but also, for example, of public services. Consider how the progressive deterioration of city

centers has weakened their capacity to act as places of social aggregation and commercial exchange. Numerous experiences at international
level have highlighted how the "branding" of a place by means of new
"urban marketing" tools has been the key to the rebirth of run-down
city centers – a case in point being Times Square in New York.[20]

Places themselves have in fact become new and powerful media
through which to build and strengthen a brand's identity. Aesthetic and
sensorial planning is the basis today for creating flagship stores: shops
in which companies produce the most exciting experiences, tying them
in with their own image and putting the best of themselves on display.
Think how all the big brands compete for the best architects and designers to create points of sale in the shopping streets of the world's major
capitals. Some companies think of them as a real "brand of communication," unconnected to business and cost forecasts. Each is no mere
point of sale, therefore, but a playground aimed at strengthening the
relationship between brand and consumers and, above all, at widening
the offer's audience by providing new brand experiences.

But what emerges as the most significant phenomenon is that the
demand for beauty is a demand which comes increasingly from all levels
of society, and no longer just from the better-off and more cultured
classes. We are witnessing a sort of democratization of the beautiful,
a direct consequence of the growing awareness across all classes at the
social level of the ugliness which surrounds us – and of the fact that this
has brought us full circle to greater need of aesthetic appreciation.[21]

In fact, beauty has today become an attribute on which the evaluation
of a brand's quality is based. A product may be unimpeachable on the
functional level, yet be seen less and less as a "quality product" if it
is ugly. Consumers are tired of products which work but are unable to
excite.

If we look at successful products today, their true strength, from
which their primary attractiveness derives, is not so much in their technology as in the fact of their being "nice" and pleasant. Taking again the
iPod, the outstanding reason for the superiority of this product, probably the most successful small consumer durable in the last ten years, is
aesthetic: its success, which has broken the mould of the music market,
is above all the success of the beautiful and only some way after that of
technological and business models.

As we saw in the previous chapter, the enhancement of aesthetics
has always been attributed to women – once almost contemptuously,
it being associated with the superfluous and useless – today as a factor

in promoting social progress. Now greater emphasis is placed on emotional design, that is the capacity of products to create a greater aesthetic resonance with their users.[22] Planning the form of a technological product, for example, today requires elaboration of a synthesis which takes into account the user's desires as much as the product's functional needs. This leads to a progressive process of humanization of objects, which while maintaining their functionality releases a powerful affective load; all this tends to confirm what has already been discussed at length above regarding attributing vitality to objects which by their nature are inanimate. In fact, if we accept the hypothesis that brands are living organisms, we cannot limit ourselves only to considering them as having personality, identity, character, but must also believe them capable of interacting with the surrounding environment via the senses.

CHAPTER 10

BRAND SENSES: THE CHALLENGE OF POLYSENSUALISM

Faced with an increasingly immaterial economy which has progressively lost physicality and where everything depends on information and its capacity to circulate, a brand, if it is to be completely understood, needs to highlight its emotional side, so that it is perceived as unique and exclusive.

Empirical evidence shows that the strategies for positioning the major brands in the mind of the consumer make more and more use of the emotions and less and less use of performance. We are witnessing a gradual process of the dematerialization of products, which are progressively changing form and characteristics but which are above all acquiring new and increasingly humanlike personalities. Today a winning product must be able to appeal not only to reason, and therefore to *what the product does, what it contains and how it works,* but also to the emotions and the senses.

Fabris maintains that the consumer has entered the era of polysensualism, in which every sense questions the world around it, gaining information about those surroundings and mediating with what is perceived by the other senses. Polysensualism consists in mobilizing and making use of all the five senses. According to Fabris, the body's new experience and a new way of posing dedicated to hedonism and narcissism have generated the recovery of lost aspects of physicality, which have become new, important references for the purchase and consumption process.[1]

The moment we consider the involvement of the five senses in planning a brand, we will be able to obtain a result which is certainly richer in experiences, thus giving birth to a vision of the whole which is much more complete than the simple listing of its attributes.

It can certainly seem paradoxical, as we have mentioned already, that in the era of artificial intelligence, neural networks and expert systems, man is tending toward a more animal, and therefore more instinctive, dimension, characterized by extreme recourse to the senses.[2] Perhaps the explanation is to be sought precisely in the reaction to the excess of rationalization, and the information surplus which characterizes modern society; this leads the consumer to look for relief and security in their most primeval component (namely, instinct) and to need interaction with the surrounding environment through perceptive activity, in the search for escape from a world in which they are more and more an automaton and a slave to technology. We are therefore witnessing a profound change in the way in which consumers relate physically to products, even changing their perception of the functional and "objective" side of the "goods." While this process was once delegated mostly to a single sense, today evaluating products is carried out increasingly by mobilizing two or more senses collectively.

Polysensualism and, more generally, this new way of physically approaching products, means above all overcoming the supremacy of sight, which tends to reduce the involvement of the other senses. All this obliges companies to rethink not only the ways new brands are planned but also how they are communicated and commercialized. The perception of a product today is becoming increasingly the fruit of a multidimensional and multisensory experience, so that the modalities vary in which the quality of the product is evaluated. Product marketing has for a long time attributed growing importance to sight, touch and taste; however, in recent years an approach which allows collective mobilization of all five senses has started to be exploited, attributing greater attention to smell and hearing. The extraordinary development which sensorial marketing has undergone in this period can be traced only in part to the incapacity of traditional marketing to consider the impulsive and emotive aspects of purchasing decisions; rather, new and "complex" needs which have emerged at a social level have intervened to determine this novel reference horizon.

We have already had occasion to highlight how the modern consumer is an increasingly "lighter" and more hedonistic consumer, moved more and more by desire and the taste for getting pleasure out of every act of consumption. Let's see how it is possible to build up a powerful positioning strategy by giving brands sensorial capacity.

OLFACTORY BRANDING

Smell has relatively strong connections with the area of the brain which is associated with memory and emotions and is therefore decisive in evaluating experience. Olfactory memory can make a person relive previous experiences or episodes from the past, and the emotions associated with them, with great immediacy.

Thus some of the houses we each of us know have, just like people, a clear olfactory identity, so much so that they can be immediately remembered, even many years after, thanks primarily to their smell.

Now, unlike sight and hearing, which stimulate the rational part of the brain, olfactory stimuli are elaborated even before being rationally codified. This means that smell dialogues with the emotional and instinctive part of an individual, and is therefore able to influence all those unplanned purchasing decisions, by acting as a generator of emotions both during the purchasing process and in the experience of consumption. Also, unlike taste, which as we will see has few variants, the sense of smell's perceptive range is vast: this means a person may be incapable of conjuring up smells again despite being able to recognize them.

The first companies which took an interest in scenting products were those operating in the field of household cleaning and personal hygiene, categories where the smell given off by the product was a particular indicator of its effectiveness. For this reason, smells have become real characterizing features of brands and have acquired growing importance among the motivations behind choice. The market leadership in the cleaning and detergent sectors has in recent years played on its capacity to propose more and more unusual scents able to evoke worlds, places and situations which have very little connection with the use of the products.

There are today many companies which have deliberately created an "olfactory logo," by which we mean a real olfactory signature for their products – think, for example, of the now famous smell which emanates from the leather of Frau armchairs. In the past, on the other hand, a few companies created an olfactory logo unawares. Studying these cases reveals some very significant data regarding the effectiveness of olfactory marketing. As a matter of fact, for the people interviewed during research, the smell of vanillin aldehyde evoked not only baby talc, but also the name Borotalco – the company which produces it; in France, the smell of cedarwood evoked the color pencils made by Crayola.[3]

Consider, moreover, the famous Barbour jacket. What most distinguishes this line of raincoats, designed originally for hunting, is the particular smell they give off, which comes from the special wax used to ensure they are really waterproof.

Then there are, of course, brands which have been able to build an olfactory logo based on non-smell – think of Geox and Febreze. Geox put a perforated membrane into the rubber sole; the perforations in the membrane correspond with the areas of the sole of the foot where the concentration of sweat glands is greatest. In so doing, the company resolved the problem of the condensation which is produced by the natural sweating of feet and which is one of the causes of foot odor. With Febreze, Procter & Gamble launched a new category of products which seek out the smells trapped in fabrics, capture them and leave only a pleasant sense of freshness and cleanliness.

In the car sector, the management of smells as a component of the product has followed two distinct guidelines. With some the aim has been to eliminate the so-called "new smell" of a car, since consumers thought it was unpleasant, and even the cause of car sickness. With others, on the other hand, the concern has been to design every single component so that it maintains the "new smell" as long as possible. In fact, some studies have shown that a new car buyer's perception of the product as exciting lasts as long as the car maintains the "new" smell and, as soon as that disappears, the product (and consequently the brand) is experienced in a more routine way and with less affection. The longer the "new" scent lasts, therefore, the greater the dilution of consumer enthusiasm, and this conditions in a more consistent way the experience of using the brand.

Moreover, there are many supermarket chains and individual shops which use smells to "mark" their sales environments, making them unique and distinguishable from the others. All this has the aim of influencing and orientating consumer evaluations and behaviors. It has in fact been demonstrated that in the presence of pleasantly scented environments, the purchaser has a reduced perception of the time spent in the point of sale, and that introducing particular aromas alters the consumer's perception of time, above all in critical moments, such as when queuing at a checkout.[4] Many retail firms, in order to provide effective responses in terms of reducing checkout waiting times, increase the number of staff, thus incurring serious costs: would it not perhaps be simpler to stimulate the mobilization of the consumer's senses to try and reduce the perception of time spent in a queue?[5]

A sales environment in which there is deliberate stimulation of the senses, among them that of smell, will influence consumers toward staying longer at the point of sale and consequently make more purchases. Thus Timberland gives its shops a connotation of naturalness by paying attention to the smells, particularly those of wood, leather and baskets of apples. Thomas Pink, a shirt-maker based in Jermyn Street, London, diffuses essences of clean washing in its shops worldwide.

At the communication level, new and interesting perspectives have been opened up by the possibility of replicating a product's smell on various supports such as paper and fabrics or emitting it via environment essence diffusers. Lickable ads, such as that for Welch's grape juice discussed below, while being connected primarily with taste branding, also leverage the olfactory element, since the senses of taste and smell are so closely linked.

The olfactory message is particularly effective because it works on a communication channel which is not overflowing with messages, and involves the receiver emotionally by working on the most remote areas of the brain, namely those linked with both memory and emotions.[6]

However, there are difficulties in using smells as a means of communication, since the physical process of decodifying and cataloging smells is rather slow, particularly compared with other forms of communication such as visual and auditory. This is particularly true if it is not accompanied by other sensory stimuli. Using only the olfactory element can therefore, as Gallucci suggests, generate what linguists define as a "blurred concept" – a phenomenon which occurs when a person remembers a letter or two but not the whole word. The risk is linked to the fact that smell stimulates something in the memory which the consumer has difficulty conceptualizing. In other words, it recalls something the consumer is unable mentally to give a form to.

Moreover, particularly when olfactory marketing is used in points of sale, there is the risk of creating an overlaying of smells; there are technological infrastructures today however which are able to define exactly the physical boundaries of propagation and thus diffuse a number of essences simultaneously without their being mixed together.

The correlation between smells and experience is influenced by various factors, such as socio-economic background, sex, age, religious beliefs and ethnic group. This means, for example, that incense will be perceived by an Oriental as a perfume linked to religion, while for a Westerner, it will evoke the image of faraway, mysterious, exotic worlds, full of fascination and atmosphere. Again, more simply, the smell of white truffles is perceived as intoxicating and enrapturing by some and as unpleasant by others.

The sense of smell is attributed with a primary function of having a positive influence on the balance of emotions. It is no coincidence that in recent years the use of aromatherapy has increased rapidly, even in working environments. A particular case is that of a Japanese firm which diffuses different essences into the workplace, depending on the time of day: invigorating and energizing lemon in the morning, cheering rose in the middle of the day and refreshing cypress after the lunch break. Smells in fact influence people's moods, and thus become an important ingredient in strategies developed to achieve a holistic state of wellbeing.

SOUND BRANDING

If smell is connected more with memory, sound is strictly linked to mood – we can affirm that sound is able to satisfy or modify moods and generate sensations and emotions. Let's think, for example, what a romantic comedy would be like without a suitable soundtrack, or a horror movie with an extremely melodic soundtrack. They would lose their capacity to both generate emotions and plunge the audience into involvement in the plot. Sound can inspire joy and sadness in equal measure.[7]

The ear is one of the most complex organs in the human body; it not only makes it possible to listen, but also performs an important role in maintaining balance, through the stability control point at the end of the labyrinth.

And today the use of audio in planning products is acquiring ever greater importance. Above all, for those products which are not visible, and therefore perceptible to the consumer, sound has been a factor which has made it possible to give an almost real dimension to something which was not real. In this regard, think about the Intel microprocessor: the brand acquired a sort of physicality thanks to the now famous sound signal which is emitted by turning on a computer which contains this component. Research has demonstrated that the Intel jingle is more memorable than, or at least equally memorable to, its logo. It should come as no surprise therefore that ten musicians were involved in composing the four notes of the Windows Vista boot jingle, nor that eighteen months were needed to do it. A decade and more before it, the Windows 95 startup boot was itself composed by the famous musician Brian Eno.

Each product has in fact a more or less marked sound dimension. Let's think, for example, of a bottle of Coca-Cola and the unmistakable sound given out when the top is opened: it really seems as if there is no other drink like it on the market. In fact, the sound of a bottle of Coca-Cola is linked closely to its formula and gaseous composition: together they univocally and unequivocally characterize the brand.

Other examples are those of the sounds of a Porsche or Ferrari motor; at BMW there are even 60 specialists in charge of maintaining the parts which emit the sounds of the German car, and each sound is linked to a particular function representative of comfort as well as luxury and quality. No detail must be ignored therefore from the exhaust note of the powerful six-cylinder motor to that of the doors closing. Each noise contributes to building the product's identity and the BMW style.

Every one of these brands has known how to build their own sound dimension, but maybe the most obvious case is that of Nokia, whose ringtone "Nokia tune" is absolutely the most used ringtone in the world, so that it has become one of the physical components of the brand. Market research has also demonstrated that the superiority of Kellogg's cereals is determined partly by the ability to be crunchable for the hearing, not only in the palate. It is in fact no coincidence that the company invests considerable sums in research projects aimed at making the crunch even more sonorous; they understand not only that the unequalled status of the product must not be limited only to the dimensions of wellbeing, taste and lightness, but also that the sound is an integral part of the brand.[8] Meanwhile, even cosmetic firms study the emotional effect created by the "plop" sound made by opening a jar of cream.[9]

As with smells, the elimination of sound can also become an integral part of a brand. Think, for example, of electrical appliance manufacturers who, over time, have created products which are quieter and quieter, or computer manufacturers, like Apple for example, who have invested heavily in reducing the noise made by cooling fans, even succeeding, on some models, in eliminating them and replacing them with heat disposal units.

After the great interest in designing forms, companies must also concern themselves more and more with the sound and music design of their products.

VISUAL BRANDING

We live in a society in which we are subject to an extraordinary bombardment of visual stimuli. Excessive exposure leads individuals to a mechanical, almost unconscious, assimilation of them, thus invalidating their motivational capacity in the purchasing process.

Although our perception of its supremacy has been challenged by the mobilization of the other senses, sight maintains an extremely important role. Above all, the use of color is decisive since cognitive and affective responses are associated with it, and these can be made to "bear fruit" as part of marketing policies.

An emblematic case is the strategic use of color by Apple computers. While all the other computer manufacturers based their competitiveness on processor speed and memory size, on available hard disk space and graphic card performance, Apple differentiated its products by launching the iMac line, which was characterized by vibrant colors able to transform a technological object that was quite ascetic from an emotional point of view into something more than a computer – almost an item of furnishing. We can say that Apple is an extremely effective example of how changing the visual angle from which an object is observed can bring about evolution of the species, as it did for the blue tits. The lesson to be drawn from the Apple experience is that functionality, price and performance are only part of the story. To put it better, they are the basis for creating a wider story, that of experience: in the case of Apple, the use of color allowed a competitive advantage to be built which has led to most of the other personal computer manufacturers following the path taken by Cupertino's company.[10]

The case of Crocs, already mentioned, allows us to understand how banal products can tell new and exciting stories, through the use of color, making it possible to build a brand identity which is increasingly disconnected from the functional aspects of the product.

Philips's "Sense & Simplicity" advertising campaign is positioned on the polysensual front, by setting itself the goal of transmitting to the market the distinctive image of a company able to carry on producing innovation and intuitive solutions, and contextually able to satisfy customers and consumers with use experiences which are increasingly richer in meaning. The communication of this campaign is simple and essential: a hand which changes shape, changing into the hand of a woman, a baby, an old person who opens a white box by touching it delicately. The use of the color white aims at drawing attention to the concept of "easy" technology; the allusion to touch brings us full circle to the accessibility of technology, indiscriminate of age or sex.

Moreover, color performs an essential function in planning sales areas, since the optical and dimensional effects it creates allow shapes and dimensions to take on different connotations. Each color thus has a precise function within the planning of the architectural sales space: red reduces surfaces and recalls the concept of "speed" (a Ferrari is red, just as red is at the basis of the logo of McDonald's – a form of fast catering); yellow reduces surfaces with "patches of color"; orange brings objects closer; green leaves dimensions unaltered; blue increases the dimensions of objects; purple limits the resolution; black takes away the sense of borders; white suggests peace, serenity; and so on.

Along with color, lighting acquires strategic relevance in planning sales areas, since it makes it possible to show up spaces, define volumes, supply heat and, above all, support the chosen theme by playing a primary role in creating atmosphere. Strong, concentrated lighting, combined with weak contrasts and light and dark tones, for example, would be the most suitable if the aim was to create an exciting atmosphere, while dynamic lighting, combined with strong contrasts and changeable light and dark tones, would be better suited to an "iridescent" atmosphere. Modern technology connected with lighting and the arrival of new professional figures such as the light designer offer important new opportunities for commerce. The use of dynamic light makes it possible to enhance storefronts and windows by adapting them, for example, to the different lighting conditions throughout the day and the changing of the seasons. All this makes it possible for the storefront to effectively perform its important role of communication and "welcome" in every environmental condition.

TASTE BRANDING

Of the five senses, taste is perhaps the most intimate one since it cannot be stimulated at a distance nor is it outwardly displayed. There are basically four basic taste variants: saltiness, sweetness, acidity and bitterness, and any taste is nothing other than the combination of these base variants. The tongue has different zones, each of which is better suited to perceiving each of the variants. The tip, for example, is better suited to perceiving sweetness.[11]

Most "taste" sensations derive from multiple sensorial modalities. In fact, apart from the taste papillae, full of tactile receivers and terminals whose task it is to distinguish flavors, the sense of smell is stimulated by the aromas and perfumes given off by foods. We can also say that hearing is important in enjoying what we eat: think of the sensation provoked by crunchy food. And as for sight, it is no coincidence that in colloquial Italian, for example, people say that food that is well presented could be "eaten with your eyes." It is therefore evident that taste cannot be thought of as a "self-sufficient" sense.

Taste and smell are strictly related to each other. When the sense of smell is reduced after a cold, the ability to perceive the basic variants of taste is compromised by as much as 80 per cent. In fact a reduction in taste capacity that is not associated with a reduced sense of smell is rather rare.

According to the anthropologist Claude Fischler, taste is a sense strongly "tinged with affectivity": for example, sweet is consoling, spicy an invitation to transgress, and bitter punitive.[12] The need for emotion and the rediscovery of the senses leads the modern consumer to a constant search for novelty able to surprise, stimulate and intrigue them. It is superfluous to underline how the component of taste represents one of the principal levers used in the development of agro-alimentary products. In fact, taste is the sense which is strongly linked to satisfying one of man's primary needs. However, what gives new importance to taste is the growing relevance which an increasingly hedonistic consumer attributes to it as a generator of psychological wellbeing. The consumer is no longer satisfied by something good, but rather wants to be amazed, excited and even provoked. Therefore, the food products currently offered by the market propose ever more bizarre and unusual combinations. Supermarket shelves are full of items characterized by unusual combinations, such as chocolate and chili pepper or green tea, or products scented with the most diverse essences. This is to say nothing of restaurant menus, which are less and less conventional and increasingly characterized by creative proposals where foods which in culinary tradition seemed incapable of going together are combined, without fear of offending the sensibilities of the consumer. Today prejudices regarding taste are gradually disappearing, legitimizing combinations which in the past were considered almost against nature or sacrilegious, but which are now becoming objects of desire for a consumer who likes increasingly to transgress and subvert the rules of tradition.[13]

Far from a heretic, then, is the famous Spanish chef Ferran Adrià, who collaborates with chemists and physicists to unite creativity and new technology in preparing foods as part of the so-called "molecular cookery."[14]

Food, as Fabris notes, represents an observatory of great interest even when it comes to understanding social dynamics, because the changes happening in people's lifestyles are reflected more immediately in eating than elsewhere.[15]

We could say that for today's consumer, with their love of transgression, the confusion of heterogeneous gastronomic cultures and suggestions also works at a psychological level, no longer as mere curiosity but also as a reassuring factor and as a way of rebalancing the synergies, anxieties and contradictions which infest, as Del Duca has highlighted, our alimentary imagination.[16] The most emblematic example of this process is certainly represented by yogurt, which had affirmed itself as a healthy element, and therefore far from the pleasures of taste. For large numbers of people, eating yogurt represented almost an alimentary constriction, a sort of food for the "sick" or "hospital" food, something which many would have willingly done without but which they were forced to eat. Today yogurt has divided itself into two dimensions, enriching itself with new functionalities. It has lost the "punitive" character which relegated it to the healthfood consumption niche and has taken on a new, more exciting one, widening the market boundaries of "health" to the sphere of taste.[17]

The food products of the future will be planned more and more to stimulate the senses and amaze the consumer, pushing research to the constant development of new associations, new combinations and new consumption modalities in the planning of foods.

Let it be quite clear that even the rediscovery of organic agriculture can be interpreted as an attempt to get back the "lost taste" of food. In fact, while the consumer may be receptive to new and unusual combinations, they are also less willing to accept products latterly deprived of their taste essence. The rediscovery of organic foods pushes the consumer toward a search for those ancestral, traditional tastes sacrificed at the altar of intensive agriculture, which privileges yield at the expense of quality. To sum up, if on the one hand there emerges a strong demand from the consumer to be amazed and provoked by food products able to present them with new associations and compositions, there is on the other hand the need to get back lost tastes. The food products of the future will be those able to satisfy these requirements.

We must not however fall into the easy misunderstanding that taste is the exclusive prerogative of food products: think of the importance taste has in characterizing products which are *not* eaten, such as toothpaste, lip balm, or even some medicines. They are however products which, in carrying out their main function, which is not linked to feeding, are able to give a less irksome character to their routine use, which through sensorial activation is often linked with an unpleasant duty.[18]

An example of the effective application of taste marketing to non-food products is represented by Listerine mouthwash. Its bad and particularly intense taste, the result of a high alcohol content, makes Listerine a unique mouthwash to which the consumer attributes extraordinary effectiveness. In reality, Listerine is no better a mouthwash than others, but its "bad" taste gives it an aura of greater effectiveness. We could say that being unpleasant it is associated with the sometimes far from pleasant taste of a dentist's medications, which patients know, however, are "indispensable"; more than a few consumers even associate the unpleasant taste with the idea of "treatment" and safeguarding the best oral hygiene conditions – the same sensations that should be felt in the dentist's chair. Listerine is a valid (if extreme) example of taste branding.

As mentioned above, in 2008 Welch's started using lickable ads as part of their communication, an example of how both smells and tastes can be reproduced on paper for marketing purposes. The full-page print ad features a picture of a bottle of Welch's grape juice and a special peel-off strip which readers are invited to lick so as to sample the juice. Lickable ads are probably still in the experimental stage, but marketers are enthusiastic about their potential, and their development highlights how important getting consumers to use all their five senses to process advertisements can be in strengthening the brand–consumer connection.

TACTILE BRANDING

The skin is a person's most extensive organ, and touch is perceived all over the body, with lips and fingertips playing a decidedly predominant role in tactile perception.

Touch represents an extraordinary means of mediating with, and learning about, the surrounding world and the objects it is made up of. Just think, for example, how the contact the newborn have with their mothers helps them approach both the world and life. Through suckling, the little one learns not only how to get food, but also how to reduce the stress of the transition from the maternal womb to the outside environment.

As Greimas in fact suggests:

> because of . . . its sensual value (sensual being the tangible culmina-
> tion of sensitivity) and the close proximity necessary between subject
> and object, [touch] has been consecrated the deepest of the senses,
> and by virtue of such depth becomes the privileged place of aesthetic
> experience.[19]

The consumer can perceive a product's profound essence by touch.
The identification of some objective characteristics such as softness,
heat and consistency communicates important information about the
product.

Gillette is a particularly effective example of how a brand can be
successful also because of its tactile content (in a broad sense), accom-
plishing a task which goes well beyond the function of shaving: beyond
the precision of its razor heads, which follow the profile of the face, the
micro-fins delicately stretch the skin to give a closer shave, the aloe
essences tone and refresh the skin and, last but not least, the special
handle in elastomero produces very pleasant tactile sensations.[20]

The Motorola Pebl is a further example of how a product can distinguish itself within a category which has a high technological content,
on the basis of elements which have little to do with technology. The
principal characteristic of the Pebl is in fact tactile: it is no coincidence
that the American company promoted this mobile by inviting the consumer "to hold it in order to discover its beauty, to discover its materials
so pleasing to touch and to caress its soft curves."[21]

It seems evident that choice of materials is important when planning
a product: a careful choice of materials can stimulate the consumer who
is in a condition of uncertainty to decide to purchase the product. By
means of tactile perception a product is able to supply information and
seduction, thus contributing to increasing its prestige and affirming
its brand image on an emotional level too. However, we must not fall
into the easy mistake of confusing the tactile aspects of a product with
those connected with ergonomics. A tactile content goes far beyond the
traditional and codified canons of ergonomics, so ascetically respected
in the world of production.[22]

Moreover, the tactile approach to marketing can transmit a promise
of the use of the product. Think, for example, of what has happened
in the car market. Scientific research has made it possible to produce
cars using lighter materials (for example, aluminium) which are equal

in their qualities to those used in the past. There have been numerous benefits from this: reduced fuel consumption, better performance and greater safety deriving from planned deformation if there is a crash. However, the general feeling is that lighter cars are less resistant to impact, and more than a few people miss the heavy car doors of times gone by.

One of the brands which has most distinguished itself from the point of view of tactile appeal is Bang & Olufsen, which produces luxury audio and video products characterized by extraordinary sound and visual performance and particularly appealing design. One of the most important innovations launched by the Danish firm was that of the remote-control unit, which made it possible to manage all the devices it produced, from the CD player through the DVD player to the television receiver. Launched in 1985, it quickly became a cult object for the lovers of high-end electronics. Today a myriad of similar products are present on the market, but no universal remote control-device has the same charm as that of Bang & Olufsen. What makes this unit extraordinarily unique is its weight. In fact, there is lead inside, which makes it particularly heavy and at the same time provides a tactile perception of great solidity. All Bang & Olufsen products are heavier and when touched give the sensation of being extraordinarily long-lasting; the weight and tactile sensation provide information which leads the consumer to perceive the superiority of the products both rationally and emotionally. It matters little that, in reality, the strength of technological products is linked to their absolutely intangible component (the software): weight promises something which at an emotional level technology cannot do. This is yet another incongruity of modernity.

PART III

THE FUNDAMENTALS OF BRANDING: SOME RULES FOR KEEPING ON THE RIGHT TRACK

CHAPTER 11

BUILDING A FRAME OF REFERENCE BETWEEN ADVANTAGES AND PARITY

A brand's positioning is related strictly to the specific meaning it assumes in the mind of the consumer. It represents the answer to the goals which motivate purchase and consumption, a response enriched by the multiple meanings attributed to those goals.[1] An effective positioning of a brand requires the systematic evaluation of some crucial elements, and is the routine followed by companies when generating and consolidating a brand. To this end, four consequential steps can be identified: identification of the brand's target, identification of the principal competitors who can allow the consumer to achieve the same goals, identifying the brand's differentiation elements, and providing motivation.

IDENTIFICATION OF THE BRAND'S TARGET

This is based on the logic of market segmentation which create subdivisions between groups of consumers who are similar, and the subsequent selection of the most suitable group or groups for the brand. The characteristics of a brand's target are identified on the basis of numerous factors which, in extreme synthesis, can be traced to the modalities with which the brand and, in a wider logic, the category are used.

The identification of the brand's target, the goals which guide its purchase and the modalities of its use provide useful instructions for building the brand's frame of reference. However, there is a circular cause–effect reaction, since defining the frame of reference can lead in turn to circumscribing or widening a target by means of more precise information about the situations in which a brand may be used. The case of Johnson's Baby Shampoo confirms this. When the product was launched it was positioned for exclusive use on babies, the use it had been created for, and its performance – its extreme delicacy and the fact it does not irritate the eyes – made it particularly suitable. The consumption experience of the product soon showed up an alternative use by people who washed their hair often and therefore needed a mild shampoo – and what can be more delicate than a baby shampoo? Modifying the brand's frame of reference led to the company reviewing its positioning, no longer limiting the shampoo to babies but orientating it toward adults too: for example, those who do a lot of sport and need to wash their hair frequently.

IDENTIFICATION OF THE PRINCIPAL COMPETITORS

Targeting a brand based on consumer goals can be extremely effective in planning a marketing strategy aimed at identifying both potential competitors who can allow the consumer to achieve the same goals and also those who are already part of the category. Marketing literature teaches us how a need can be satisfied in different ways and with different products, sometimes in a very different way or ways.Think of the need to refresh oneself with a drink. This need is traditionally associated with the soft drink category, where products have the characterizing feature of being refreshing and the role of relational catalyst (think of a party or a pizza with friends). These goals are in part achievable by using other product categories – from bottled water to sports drinks, which not only refresh but also restore the minerals lost during sports activities, something which helps people to cope with higher temperatures more easily and makes the drinks particularly effective in refreshing.

Also think of how many product categories can be used for female hair removal: waxing, traditional shaving systems, creams and strips, electric shavers and so on. What is more, the same need can be satisfied directly by the consumer, by using one of these products, or she can call on a specialist operator, for example, a beautician. Limiting a brand's frame of reference to direct competitors in the category would certainly be going astray. Gillette Satin's competitor is not only Wilkinson Intuition but also the local beautician.

When, toward the beginning of the 1990s, a few of the main American supermarket chains found themselves faced with a significant drop in sales turnover, they initially attributed the phenomenon to the increased competitive pressure which characterized the sector. So they adopted more aggressive pricing policies and widened the services they offered. Sales continued to go down, however. Only when they realized that the problem was not horizontal competition from their direct competitors, and widened their frame of reference, did they have a clear idea of the situation and the road to follow. In fact, they became aware of how a growing proportion of food consumption was gradually moving toward catering or toward sales outlets with a strong connotation of proximity, often open twenty-four hours a day, as in the case of minimarts linked to petrol stations. The number of consumers' stomachs being satisfied by US retailers was smaller and smaller, while contextually the quota satisfied by the most disparate forms of catering, in particular fast food or takeaway, was growing. Only by identifying a larger competitor framework were they able to review their own offer dynamics, and, by introducing new processes and new product categories, to stop the serious hemorrhaging of turnover.

IDENTIFYING THE BRAND'S DIFFERENTIATION ELEMENTS

Once the brand's frame of reference has been defined, it is necessary to spend time considering the brand's capacity to achieve success within the competitive arena and, consequently, identify the differentiation elements it has.

PROVIDING MOTIVATION

Finally, faced with a clearly defined frame of reference and the construction of differentiation elements, a brand must be armed with a deep motivation which encourages consumers to believe in it, and so prefer it to other possible alternatives present on the market.

To make the above process more understandable, let's look at the case of Vorwerk. Thermomix is a food processor manufactured and distributed by Vorwerk, a company which makes high-quality electrical appliances and is unusual because of its choice of distribution strategy: direct house-to-house selling. Although outside the traditional commercialization channels of white and brown goods, Vorwerk has been able to make itself very well known among the Italian female public. Thermomix is a particularly powerful food processor which allows women with little time or limited culinary skills to prepare dishes they would normally not be able to make. Thermomix's owners also find it extraordinarily easy to use and clean. Furthermore, with Thermomix, ingredients can be economized, and particularly tasty and elaborate dishes prepared. With just one bowl and a limited selection of interchangeable knives, Thermomix grates, grinds, minces, makes juices, cuts into pieces, mixes, kneads, weighs the ingredients and leavens, but above all, it cooks and even steams. All you have to do is put all the ingredients in the bowl, follow the instructions in the recipe books which can be bought separately, program it and, in a short time, the dishes are ready. In the case of Thermomix, the reference target is all those women, mainly young, who have little time or who are not very good at cooking, but who still want to have the pleasure of preparing varied, attractive and creative meals quickly for their families and friends. The product's frame of reference is also represented by all those machines, defined as food processors, which make it possible to carry out certain domestic activities quickly and easily.

Thermomix's differentiation element and its real "reason why" is its capacity to perform the functions traditionally carried out by a food processor, but more quickly and with greater power, and above all to do something no other food processor can: cook. Moreover, a wide series of recipe books are available for Thermomix, with different thematic contents, such as for example party menus, baby food or finger food.

Whoever purchases Thermomix becomes part of a community where experiences, gastronomic secrets and inspirations are shared. In recent years, Thermomix has affirmed itself as a sort of urban legend for young women, becoming a rather frequent topic of conversation. Extraordinary functionality and entry into the Thermomix owners' community (with a related sense of exclusion being felt by non-owners) are the two main motivations for purchasing the brand.

There is a wide abundance of literature available on defining targets and segmentation strategies which we would invite the reader to refer to; it is important now for us to concentrate on the need to build a solid and realistic frame of reference for the brand. The representation of this framework can come about in numerous ways; we believe that the prevalent means of classification is the performance offered by the product and the other requirements of a more abstract nature which guide consumer choice.

There are many cases in which a brand can establish an effective frame of reference by claiming membership of a category in such a way as to make the consumer understand that it can achieve the aim associated with its purchase or use. Coca-Cola, for example, identifies the soft drink category, associating the brand with all those pleasant-tasting drinks which go well with informal meals and are very refreshing.

This classification modality can also be achieved by choosing a specific competitor whose performance exemplifies and represents the aims a brand wants to satisfy. We will see how, in an advertising campaign, Subaru associated its image with that of Volvo. Clearly it did not present itself in this way in order to subtract market share from the Swedish company, but rather to associate its own image with that of a company which was considered "best in class" when it came to safety.

Let's also think of how Visa modeled its profile by positioning itself against the premium credit card, American Express. Visa's direct competitor was MasterCard; the two credit cards were equal in all dimensions: the large number of shops which accepted them, attributes, issuing banks, socio-demographic characteristics, target and, last but not least, market share. In practice, the two products were so identical that consumers had developed the same associations about them. For Visa, competing with its twin was certainly difficult and made identifying net differentiation points highly problematic. So it decided to widen its frame of reference to include American Express, with which it was not in direct competition and which the consumer perceived as the quality leader of the category. A weak point of American Express compared with Visa was discovered (the fact that it was accepted in fewer shops), and a campaign was launched which highlighted the contrasting omni-pervasive presence of Visa by means of the claim "It's everywhere you want to be." The results of this repositioning of the brand were extremely interesting: in fact Visa had taken away market share not from American Express but from MasterCard, succeeding in a task which, had Visa used direct comparison, would have seemed almost impossible.[2]

Classification via a category or a competitor implies that the brand has expressly chosen to compete with other brands with which it shares concrete performance. With regard to this argument, Keller talks about elements of parity or, to be precise, associations with the brand which are not necessarily unique but which can be shared with other brands.[3]

The elements of parity with a category legitimize, in the eyes of the consumer, the brand's belonging to that category and assume particular relevance in cases of brand extension, where a brand which is already successful in one or more categories decides to enter into a new one.

Category associations therefore represent a sort of "entry ticket" for taking part in a competitive game. In other words, it is through points of parity that a brand is legitimized as credible in the eyes of the consumer.

In many cases, these associations are based on an attempt to deny the existence of competitors' differentiation elements. It is precisely by highlighting points of parity that a brand tries to make competitors' efforts based on differentiation elements ineffective. It is no coincidence that the proposal of elements of parity is often done by consolidated brands who have a strong market position, so as to use them as a sort of barrier against the entry of new brands or the repositioning of others.

An emblematic case in this sense is represented by the campaign launched a few years or so ago by Burger King, in which it claimed that the potato fries sold in its restaurants were tastier and crispier than those sold by McDonald's. The vast advertising campaign was launched with the claim "Better taste" but the results were very different from those hoped for. In fact, rather than convincing consumers of Burger King's superiority, the claim "Better taste" had the effect of reawakening in the consumer associations linked to taste in respect of McDonald's. McDonald's, to reinforce this association, launched a reply campaign with the claim "Equal great taste"; by not claiming elements of superiority over its competitor in the campaign, and thanks to the strength of the brand as a result of the favorable consumer associations with taste, McDonald's practically repudiated its rival's promise. McDonald's therefore did not need to differentiate itself from competitors and understood that it was sufficient to reactivate every now and then what was already present in consumers' minds, namely the brand's superior taste.[4] Moreover, Burger King's campaign used as an element for promoting the brand the superior quality of a product, its french fries, which no longer represented an important element in choosing one chain as opposed to another. What in the United States was called the "French Fries War" had the sole effect of increasing consumption in the category, leaving market shares more or less unaltered.

Proposing a brand by means of the elements it has in common with competitors makes it possible to attribute further meaning to the frame of reference, particularly where there is a target which gives special attention to a product's performance and identifies such performance with a specific category in which the brand is not very well known. The need to concentrate on points of parity is even greater the further along the line products are in the successive stages of their life cycles. In fact, the nearer the product is to maturity, the greater is the number of competitor brands in the category, and therefore the greater is the homogeneity between products. The distinctive element tends in fact to lose its function with the category's maturity owing to the minor importance it assumes in the choice process, which progressively focuses more on the common aspects than on the differentiating ones.

When a brand has none of the attributes which would normally legitimize its belonging to a specific category, using points of parity in the frame of reference process is, quite evidently, unlikely to be achievable. Claiming that a product is something which it actually is not by aligning it to a category is obviously not advisable. There are circumstances however in which a brand which does not possess the recognized attributes of a category can gain benefit from association with that category if there are low points of overlap. The aim of such a frame of reference is to highlight the goals which the consumer can achieve by using that brand. Think, for example, of the case of PDAs or smartphones presented as if they were small computers. Presenting a telephone by associating it with a computer, and therefore as having a processor, operating system and the possibility of using software normally installed in a PC, makes it possible to propose new reasons for buying products which, however technological they may be, have more and more come to be seen as mere commodities.

Finally, it must be stressed that the frame of reference must provide strict boundaries within which the brand can move. Even if a brand has a multidimensional connotation, it cannot be everything to everybody, and it is therefore necessary to avoid attributing too many qualities to it: too long a list of elements could make the brand lose credibility by making it appear incoherent and false.

Differentiating elements, on the other hand, are (again according to Keller's definition) strong, favorable associations unique to a specific brand, and which can be based on any type of attribute or benefit connected with the brand; these associations can be functional or abstract.[5] Basically, these elements indicate the superiority of a brand compared with others in the same frame of reference, and can be expressed according to different levels of abstraction: some brands therefore can claim concrete superiority based on the functional aspects, superior performance and good value for money, while others promise something more abstract, such as emotional benefits associated with their purchase and consumption.

Superiority based on functional elements acquires credibility when it is supported by induced motivation. The non-technologically relevant attributes may thus sometimes become the reason for believing in a functional benefit.

Such superiority can be effectively built by representing those who use the brand and the related occasion of consumption. Think how important a testimonial is in the case of sports products. Tiger Woods has attributed to the Nike line of golfing products a superiority which does not derive from the brand's history in that category. Because of its lack of tradition in a sport in which tradition is everything, before the young champion's affirmation, Nike was not legitimized as a brand for golfers and so could not successfully compete with Callaway, Taylor Made and Mitzuno.

Functional benefits are almost always correlated with the benefits of a more abstract nature, which represent an important basis for achieving an emotional connection with the brand on the part of the consumer. McDonald's promotes the taste of its food as the basis for developing a further association with the play-like character that a meal in a fast food restaurant can acquire. Lunch or a snack at McDonald's can thus be an occasion for consuming a cheap, quick and tasty meal and letting the children have fun.

The emotional resonance is very often completely independent from the functional benefits offered by a product, and proposed as an element of differentiation. The emotional element increasingly constitutes a brand's real factor of differentiation. Think of those brands which sell access to worlds and communities and which, as we have already highlighted, take on an almost mystic and religious aura; or think of the brands focussed, instead, on aspects which are linked more to interiority such as, for example, the desire for self-expression, individual growth and overcoming personal limits.

Modern technologies linked to the web have significantly increased the capacity of firms to create real communities around their brands. More than 200,000 athletes visit the Nike Plus site daily, where it is possible to communicate using the Apple iPod. The site allows runners to download and compare their respective performances and more than half of the members visit it at least four times a week.[6]

In the Adidas "Impossible Is Nothing" campaign, thirty internationally famous athletes and simple fans tell their impossible stories through freehand paintings and drawings: encouragement to overcome obstacles and limits in order to achieve the goal, the dream. At the presentation of the campaign in Rome, Eric Liedtke, one of the top managers of Adidas's Global Brand Marketing affirmed:

> When you witness a victory, a final result, it is not always obvious how the athletes got there or what obstacles they have had to overcome on the way. Sharing the journey, and more precisely the challenges, that they have had to face allows us to observe an enchanting aspect which is often ignored. We are convinced that observing the backstage life of these athletes will stimulate people to undertake their own journey.[7]

In fact both emotional and functional benefits are equally correlated to the people who enjoy them or use them.

Häagen-Dazs, a famous US brand of ice-cream, came up against notable difficulties in increasing its penetration toward the adult public. So, research was commissioned to identify what the barriers were which were conditioning behavior and what meanings adults attributed to consuming ice-cream. What emerged from the research was that adults thought of ice-cream as something children consumed, or at the most as something to be limited to a dessert at the end of a meal on special occasions – festivities and other particular moments. Just like their children, they needed to have permission to eat ice-cream outside these occasions. The company therefore decided that sensuality would be the key to unblocking adult consumer reticence, and to this end it realized a campaign which was strongly centered on this theme: pairs of lovers were shown in the "moment of sharing" – through ice-cream. The campaign was so incisive and "cheeky" that the results were not long in coming: in a short time adult consumption increased rapidly.

In choosing elements of differentiation, it is necessary to take into account how desirable the consumer considers them to be, and to what extent the consumer thinks the company is able to maintain its implicit promise – in other words, what their *relevance* is.[8] Relevance represents the degree of importance the consumer attributes to the element of differentiation and therefore the effective value this assumes.

The concept of relevance, in an economic framework such as the current one, characterized by an extraordinary surplus of offerings, has changed its meaning substantially. Firms think too often that adding an ever increasing number of attributes to a product leads to the product differentiating itself more from the other competitors and therefore to taking on greater relevance. Think, for example, of the world of consumer electronics. How many of the functions present today in a computer, in software, a DVD player or a microwave oven are effectively used by consumers? In the best of cases, that of "expert users," maybe 20 per cent? All those functions not used have in fact low relevance; they are elements which are scarcely effective in conditioning the process of brand choice, since they do not attribute a brand with a distinctive character. The only real aim correlated to building a default offer which is richer in attributes can be that of creating, through the addition of non-relevant functions, a greater "technological" aura. The longer the list of functions the more "technically muscular" the brand appears to be.

This reflection leads us to consider how important the identification of user and occasion of use is in defining a brand's frame of reference. It is indispensable that the points of differentiation acquire relevance, both in terms of desirability and in terms of utility, in a variable way depending on the product user and the occasions and modalities of use.

To make this concept more comprehensible, let's consider the example of a discussion we happened to witness between a couple of friends. The subject was choosing an oven. The husband, at all costs, wanted to buy a highly technological product with an infinite number of functions – among them the possibility of steaming. His wife, though, had decided to opt for a product which could do fewer things and did not have the steamer function. In the husband's opinion, the fact that the oven did not have this function plunged the brand his wife had chosen into an area of technological mediocrity. The concept of relevance, correlated to the principal user of the product, won: the wife in fact was the user of the electrical appliance and attributed little importance to the steamer function, which was scarcely relevant for her. This conversation further reinforces the idea that the emphasis placed today on the need to build elements of differentiation is dictated less and less by the real needs of consumers than by the needs of communication – men in constant search of something different to talk about in order to get brands out of the nebulosity of indifference generated by the surplus of offers and the correlated information overload.

Brands are gradually losing their original function of identification and their initial ability to orientate choice, and are taking on a new one, which is aimed at capturing the real essence of a product by creating an attractive personality, which is rich in meaning and makes it possible to connect with consumers on an emotional level by supplying something between the magical and a diversion.

This does not necessarily mean a brand giving up the traditional informative function carried out by it or radically rethinking the process by which it is positioned. However, what the product does and what the product offers are elements which have become more and more standard, and are not sufficient to differentiate it. A brand must be able to seduce, and it is in seduction that purchase motivation can be increasingly found. The concept of seduction is undoubtedly subtler, more complex and more difficult to manage than the brand's informative capacity, but it is precisely the capacity to supply information, which in reality today's consumers are submerged in, that has determined the phenomenon of turning brands into mere commodities.

No longer is it enough to convince a consumer of what a brand can do and guarantee, or of the distinctive elements it has compared with other brands; what counts is seducing. The market is characterized increasingly by the presence of products which have conquered the mind of the consumer, are recognized on the shelves, have high brand recall and brand recognition, carry out their tasks well and maintain the promises made – yet still do not evoke an impulse passionate enough to drive the consumer to choose them.

We would like to make it clear that it is not our intention to claim that everything which is able to seduce can be a brand; we want, rather, to highlight how a brand's differentiation capacity is linked increasingly to its capacity to seduce. A brand which has a seductive ability has an emotive load which can make it stand out from the crowd and emerge in respect of the frame of reference, in short *differentiate itself*. All this must take place in a context in which the shelves tend to fill up with brands that do not represent anything, have no relevant meanings and are perceived more and more as commodities.

The challenge has thus become that of knowing how to position oneself not only in the mind of the consumer but also in their heart, and this sometimes makes it necessary to force the frame of reference, and break the rules of the category's competitive game. Brands must sometimes *rethink themselves* by affirming a new mentality which allows them to go beyond the evidence of the facts, the state of the art and the status quo of the category. Think of Absolut Vodka. When the password in the vodka category seemed to be the product's origin, based mainly on its nationality and the modalities of production, Absolut had the courage and the ability to break the rules, focusing attention not on the product, but on the container, the bottle.[9]

It is evident therefore that when defining elements of differentiation, not just great attention to detail must be developed, but rather an authentic obsession with it, since it is precisely from the ability to propose recognizable details with a strong emotive impact that effective informal communication mechanisms are generated, mechanisms which are able to lead the brand "out of the crowd."

Consumers want products and service which are not only functional but which satisfy other specific needs, and it can be seen that to achieve this they are willing to buy a product which possesses even only one small style detail more than the previous line.

We must see that for a long time, a large number of businesses have been obsessed with the need to build elements of differentiation for their products. Historical experience has however shown us that only a few brands have been able to build and consolidate over time a strong differentiating capacity. The elements of differentiation are today more than ever the object of imitation by competitors able to copy them more and more easily and quickly.[10]

There are very few companies which have an internal and organizational vocation for continual innovation which allows them to propose elements of differentiation without dissolving their continuity, thereby performing the concrete role of captain of the category, such as Gillette does for shaving systems; most brands have difficulty building a lasting competitive advantage based entirely on the identification of elements of differentiation. The same propensity for continual innovation is not always able to guarantee an ability to produce significant differentiation.

It therefore appears evident that the presence of differentiation characteristics can undoubtedly represent a useful element, able to influence brand choice, but that it does not always help to confer an aura of superiority on the brand. Moreover, elements of differentiation cannot be defended forever. Points of differentiation are often not enough to sustain a brand in the competitive evolution of markets, even though in most cases they are elements which contribute to increasing fame. An effective brand strategy must not limit itself to listing the elements which differentiate its product from that of competitors, but must also highlight what the brand has in common with competitors.

For years, Audi was one of the few big car manufacturers interested in four-wheel drive. When consumers thought of Audi they thought of elegant, high-performance and robust cars which, compared with their competitors, had the added plus of all-wheel drive, something seen as an additional safety factor which made it possible to drive the vehicle safely in all road and weather conditions. The image that the consumer had developed of the German brand was not however connected only to this specific equipment, but also to the pleasure of driving, to comfort, and to the status statement which purchasing an Audi allowed them to make.

If Audi had allowed itself to rest on the four-wheel drive element of differentiation only, with the arrival of SUVs the brand's distinctive character would have lost a large part of its effectiveness, centered as it was on a technological quality now adopted by the majority of its competitors. While consumers previously chose Audi cars because they had four-wheel drive, today that plus factor would no longer influence the choice, as numerous models with that specific technology are to be found in the ranges of other makers. The proof is in the fact that, unlike Subaru, which had centered its positioning exclusively on the differentiating element of four-wheel drive, the Audi brand continues to be up-to-date and have success in the market, even though it has lost its important distinctive character. The case of Audi is an effective example of how a brand can continue to be a winner even in the absence of elements of differentiation. Undoubtedly, the intuition Audi had about four-wheel drive attributed a temporal transcendence to the brand in terms of competence in this technological sphere, assigning it the best-in-class role for that specific functional attribute. Currently, Audi's strength consists however in affirming the points of parity it has with its two main competitors, BMW and Mercedes, being able if anything to boast of a greater technological tradition than these two, in terms of that specific attribute.

A further problem is posed for those products which have a strongly innovative connotation and for which it is therefore difficult to define a frame of reference. The temptation is to build an abstract one, since the obvious and natural lack of points of parity, and therefore of the possibility of being collocated in a specific category, results in a lack of operative and strategic reference points. While we would tend to discourage the use of an abstract framework, believing that a brand which possesses a strong connotation of innovation has the moral duty to promote it, this method may in a limited number of cases be justified.[11] Classifying a brand by using other products and correlated services can in fact be effective in developing a *familiarity* character in a new brand. When US Robotics launched Pilot it was important to make the

111

consumer understand what the principal function of a personal digital assistant (PDA) was. The firm decided not so much to position the brand in the personal computer category, thereby exalting its technological potentialities, as to link it to the need to manage personal contacts and appointments in a more efficient way than using a common paper diary could. It was necessary to make the consumer understand what the benefits of changing from a paper diary to an electronic one were, and it mattered little if this aspect was not the most innovative or advanced technological function of the Pilot. Creating the category obliged US Robotics to develop an abstract framework because they had sensed that it would be a more effective way of making the consumer understand the benefits it offered, and avoid the product's being perceived as a "second-class" computer.

Framing which is centered only on differentiating elements and ignores category associations can create more than a few problems in understanding, particularly in the case of brand extensions. When Nivea decided to enter the deodorant market, it did so by launching its products with the claim that they were "delicate and protective," something which had always been associated with the brand; Nivea had built up a strong reputation through its moisturizing skin products, with delicateness and protection important elements of distinction for the brand. The same brand associations however were not so effective in the new category. Nivea in fact proposed the introduction of a product which was differentiated from other deodorants by its ability to protect the skin, playing on the brand's "halo effect." It was simply a matter of moving the associations of one category into another one, and what is more, the two categories were not too far apart. Empirical evidence showed however that Nivea had forgotten to "detach the entry ticket to the category" by highlighting the points of parity which legitimized its belonging there. People who purchase a deodorant want a product which gets rid of BO, and only later in their decision tree do they evaluate other aspects. It was necessary to make it clear to the consumer straight away that the product was effective in solving the problem it was required to solve. It would have been enough to communicate the points of parity and contextually highlight the elements of differentiation in order to achieve a less turbulent introduction onto the market of the new product.

iPhone, the new Apple mobile, on entering the mobile phone market, and despite having strong elements of differentiation from other smartphones available, "knocked" to ask for permission to come into a category it feared it was not legitimized to enter. The first act in the iPhone launch campaign was that of identifying the brand with the category, by a campaign centered on the claim "Just say hello." The fact that iPhone proposes sophisticated software never before seen in a mobile, and that it redefines what users can do with a portable device, could have created the perception of it being too complicated to be a mobile phone; dispelling the doubt represented the first act to perform for its launch.

We do not intend by what we have said to affirm that building a series of differentiating elements for the brand should be ignored. Having a distinctive character still remains a vital need for a brand and an indispensable element in its positioning, but focusing exclusively on this must be avoided, and awareness acquired of the fact that the temporal consistency of differentiating elements is extremely variable.

The times are long past in which Rosser Reeves created the famous and contested USP (unique selling proposition) formula, on the basis of which he claimed that every publicity message should present an exclusive offer, and therefore something which other competitors could not propose. Reeves believed strongly in the possibility of making his products fight the hard battle of benefits and that they had to be characterized by a strong element of differentiation.[12] If, of the many things said about a product, people remember only one at best, this had to be strong, significant and well argued, so that it seemed unique. The same principle maintained that the reason a consumer should use a product had to be clearly shown to them: just one reason, capable of convincing them, without distracting them with other argumentation. But in modern competitive scenarios, we believe, a brand must assume a multidimensional connotation; it cannot limit itself to excelling in a single dimension and simply link its communication processes to that – even if it is that on which it has built its reputation.

In some cases, elements of differentiation can also produce negative effects in relation to collocating a product in a precise category. Think, for example, of when Apple launched the Mac. The authentic element of differentiation was represented by its ease of use; in short, the Mac was a product everyone could learn to use without needing a special information technology background. They were however the times in which information technology had an almost esoteric aura, considered something for the elite few: more accessible technology which was easier to enjoy risked being perceived as a low performer. In other

words, the element of differentiation risked not making the collocation of the brand in the category credible. In reality, the real revolution
started when Apple intended making a technological object easier to
use without sacrificing the product's performance or power. The Apple
lesson teaches us how for products which present a high content of
innovation, the management of elements of differentiation can be a
double-edged sword.

CHAPTER 12

PERFORMANCE ANXIETY AND THE ILLUSION OF QUALITY

There are three elements which all brand definitions have in common, and they are the functional and emotional attributes and the promise offered by the product, understood in terms of expectations, guarantee and safety.

In the classic approach to brands, the functional benefits represented a brand's reason for being. People bought Tide in order to succeed in winning the war against dirt without compromise: every housewife wanted washing that had "outstanding whiteness." Tide assumed a highly technical connotation, giving itself the airs of a "little washing-machine." In short, a white powder for washing clothes promised to become a domestic ally in the fight against dirt, which was incessantly proposed, in a communicational key, as an authentic phobia. We could say that all this was the "domestic reflection" of the social context which saw the family and the home as a happy island in a world which was progressively taking on a connotation of "ugly," "amoral" and "difficult" – in other words, a "jungle" with which the concept of dirty was naturally associated.

Volvo has led the way when it comes to building a brand by defining a promise which is correlated to the product's functional benefits. For years, Volvo was synonymous with safety. If you wanted a safe car, a real protective shell for you and your loved ones, Volvo was the answer. The physical protection of the passenger was an authentic mission for Volvo, becoming a sort of strategic obsession. A large part of its investments in research and communication were thus focussed on the theme of safety. The prestige taken on by the Swedish manufacturer as a result could even be the cause of a certain sense of guilt for more "sporty" dads, who preferred to purchase fast cars or those with more persuasive lines and for whom the safety factor took a back seat in the choice process. And Volvo's communications, like the spot which showed the effects of an accident on a child passenger in the back seat without safety belts, could be configured as acts of real psychological terrorism, however coherent with the role of "safety paladin" that the Swedish manufacturer had decided to assume, even to the point of taking on a role of civic educator.

The history of Volvo went well until the beginning of the 1990s, when other car manufacturers started to include in their standard equipment the same technological safety devices and to orientate growing budgets toward research into active and passive safety. Suddenly safety became a benefit which the consumer took for granted in a car and the appeal of the firm's communication, based prevalently on this factor, lost its effectiveness. The brand found itself having to cope with a sudden identity crisis: it had built its reputation on doing, on knowing how to do, how to guarantee, but it had worked on only a part of its character; if we compare the brand with a human being, we could affirm that it had known how to build a reputation as a reliable person, but not a particularly sparkling or attractive one.

What the brand was missing was the capacity to guarantee real driving pleasure – the promise of living those experiences at the wheel which other brands promised and guaranteed (without, however, compromising safety) was missing. Instead, Volvo's promise had progressively lost relevance and up-to-dateness. People who buy a BMW today do so for the pleasure of driving, the beauty of its form, the elegance and modernity of its interior. It is obvious that a BMW has airbags, an intelligent braking system, dynamic traction control and everything else, but these are not the choices of the drivers – if anything they are standard equipment which a BMW customer takes for granted, not an additional benefit. Today, Volvo has clearly understood that the competitive challenge is no longer based on the guarantee of safety and that what was once a benefit which allowed it to have a strong differentiating capacity has in recent years become a standard component in the offer of products in the car market.

Many brands that, like Volvo, today find themselves having to build a new identity must deal with the multiple (and simultaneously expressed) requests of an ever more variegated and complex public. Consequently, a brand must assume a multidimensional connotation and it cannot level itself on primacy in one field, even if it is on that which it has built its reputation. In short, it is necessary to create new motivations for its purchase, which go well beyond the promised performance. In a recent campaign, "A Little Less Hurt," Nike did not limit itself to making its athletes and its products work, exalting their performance and victories, but it showed their defeats. So, in the spot athletes can be seen falling over, crying, suffering, even with clothes ripped after a fall in a cycle sprint, but dressed by the real spirit of sport, something no longer represented by the goal of winning and the obsession with performance which is typical of contemporary society. What counts in fact is not the final result, strictly reduced to agonistic performance, but the spirit which animates it: a real passion for sport which is able to annihilate the fear of defeat, even to the point of exalting it; the athlete is encouraged to do – in the same vein as other past campaigns, "Just Do It" and "Test Your Faith" – because the brand associations are multiple and not limited to performance. With the claim "A Little Less Hurt," Nike does not exalt the quality of its product in guaranteeing the best sporting performances, but presents an identity which on the surface almost totally ignores the functional pluses so as to exalt others which are linked to emotivity, values, sentiment and confronting human fears. In the past, Nike had already abandoned the theme of performance since it was unable to connect the brand with the female public. In fact, shoes which guarantee better results had a temperamentally aggressive trait which was too masculine and did not satisfy the needs of a female public which was looking for values in the product completely different from effectiveness and strength.

It seems that today it is necessary to associate with a brand elements of differentiation which go beyond the expected functional benefit, thus creating new reasons for purchasing it. The more material vision of brands must be overcome in order to affirm a more immaterial one, linked increasingly to values and emotions. A brand's identity has become centered more and more on new meanings, made of tangible and intangible associations; to this end it is necessary to generate affective reactions, sensations and polysensual perceptions, coherent with the meaning the brand wants to assume in the consumer's mind. Only then can the consumer's response be translated into a relationship with the brand.

Associations, both favorable and unfavorable, assume different characteristics depending on the product. Associations play a decisive role in rendering a product desirable, and therefore in building a brand's relevance. We would like to make it clear that we do not underestimate the importance of functional benefits in the choice process, but simply wish to make it understood that this is not necessarily enough to attribute the brand market supremacy.[1] A brand must build itself a distinctive capacity which cannot be limited to satisfying the primary need but does incorporate all the expected benefits and is thus able to provide a further reason for purchasing. Berthon *et al.* propose a theoretical model of brand analysis based on the concept of brand space.[2] The approach followed by these authors is different from that proposed by some minimalist visions – which limit a brand's meaning to its effective functionality and its distinctive capacity – and promotes a new one, that of a *symbol* around which experiences and relationships can evolve. The authors maintain that a brand's space is defined by two dimensions: the degree of abstraction and the degree of enactment.

– *The degree of abstraction* represents the process of movement from the physical, tangible and concrete toward a realm of thoughts, ideas and sensations. In practice, abstraction represents the passage from the objectivity of the product to the subjectivity of experience and culture.
– *The degree of enactment*, on the other hand, represents the process by which individuals tend to build their own reference contexts, linked to modalities of brand use and to experiences lived. Via enactment, therefore, the aim is to develop the intention to act, create, do and build in contrast to passiveness and acceptance. In other words, enactment aims to go beyond the self-referential vision of the brand in order to affirm a new, deeper one, where dialogue and dialectics prevail.

In the classic approach to brands, there was a low level of abstraction: it was simply a matter of affixing a name, often representative of origin or provenance, not so much to a product as, if anything, to a functional benefit. Slowly, and above all as a result of policies of extending a brand via attributing to it new categories and therefore new functional benefits, brands started to take a progressive level of abstraction until, in some cases, they lost their association with the original product or category, even if they kept their consistence, as in the case of Virgin, for example. The more abstract a brand, the more it becomes independent from the product; the less abstract, the more it becomes identified with the product. Think of how Apple is today a brand which is associated more with the world of music than with that of information technology.

Enactment, on the other hand, is connected to functional performance, representing what a product can do compared with the meaning it assumes for the consumer. The less enacted a brand is, the more it focuses on meaning rather than what it can do; the less abstract, the more it focuses on what it can do rather than on what it means.

It is almost superfluous to point out that the ideal situation a brand can find itself in is that represented by a high level of abstraction and enactment. This situation in fact offers the company which owns such a brand the greatest flexibility, generating a strong sense of belonging in the consumer, a feeling which can become so strong as to lead to the self-attribution of an emotional property right. This condition can, paradoxically, transform itself into something which severely restricts brand management flexibility, as is said to have happened to Coca-Cola when it tried to change its formula and style with New Coke.

Marketing literature has always identified *guarantee of quality* among the principal functions carried out by brands, affirming that brands are *condemned to quality.*

In this chapter we will attempt to question, at least partly, this founding principle, by looking at it again from an approach which, while not developing in the opposite direction, is put forward to affirm a new vision of the phenomenon.

We believe in fact that there is not always a direct correlation between a brand's market success and the quality of the products associated with it. According to the classical approach to brands, the consumer purchases a brand because they are convinced it offers them a service or benefit which is (in certain aspects) unique. This conviction is often induced by the degree of fame the brand has achieved. Think, for example, of car rental: the consumer's choice initially regards Hertz and Avis, not so much because these two operators offer a better service than other companies, as because, if anything, these two brands identify the category in a certain way. They are the brands which compete for "top of mind" fame, thus becoming a sort of visible and verbal marker of the category itself.

A strong brand often becomes the default choice for a consumer, who is having to scan an ever longer list of alternatives among which the elements of differentiation are less and less perceptible. Strong brands are enveloped in a sort of aura of quality which other brands do not have and which allows them to conquer a position of superiority in the mind of the consumer – and it is of little importance whether this is a mere illusion.

Moreover, a recognizable brand becomes a guarantor of effectiveness, simplifying the choice process for a consumer who, above all when purchasing banal goods, has neither the time nor the desire to start comparing the performances of different brands when they make their purchases and routine choices.

Creating elements of differentiation compared with other entities which satisfy the same needs does not necessarily require effective qualitative superiority. Not always, therefore, does the presence of superior quality allow the brand to be victorious against the plethora of other brands which also claim to satisfy the same need. The real challenge therefore consists in building the perception of a brand's superior quality in the mind of the consumer, by means of elements which are not always correlated directly to the effective performance of the product.

Think about choosing a watch. A person buying a watch today does so less and less because they want an instrument which allows them to tell the time precisely. Watches have in fact become a fundamental element in our customs. Models which are more and more stylized, straps which are interchangeable to go with the color of clothes you are wearing, new materials and new colors have changed our way of seeing watches – more and more as accessories and less and less as a measuring instrument. A product's technical supremacy and performance have thus become less and less relevant in the choice process and, consequently, in that of communication. In order for this to acquire new relevance, new roads must be traveled.[3] Rolex has always been the brand synonymous with luxury watches. The question of whether it is the best watch from a quality point of view arises spontaneously, therefore. Certainly Rolex produces watches which are manufactured to a high quality and have extremely sophisticated mechanisms; however, other less "titled" competitors are also able to offer the same quality of manufacture and the same performance. People who buy a Rolex do not do so to be more punctual than those who buy a Zenith, for example; they buy a Rolex to show others that they can afford to, to affirm their status, maybe also because they are convinced they are buying a better watch simply because, being more solid and heavier, it seems to be more reliable. The success of Rolex in a sector like that of high-quality watchmaking can, in part, be explained by its capacity to "psychologically" build the product's technical supremacy through more solid and heavier cases. Rolex has known how to give its products an image which is distinct from the concept of precision alone and puts them in a more complex dynamic, presenting them as structurally more robust watches, which can be subjected to a more "stressful" life, therefore, responding to the needs dictated by lifestyles which are characterized more and more by the concepts of stress and speed.

There is an abundance of brands on the market which, like Rolex, have been able to build an image of superiority at an emotive level and therefore, in the mind of the consumer, by understanding that improving performance is not always enough to attract the consumers of other brands. The case of Listerine is rather representative in this sense. Listerine convinced its consumers that its bad taste was the element which guaranteed the greater effectiveness of its product, recalling, as we have already noted, a "paramedical" connotation in the consumer's imagination. This superiority was achieved simply by adding a larger quantity of alcohol to the product compared with other mouthwashes.

In the car sector, sports utility vehicles (SUVs) represent a further example of how "emotive superiority" can be built in one segment of the market compared with others. SUVs represent a segment characterized by its highly hybrid nature: we are not talking about a sedan car or an off-road vehicle, but something which combines the advantages of both. In other words, an SUV makes it possible to travel as comfortably as in a saloon car while being able to cope with the bad weather and road conditions which only an off-road vehicle made it possible to cope with before. The value of an SUV is traceable to its driver's "trucker syndrome": being able to look down on other car drivers from above, the SUV driver is often convinced they have the better of anybody else when it comes to performance.

The market is full of successful products which have known how to build a qualitative superiority in the mind of the consumer therefore consists in seeking out those elements simply by linking it to the concept of *more*. Häagen-Dazs ice-cream has a formula which has a high butter content to which a small quantity of air is added; Montblanc was able to revitalize the exclusive writing tools market by proposing "chubbier" models; Callaway innovated the world of golf with the Big Bertha driver which was characterized by the head of the wood being significantly bigger than those of competitors, thus promising greater power and control when hitting.

The challenge of modern brands therefore is to seek out those elements which can bring about a solid collocation in the mind of the consumer by recalling the concept of superiority, and it is of little importance if these are founded on assumptions not of real functionality in the field, but rather of ideal satisfaction *in the minds of the users.*

CHAPTER 13

BRAND AND CATEGORY: A COMPLEX RELATIONSHIP

The relationship between a brand and the category it belongs to is a particularly critical and complex factor.

Often in managing a brand the task that predominates is attempting to make it stand out from the plethora of competitors which crowd the category, and thus rescuing it from the anonymity of the shelf. Two questions arise spontaneously, however. The first, for a new brand, is: is there any sense in entering a category already heavily crowded with brands? The second, for existing brands, is: is there any sense in staying in a category where the brand does not have sufficient personality to stand out?

In many cases, entry into a category is the fruit of brand extension policies which do not have winning a significant market share as a primary objective. The important thing is to be present within the category. This is not just so as to achieve significant sales volume; it can also strengthen a brand's positioning and have important positive effects at the level of communication: it is easier for a consumer to perceive of a brand as satisfying a specific class of needs when the brand is present in the category they associate those needs with. However, this continual process of reference multiplication is in contradiction to the expectations of clarity and choice simplification. Consumers expect big brands to play a rationalizing and regulating role in a market which is increasingly intrusive, abundant and opaque. Consumers tend more and more to reject brands which offer overflowing ranges in favor of others which are able to offer ideas, creativity, meaning and plans. The best way today to have effective publicity exposure depends more and more on the capacity to create new categories or to be the first mover within them. Empirical evidence shows us in fact that only 6 per cent of new products can really be considered innovative, while the remainder are line extensions.

Many leading companies do not understand that it can be more effective to concentrate on promoting the category rather than the brand.

At the same time, on the other hand, those companies in a weak market position do not understand that rather than promoting the brand it is cheaper to exalt its belonging to the category. Paradoxically, it is often the growth of the category which makes it possible for a brand to acquire consistent awareness. A brand leader today has the "moral duty" to take on the task of promoting the category, and those brands which want to become leaders cannot refrain from this behavior. Above all, when the category is relatively new, a brand which fossilizes by promoting only itself can paradoxically limit growth potential.

To clarify this concept we will again use a number of cases which show how important it is to concentrate on the promotion of the category rather than that of the brand. Think of the category of chilled snack cakes created by Ferrero with the introduction onto the market of "Kinder Fetta al Latte." Launched in 1991, it was the very first experience on the Italian market of producing and commercializing a fresh child snack cake. It is a between-meals snack cake, sweet and fresh, fills that little gap in the stomach, is simple, light and represents a modern interpretation of milk.[1] As soon as Kinder introduced Fetta al Latte onto the market it had immediate success and very soon other competitors, such as Nestlé and Danone, entered the market. Like a good captain of the category, Kinder understood that the company's strategic objective should be aimed at increasing the penetration of a category which had strong innovative traits and was revolutionizing the world of snack cakes for children. Defending its own share in a market that had yet to develop was secondary compared with growth in the need for the category. In short, share points could and had to be sacrificed at the altar of the category's greater penetration. Even now, Kinder exalts the benefits of a fresh child snack cake made from pasteurized milk in its communication, emphasizing the nutritional aspects compared with the brand image. Nevertheless, it is precisely thanks to its role in promoting the category that Ferrero has led the consumer to associate the category with the brand, and the company's share has been considerably strengthened in this market, far beyond what the company could have imagined in 1991.

Danone did the same thing when it launched the probiotic yogurt Actimel on the market. The main objective was to develop the primary demand by promoting the need of the category, even before the brand's awareness. It was necessary to make consumers understand that daily consumption of the product could strengthen their natural defenses. Moreover, it was necessary to make them understand that it was not a product for sick people, with an almost medical aura about it, but a habit for healthy people looking for a healthier lifestyle: in short, not a medicine but a functional product. The challenge consisted in making consumption of the product, not just of a brand, part of the target's daily routine. In order to do this, Danone had to illustrate the benefits and thus promote the need for the category; they had to convince consumers that consuming probiotic yogurt was an important daily gesture which could contribute to a healthier life.

In the history of brands, there are more than a few cases of companies which have achieved resounding flops precisely because they have not followed this approach but have focussed exclusively on promoting the brand. The world of electronic consumer goods provides us with numerous cases of such debacles dictated by the fact that the closure of the proprietary standard, and the related ineffectiveness in promoting the category, have constituted the main cause of many new products imploding.

Thus, when Sony, despite the mistakes made with the Super 8 standard, decided to launch the magneto-optical MiniDisk, it was convinced it was defining the new technological reference standard for music, through the use of a magnetic medium which, being more evolved than a tape and more flexible than a CD, was to lead music toward the digital.[2] The company believed in the product so much that the MiniDisk became a sub-brand with widely independent management spheres. Although it was thought of as the digital successor to the music cassette, the MiniDisk did not enjoy vast circulation.[3] The result was not what Sony had hoped for, and the reasons for the failure are easily identified in the closure of the standard and, consequently, the lack of promotion of the category.

For a form of technology to become the reference standard, it must be circulated and it cannot be the exclusive property of one brand. Sony did not promote a new technological *standard* as JVC had done in the past with VHS, but promoted the MiniDisk *brand*. The result was that they failed to make the category take off and when they understood their mistake, music was already entering into the MP3 era. If Sony, rather than promoting the brand, had promoted the technology and opened the standard to other competitors, the story of this brand would probably have been very different from being confined largely to musicians and audio enthusiasts.

Apple, which has always made its niche positioning and proprietary standard a part of its identity, understood that it was necessary to review its traditional business model, based on the almost ideological dualism between it and Microsoft's operating system, in order to develop iPod and iTunes sales. Today, iTunes is a multiplatform software which runs with both Mac and Windows. The growth in Apple's penetration into the computer market was not by chance helped by the possibility of making the Microsoft Office suite of programs run on its own operating system.

Promoting the category, we see therefore, becomes a must for a leader or for those who want to become one, and this rule is even more important for those innovative products which create the category. Paradoxically, promoting the category allows the pioneer to strengthen its brand by creating ever stronger links and associations with the category. Moreover, it makes it possible to create entry barriers for new competitors, who should be seen however as a further factor of propulsion for the growth of the category rather than as a threat. Greater crowding often means greater visibility of the category on the shelves, with benefits for everybody. When Kinder introduced Fetta al Latte, the category had low visibility, squeezed as it was between yogurt and cheeses. The presence of numerous competitors has allowed the category to create an important display window for itself, thus increasing visibility and, consequently, the propensity for impulse buying.

Moreover it is also important to remember that consumers are moderately attracted by new products, but very attracted by new categories and the promotional innovations which mark their natural evolution. It is no coincidence that line extensions have never had massive effects on sales, and often have only the aim of strengthening or increasing a brand's leadership within the category by increasing its visibility. When it comes down to it, consumers are interested in new solutions, not old and new brands. Many managers think that by increasing line extensions they can increase a brand's profile and appeal. However, while on the one hand these policies allow a brand to increase its visibility space at the moment of purchase, on the other hand they can, if there is an excessive proliferation of the extension, lead to every product becoming more banal, thus threatening a brand's level of trust. A brand is like a piece of elastic: there is a limit beyond which it cannot be stretched without breaking.

Any difficulty in putting brand extension policies into effect lies in a company's inability to transfer the associations which the consumer attributes to the brand from the original category to the new one.[4] In the processes of line extension, particular care must be taken not to cause the brand to lose consistency. There are few brands which are elastic enough to move into new categories, even when commercially distant from each other. Virgin is one of these, and represents an effective example of how a name can extend itself from music to travel without losing its consistency. But the success of Virgin is linked strongly to the mystical personality of its founder, Sir Richard Branson, one of the most charismatic and charming characters ever to have dominated the world of entrepreneurism and communication. It is not by chance that Branson is often compared to Steve Jobs, since both are entrepreneurs able to develop business by creating something to believe in, rich in meaning and, not least, able to improve the existence of individuals and the collective. The case of Virgin is further confirmation of what has been repeatedly affirmed: brands which can build their own creed are helped in the processes of extension as long as these happen without the creed being depreciated or weakened.

In some cases, it can be effective to launch a sub-brand which uses the name of the mother brand to support its attractiveness. This is the choice of, for example, Marriott.[5] Starting from the assumption that people who book a hotel often tend to have very different needs and reasons for doing so, Marriott understood that its structures were not able to satisfy all of them effectively. The problem stemmed however from the company's desire to use the Marriott brand name without diluting its awareness. Marriott had to satisfy different clients with different needs, without however giving up its own brand identity. The company decided therefore to divide the brand into four different types of hotel:

- Marriott (full service hotel).
- Court Yard by Marriott.
- Fairfield Inn by Marriott.
- Residence Inn by Marriott.

The full-service hotel type represented the classic Marriott product, aimed at a general target with a medium–high price positioning. This type of hotel is suitable for the needs of both businessmen and families, and provides a wide variety of services, such as conference rooms, exhibition spaces and business centers, restaurants and spas. It is also characterized by ample lobbies, and the various restaurants satisfy diverse needs, with proposals which range from a grill to *nouvelle cuisine*. Marriott Court Yard is also aimed at a general clientele: families and businessmen who are looking for a reasonable standard of quality at a lower price than that of Marriott Full Service. The client of this type of hotel is not particularly interested in the presence of business services nor in restaurants, and they find no emotional gratification in vast and luxurious lobbies, since they do not look for particular ambiance in the public areas of a hotel. However, they do want a fast breakfast included in the price. Fairfield Inn by Marriott is aimed at a clientele with a restricted budget: the quantity of services offered is less, although the rooms are pleasant and welcoming. Breakfast is not included in the price. Finally, Residence Inn by Marriott is an all-suite hotel type, of particular interest since it identifies as its main target women travelling for business (confirming what was previously said), responding in an effective manner to the very precise needs deriving from the new role of women in society. Besides businesswomen the target includes families, and the structures are characterized by being small two-bedroom apartments (each bedroom equipped with television), with a living-room/kitchen area, which are suitable for rather long stays.

Today, Marriott represents the most successful experience of segmentation in the hotel industry in the United States, above all since its brand awareness has been strengthened by not being diluted into different brands.

A further approach to extension can be represented by the use of a brand which differs from what it was originally created for, and which allows it to cross the boundaries into new categories. Consider, for example, the sports drink Gatorade, created to replace the minerals lost during sports activities and also promoted as being able to re-establish liquid levels after a bout of flu. Think also of Kellogg's Special K, eaten as a light and nutritional afternoon snack, far (in ways and time) from the breakfast experience. It is no coincidence that Kellogg has recently launched single-portion bags of Special K, designed for consumption as a snack, and not necessarily accompanied by milk.

In the case of any of the weaker brands – those squeezed hardest by the crowding of a category – strengthening the sense of belonging to the category can be extremely useful. Insisting on trying to make the brand get through the crowd by pulling it out of anonymity, in the hope of making it more famous and increasing its possibility of being chosen by the consumer, is often useless and expensive. It is undoubtedly more effective instead to inform the consumer that the brand belongs to the category, in this way exploiting the work of the leader and benefiting from the "halo effect." Simultaneously with being identified with the category, which must be the primary element of positioning, the brand can illustrate any extra benefit it has, even a purely induced one. In short, it can declare it is part of a group, but at the same time show it is different in something.

When Subaru was being introduced to the American market, it launched a campaign in which it compared itself to Volvo. The comparison was simply to define its belonging to a precise category of cars (those which guaranteed greater safety standards) by associating itself with the make which represented the most credible member of the category. Subaru added that something extra that the others did not have, namely four-wheel drive, thus trying to differentiate itself from the other competitors. Subaru did not want to take away market share from Volvo; it was not its intention to enter into a choice niche (consumers for whom safety was the decisive factor when purchasing a car), but it just wanted to create an element which allowed consumers to identify it initially. It is often more effective for a brand merely to identify itself with a category than differentiate itself within it.

The leader often makes identification, even visual identification, of the category easy. Consider, for example, the consumer processes of identifying some categories in points of sale. Somebody looking for soft drinks instinctively looks for the red of Coca-Cola. Not by chance did Coca-Cola try in the past to affirm the concept of "corporate block" by proposing to distributors display solutions which defined a "window" where all the Coca-Cola products could be concentrated, thus trying to strengthen the image of the category with the brand.

In marketing literature, this concept can be identified as "category destination."[6] In this case, the use of the concept of destination is different from that in category management.[7] If in category management the category which has a destination role is the one which guides the consumer's choice at the point of sale, in the complex universe of brand management it is an element of attraction performed by a brand in respect of consumers of a category.

Think of the case of theme restaurants. In the majority of big cities, Hard Rock Café, Planet Hollywood and Rainforest Café are collocated in the same geographic area, in some cases next to one another. The question would spontaneously arise of why the managers of these companies decided to position their restaurants so near to their direct competitors. The answer is simple: in this way a destination area is created for all those who are looking for a theme restaurant experience, thus widening choice alternatives and making the choice of the category prevail. The consumer's need for a meal and the different reasons which determine that need can in fact be satisfied with modalities which are profoundly different from each other and range from a fast food restaurant to a Michelin-three-star restaurant, considered as – and why not? – a theme restaurant.

The problem is not that of choosing to go out to dinner at a Hard Rock Café or a Planet Hollywood, but more that of choosing a theme restaurant rather than a conventional one. The concentration of a number of theme restaurants in a specific geographic area allows the consumer to have a range of restaurants to choose from, making the choice of a form of theme restaurant prevail. Moreover, the presence of various theme restaurants in one location makes that location more attractive, allowing the consumer to have an exciting experience outside the restaurant too.

CHAPTER 14

BRAND PERCEPTION AND THE POWER OF THE SUBCONSCIOUS

There are a myriad of associations consumers can develop about a brand; these go far beyond their awareness and are activated following exposure to the brand, or its use. This means that some associations can indeed emerge in a specific context and remain submerged in another. In other words, the consumer tends to develop awareness of a brand both at a conscious and a subconscious level, reactivating that awareness from an area to which it has been "distanced" as the result of a precise stimulus.[1]

These associations, which may be more or less conscious, are often the fruit of exposure to the brand and are linked, for example, to seeing advertising spots, street posters and press advertisements, and also, last but not least, to consumption of the brand. The perception of a brand is in fact the fruit of a complex process of gathering and elaborating information acquired in a way which may be more or less conscious depending on whether the exposure to the brand is direct and therefore aware, or indirect and therefore unaware.

So there is a core of associations always present in the consumer's judgement and another one connected to the activation of areas of memory occupied by information not effectively perceived but equally efficacious.

In psychology, an important distinction has been traced between explicit and implicit knowledge.

The first concerns what the consumer thinks they remember about a brand, their fruit of experiences and their past reminiscences. In contrast, implicit knowledge concerns the cognitive associations held by the consumer between two constructs which exist outside their conscious awareness. A consumer can thus develop associations about a product whose existence they are unaware of but may have a positive propensity to purchase. Let's think, for example, of a man who finds himself having to purchase a brand of detergent; his choice could be

Tide only because his mother used to use that brand, even though he does not actually remember her using it. The simple use of a brand by his mother represented a form of exposure for him, generating information which was deposited in his brain.

In order to better understand the practical differences between implicit and explicit knowledge of a brand, it may be useful to consider how these are differently measured. The measurement of explicit knowledge is widely used by marketing men: think of those research surveys where consumers are asked if they like a particular category of products, what they think about a brand and what associations they show toward it. The methodology of investigation is fairly simple: the consumer is asked to freely express their judgment about a product or a brand, without the possibility of choosing from among various alternative answers formulated by the interviewer.

Research aimed at measuring implicit knowledge is less direct and is based on behavioral observation. A method frequently adopted is that of using a primary paradigm which precedes the objective stimulus, thus acting as a primer. The first stimulus provided is conceptually correlated with the target stimulus, in order to put the consumer being interviewed in a condition to answer more quickly. Let's suppose, for example, that we show the interviewee a picture of a can of Coca-Cola and immediately afterwards two adjectives, "refreshing" and "nutritional." The consumer will quickly answer choosing the adjective "refreshing" since the choice has been primed by the picture of the can.

This research methodology also makes it possible to measure the strength of the associations among a series of objective concepts such as, for example, flowers and insects, and negative and positive concepts such as pleasant and unpleasant. This type of analysis is used to observe a series of stereotypes and implicit associations in a wide spectrum of reference contexts. In this way it is possible to discover at which level the associations relating to the brand being investigated are more or less positive compared with those of competitors, and how some of these are more linked to one brand compared with another.

To understand this concept more fully, let's analyze the case of the famous mint Altoids. Born in England in the nineteenth century as a product for calming the stomach and regulating the intestine, with time, Altoids became a product which guarantees fresh breath.[2] When Kraft bought the company in 1993, it quickly realized that the brand's market penetration was extremely low, with the one exception of the city of Seattle. So the company decided to commission research to investigate the reasons for the brand's success in that specific geographic reality.

Despite the brand's extremely classic image, the research highlighted a rather surprising consumer profile: a young person between 20 and 28 years old who worked, had an intense social and relational life, smoked and drank coffee, ate frozen pizzas, had at least six cans of beer in the fridge, did not have stable relationships and was not against casual sex. In order to understand this target's associations with the brand, a panel of consumers was created; the members of the panel were shown magazines and asked to indicate the photos which were associated in some way with the product. The two photos indicated most showed Charles and Diana, who referred to the product's British origin, and a waterfall, which was associated with the concept of freshness; the third photo however showed a woman dressed in red, looking provocative and sexy, and this revealed a link, which was difficult to predict in advance, based on sensuality. Freshness and Englishness were therefore the explicit associations with the brand, while sensuality was the implicit one, which was drawn out by the primary stimulus of the photo of the woman in red. The campaign to relaunch the brand was therefore elaborated by developing the concept of transgression and anti-conformism, coherent with the target, and that of sensuality, coherent with the implicit associations which came out of the research. Even today, Altoids's communication is characterized by campaigns which make ample use of the sexual lever, all dressed with nice double meanings and stinging humor.

This type of analysis applied to brands also makes effective forms of comparison possible regarding the positive and negative associations correlated with various brands; it could be possible to analyze whether a specific attribute can be more greatly associated with one brand rather than another, thus discovering, as in the case of Altoids, whether a brand possesses an attribute which its creators/managers did not think it could possess; if different emotions are associated with a brand according to the age of the consumers; and so on. This also makes it possible to retarget the whole communication linked to the product by exalting an attribute which takes on new and greater relevance, in some cases, completely upsetting the original vision of the brand.

Another example of the phenomenon we have just described is that of Müller yogurt. Born as a price product originally aimed at discount supermarkets, within a few years, Müller became market leader in Italy.

Müller's rapid growth was even more significant in a market (that of yogurts) previously considered saturated and characterized by static competitive dynamics: the market had already rejected the entry of some competitors, not least Yoplait, the market leader in France, a country which had the highest European consumption rate in the category. Müller's special formula of cream of yogurt enriched with grape sugar imparted a distinctive flavor to the product and caused it to be perceived immediately as an element which broke with the past in a category which seemed to have little to say in terms of innovation.[3] Müller very soon understood that the associations which the managers thought would be prevalent for the brand – such as cheapness – did not represent the effective perceptions of consumers at all, which were concentrated prevalently on the concept of *creaminess*, taste and sensuality. It is no coincidence in fact that Müller has redefined its entire communication and market positioning through its "Make Love With Taste" claim, which is more coherent with the way the brand is perceived as being different from the *healthy* image which characterizes the category.[4]

The examples just cited show effectively how measuring knowledge of a brand makes it possible not only to highlight its real aptitudes but also to predict, with reasonable accuracy, consumer response to precise stimuli. Moreover, it can lead to greater understanding of the meaning the consumer attributes to a brand and the quality of the relationship established with it, thus supplying a fairly clear picture of both the product's aptitudes and consumer preferences.

Social psychology has for a long time been investigating how the information which a consumer has without being aware of it can influence their behavioral modalities. Borstein *et al.*, for example, have demonstrated that individuals tend to prefer objects they have previously seen, even in the absence of *complete* awareness of having seen them. These results derive from a study in which the researchers showed pictures of polygons for such a short time that it made the vision imperceptible. Subsequently, more pictures of polygons were shown and the interviewees showed that they preferred those they had previously been exposed to, even though they had not been able to recall the vision.[5]

Individuals tend moreover to remember things for a longer time than we might expect. A study has demonstrated how the people who were asked to represent an apple graphically developed greater predisposition toward buying apples. Not only did they have a greater propensity to add them to their shopping list, but they also tended more to remember them as soon as they were faced with a choice about what to eat.

These last considerations suggest that inducing the consumer to imagine the brand can be strategically important. Imagination – or subconscious knowledge of the brand – in fact performs a powerful recall function in the choice process.

The imagination can be used to make a product more desirable. Let's consider, for example, an advertisement for a beautiful holiday location – say Cabo San Lucas. Looking at that advertisement, the consumer starts to think how fantastic it would be to be on holiday. They imagine themselves basking in the sun, drinking margaritas under a palmtree, maybe reading a good book. The creation of this imaginary vision means the advertising message has been successful in creating problem recognition, inducing us to think how much we really need a holiday and what a fabulous choice Cabo San Lucas could be.

The imagination involved in experimenting with the advantages of a product and therefore of a brand is much more convincing than imagining the product itself. Think, for example, of those advertisements for cars which show people driving who are confident, having fun, serene and so on – nothing to do with the mood of a Los Angeles car driver in a jam on the highway. The consumer is thus involved not only in imaging a product itself, but also in its enjoyment.

A person's imagination can influence expectations of a brand and, very probably, their decision to purchase it. It is via the imagination that the psychological superiority of a brand can be created; the real conviction that a brand has superior characteristics develops in the consumer's imagination. It is, however, necessary not to exaggerate in generating an imaginary vision of a brand which is too far from the effective intrinsic capacity of the product. Imagining a product without content puts the consumer's personal satisfaction at risk, when the consumption experience is too far removed from the brand's promises.

Finally, it is necessary to underline that both empirical evidence and research carried out show how communicating via proposing incongruent information can increase both brand awareness and the attitude of an advertising campaign. This is particularly valid for those brands the consumer has become progressively familiar with over time. If in fact brands which boast high levels of awareness are less sensitive to competitor attacks and are intrinsically equipped with a greater persuasive capacity, the campaigns correlated to them have a life cycle which is on average shorter and are often subject to wearing out quickly. Precisely because these brands are socially accepted and recognized, they risk boring people, and the messages connected with them run the risk of wearing out and thus losing their effectiveness. For a brand which is known and collectively accepted, the proposal of something strange, outside the norms and therefore unforeseen – in other words, incongruent – can break the monotony associated with it, thus increasing the effectiveness of the investments in communication and, moreover, making it possible to generate a more intimate and less ascetic relationship with its public. It can also strengthen recollection of the brand, increase its memorability and allow greater argumentation of its attributes.

Consumers have developed a system of elaborating information which is particularly sophisticated in respect of familiar brands and this information is retrieved more quickly and easily than is the case where a brand is less familiar. This means the consumer, when exposed to a conventional advertising message, has always the same perception of a brand. And this is precisely why the consumer experiences familiar brands as a routine, since the process of extracting information becomes almost automatic, often without the consumer being aware of what they are doing; sometimes the process becomes boring. This is why, in some cases, it can be effective to force the human mind to go beyond the framework, get away from conventionality and send the preconceived routines into a crisis. The message associated with a brand must therefore disassociate itself more and more from the routine in order to subtract itself from indifference and generate memorability.

When the information contained in a message does not coincide with the elements contained in the consumer's preconceived framework of analysis, the consumer is forced to elaborate the message and, consequently, invest it with greater relevance and meaning. It is fairly evident that this reasoning is particularly valid for those brands which are highly familiar and for which the consumer has developed a scheme for understanding them; contextually, the effectiveness of this approach is in putting that framework into crisis. Where such a framework does not exist, incongruence does not perform a function of breaking with preconceived ideas but generates mainly confusion. The most obvious consequence, as the study conducted by Lange and Dahle'n shows, consists in the fact that incongruence makes it easier to remember brands, by forcing the consumer to elaborate information with greater attention, paradoxically activating the information about the brand contained in the brain.[6]

PART IV

THE BRAND AS A CITIZEN OF THE WORLD

CHAPTER 15

DEVELOPING A BRAND IN DIFFERENT CULTURAL CONTEXTS

Faced with a progressive saturation of offerings in local markets, or at least in those most evolved, modern business organizations increasingly feel the need to develop their business in new countries. Although in the international market many physical barriers have fallen there are still profound differences between countries and different cultures which can, if not opportunely considered, condition the success of a brand. Therefore, the need has grown to understand the affinities and differences between the markets of the world, particularly when these influence a brand's commercialization.

Brands find themselves having to face new expectations and this means they must review their management modalities so that their consistency remains not only in time but also beyond the borders of origin.

The dominant paradigm which for a long time characterized the processes of internationalization was based on the assumption that these could be carried out by standardizing products, packaging and modalities of communication – in short, by a strategy aimed at reaching a *common denominator* by means of which a brand would be effective in every national context. This all translated into a sterile vision which considered global brands in a merely economic logic aimed at obtaining economies of scale at production level as well as at the levels of communication and commercialization. Global brands were thus developed on the domestic market and launched on international ones in a way which proposed the uniform image the company wanted to affirm in every market in which it was present.[1]

Operating reality has however highlighted the fact that consumers have difficulty accepting products which, in order to be suitable in every situation, are extremely generic. Moreover, in those countries whose reference culture is profoundly different from that of the country of origin, brands can be perceived in ways very different from those envisaged by their creators. Companies soon understood that it was necessary to make a greater effort in trying to adapt their brands to local markets, thus giving rise to the process better known as "globalization." In planning a global brand, it is necessary to take into account how brands are interpreted always through the lens of cultural values, and that these values, particularly in emerging countries, may be in continual evolution; consequently, in time, a brand's meaning, which is linked to the cultural markers it evokes in a specific usage context, may also change.[2] Marketers must pay great attention to the social and cultural connotations that a brand acquires in a specific geographic and cultural context, and to how these can change as a result of that context's evolution. This is even more evident for those high-profile brands which represent a style of life and alternative experiences in countries such as, for example, China, where values are continually changing or the emphasis put on consumption has a strong social value.

We feel therefore that we must disagree with those arguments which aim to affirm that, with the extraordinary proliferation of media and the internet, and freer circulation of people and information, the cultural differences between countries are becoming so slight as to be of less and less importance.

The spurs which model needs and determine purchase and consumption decisions can in fact vary from country to country, if not from region to region within the same country. What is desired in Hong Kong is not necessarily desired in Shanghai or Beijing. The inhabitants, for example, of the regions of northern India are profoundly different from those in the region of Goa, where the reference culture is strongly influenced by the past presence of the Portuguese. This is not to mention the fact that large areas of India have been heavily influenced by centuries of English colonialism. It seems obvious that considering India as a single indistinct market without considering the cultural and linguistic differences between regions would be a grave error.

For decades, processes of communication were promulgated mainly inside borders, contributing to building increasingly strongly rooted national cultures. Toward the end of the last century however we witnessed a progressive globalization of the "prevalent" culture and a consequent homogenization of models of life and consumption.

Although we agree with Nicholas Negroponte's statement that in the future, communities formed on the basis of culture and ideas will be increasingly stronger than those founded on physical proximity and that children will gradually lose the sense of nationalism,[3] we believe however that that future is still a long way off. Undoubtedly, the gradual process of national economies integrating on a global scale, the greater propensity to travel, growing labor mobility and the advent of new media which allow virtual access to every remote corner of the world have contributed remarkably to this process. This has forced individuals to relate to other cultures rather than their own in ever growing measure. However, while this does not mean that we are looking at a single market in which everybody tends to have the same tastes and the same values, we cannot however ignore the fact that, albeit from different points of view and from cultural models which are often conflicting, the citizens of the world communicate using some common symbols, among the most important of which are brands. Brands, as Holt points out, have really become a sort of lingua franca for consumers throughout the world.

Research conducted by Holt *et al.* confirms this. The research was aimed at verifying which associations consumers in twelve nations developed toward global brands; three principal associations emerged, namely quality, global myth and social responsibility.[4]

QUALITY

Interviewees attributed not only a higher level of quality to global brands, but they also highlighted the conviction that global brands develop innovative products and breakthrough technologies much more quickly than their rivals.[5] A further element which emerged from the research was the progressively minor importance consumers give to the national origin of a product; while maintaining a certain relevance, this contributes to defining the perception of global brands for only a third of those interviewed. However, we must not fall into the trap of seeing nationality as a second-rank element. While it is in fact true that a brand's global character represents an indicator of greater quality for the consumer than does its geographic provenance, consumers continue to prefer brands which come from countries which have specific expertise in a particular sector; think of the value of "Made in Italy" for fashion, "Made in France" for cosmetics and "Made in Germany" for cars. In these cases, companies must manage their national identity wisely as one trait of their global character.[6]

GLOBAL MYTH

Consumers look at global brands as symbols of cultural ideals and through these they develop a global identity. So, transnational companies find themselves having to compete not only on the intrinsic value of a product but also on its capacity to diffuse cultural myths which have a global appeal. It is also by purchasing and consuming brands that individuals feel they are citizens of the world, and in less industrialized countries a sense of belonging to something which is bigger and more important is developed. With the consumption of global brands, individuals satisfy their desire for what they would like to be and what they would like their country to be. Consider, for example, what happened at the end of the Second World War when brands like Marlboro, Levi's and Hershey represented much more than simple cigarettes, jeans or bars of chocolate; they represented hope of rebirth and reconstruction after years of horror and devastation. Even now, Europeans who were children during the war remember a brand of chocolate – Hershey – handed out to children by the American soldiers in the Allied forces that liberated occupied Europe. Consequently, that chocolate represented something more than a product and became the conveyor of a myth: the American myth.

SOCIAL RESPONSIBILITY

As we have already observed, the public see global brands, for better or for worse, as having an extraordinary influence on the wellbeing of society. So, consumers expect them to give greater attention to social problems and not limit their interests exclusively to the products they sell; in short, they must act as a guide toward the resolution of problems which involve public health, social rights, safeguarding the environment and respecting human rights. This pressure from consumers is becoming greater and is aimed at global brands more than at local ones. Today, the possibility of accessing an increasing amount of information, even in the most remote places in the world, makes companies' behaviors progressively more transparent, and less and less impervious to collective judgement when these behaviors do not correspond to codes of ethical conduct.

Global brands often find themselves having to compete among themselves, and this obliges the companies which own them to not limit their efforts to building superiority on traditional levers, such as price, performance and image, but to concentrate on building their global character. This means that companies must *think globally*. It is not an easy challenge, and the presence of many people in the world who do not like big transnational firms certainly does not help its achievement. We believe however that a brand's global character also shows itself in the way it manages dissent and non-acceptance. It is therefore necessary to learn to take part in the dissent debate, and try in some way to influence it and benefit from it.

A further obstacle to developing a global branding strategy is also represented by the unstable nature of global culture. The executives of big companies must review the paradigms they use as a basis for viewing global brands, overcome the vision characterized by the common denominator principle and affirm a new one which attributes the status of global symbols to brands.

In this context, advertising tends to play a fundamental role of transferring meaning which contains within itself both the physical element of the product to be consumed as well as what a brand represents in terms of meaning within a culture; this creates a potential and paradoxical relationship between the representation of the product and the representation of what a brand transmits within a culture.[7] Modern advertising campaigns are thus conceived by creating a central theme from which many different expressions unravel in order to be able to adapt the theme to individual local contexts. Big global brands are proposed more and more in regional markets with specific creative contents. This does not mean that there are no companies which successfully promote their products without particular adaptations for local contexts; Absolut Vodka is an example of effective advertising communication planned to have international appeal by playing on the cultural pull which the brand has.

A study conducted by Jennifer Aaker and colleagues at Stanford University analyzed the different responses by consumers in three different cultures – Japan, Spain and North America – regarding the characteristics of a few brands. The study highlighted how, for example, both Japanese and US consumers thought the key dimensions of a brand's personality were being exciting, competent, sophisticated and sincere. At the same time, the Japanese consumers highlighted a trait which was more or less absent in the American ones: serenity. In contrast, the American consumer identifies themself particularly with the trait of irregularity, which was not highlighted by the Japanese consumer. In Spain, as well as the common traits highlighted in Japan and the United States, the consumer appreciated another trait – passion – represented both through emotional intensity and spirituality and mysticism.[8]

Aaker's study is further confirmation of how a product may be created to be global but cannot ignore its indigenous meaning. This does not mean however that it is necessary to marry *tout court* the "Think global, act local" principle, according to which a product is developed at a strategic level to be global but adapted at a tactical level to adhere more to local markets. The results of Aaker's research suggest, if anything, that a brand can have a common meaning which guides every level of its planning through different cultures.[9]

The relationship between a brand and consumers in a specific cultural context must be looked into in depth, thereby consolidating the specific cultural significance a brand is founded on. Let's take the example of Benetton. The associations linked to the brand, such as being young and witty, can be used in all cultures, but the unique and independent trait may be highlighted more in the United States, and that of being funny and optimistic in Japan. It is therefore by understanding the relationship which exists between *universal value* and *indigenous value* that it is possible to achieve the objective of creating a global brand effectively.

A study conducted by Professor Geert Hofstede for IBM in 64 countries has made it possible to highlight and confirm five dimensions independent from each other which allow us to describe and measure the tendencies of one culture compared with another, thus providing useful guidelines for planning the global character of a brand; they are distance of power, individualism versus collectivism, masculinity versus femininity, escape from uncertainty, and long term versus short term.[10]

DISTANCE OF POWER

This represents the limit within which the less powerful members of organizations and institutions accept and expect that power will be distributed differently. In other words, it represents the level of inequality accepted, but defined from below and not from above – what a person is willing to accept and not what is imposed on them. There is a distance of power in every situation where there is an authority and a subordinate. This component analyses how power is distributed and accepted in a society and how these inequalities are managed. In approaching international markets, it is necessary to pay attention to the fact that while all societies are different, some are – excuse the expression – more so than others. Under this profile, it is necessary to consider how the progressive passage of some economies from a strongly centralized structure to a decentralized one has considerably influenced the way of working and consuming in those countries, making it possible for people to develop freer behavior and be less subject to the coercive influence of society. In a globalized society, we are in fact moving from hierarchies to networks and this process is considerably facilitated by the increasingly more frequent, more continual and quicker exchange of information. When some societies were still centralized, acceptance of power came about by information being controlled; as the circulation of information was gradually liberalized, this upset not only the modalities in which power was managed, but also those in which products were evaluated and consumed.

INDIVIDUALISM VERSUS COLLECTIVISM

This represents the level of aggregation in groups of individuals. On the side of individualism we find societies where links between individuals have been weakened; everybody thinks about themselves and their immediate neighbor. In societies with a greater collective vocation, a person is integrated from birth into a wider, stronger and more cohesive group which continues to protect in return for unconditional loyalty. In this way, each person is part of a group in which individuals are led to think of others and to share their own experiences to the group and the community. The dimension of individualism defines a society in which the individual tends to be favored rather than the collective; an individualistic society leaves everyone to look after themselves, and any offer by another is seen as interference into private affairs. In contrast, a society with the opposite, or collectivist, behavior makes the population feel like a united and supportive group, but closed to the outside; the family is extended to relatives near and far.

MASCULINITY VERSUS FEMININITY

This concerns the distribution of roles between the sexes. This trait represents an element which strongly differentiates one society from

145

another; basically, we are talking about the (enormous) difference between how female and male values are considered. Results and success are those values dominant in what Hofstede calls "masculine societies," while quality of life and care of fellow humans are elements dominant in those societies which the scholar defines as "feminine." The more societies tend toward the feminine, the more, as we have already noted (Chapter 8), we witness a progressive homogenization of values between men and women, which reflects on the sexual identity a brand must assume.

ESCAPE FROM UNCERTAINTY

This evaluates the degree to which members of a group feel themselves threatened by situations which are unknown or which create uncertainty. It indicates the capacity of a culture to "program" its members to react in structured or unstructured situations. Cultures which avoid uncertainty have strict rules and laws and notable security measures. Cultures which accept chance more are, on the other hand, more tolerant toward the opinions of others, and try to have fewer rules and laws.

LONG TERM VERSUS SHORT TERM

The values indicated by the dimension of short-term orientation are respect for traditions, sense of duty regarding social obligations, and care of one's public image; the values included in long-term orientation are, on the other hand, perseverance and parsimony.

Attributing points for each of the five dimensions to 23 countries, it emerged that, for example, distance of power obtains a high score in Latin America, Asia and Africa, but a low score in Germany. Individualism prevails in Western countries while collectivism prevails in Eastern countries, with the exception of Japan which is halfway between the two. Masculinity is high in Japan, but moderate in Anglo-Saxon and Scandinavian countries. Evading uncertainty is high in Latin countries, and in Japan and German-speaking countries, but has a low score in Anglo-Saxon and Scandinavian countries and in China.

It is interesting to note that all Latin countries have relatively high scores in the dimensions of distance of power and escaping uncertainty.

The countries whose languages derive from Latin underwent, in some way, the influence of the Roman empire, characterized by centralized authority in Rome and a legislative system which was binding for its citizens in every region of the empire. This led to a system of thoughts and values which still shows its influence today. The Chinese empire was also based on centralization, but there was no stable legislative system. The Chinese empire was in fact governed more by men than by laws, as Hofstede underlines.

It is precisely in long-term orientation, together with a method of routine and automatic work, that we can find one of the determining principles of the extraordinary economic growth over the last twenty-five years of all the countries in the Far East, whose economies have been focussed on an orientation toward the future through saving and perseverance.

Procter & Gamble is a classic example of a company with a strong vocation for internationalization, the fruit of an analytical approach which leads to seeking out the deepest knowledge of consumers, the cultural and social environment in which its brands find themselves operating, and the related modalities of usage. It has well understood that it is necessary to understand individual countries, and often the regions within those countries, before introducing its brands on to the market. There are, for example, many areas in the world where clothes are still washed in cold water, often in rivers, and in these countries, Procter, the world leader in washing-machine detergents, communicates the importance of washing by hand in cold water by developing products dedicated to this purpose. Consider therefore how out of place it would be to think of an American woman as being the same as an Indian woman in the use of hygiene products.

A country's cultural attributes determine how the people, the society and the institutions interact with each other. Language differences, religious belief, race and social norms as well as economic and political factors undoubtedly represent obstacles to the development of global branding, and particularly development according to that approach based prevalently on product standardization. The world of cosmetics provides us with an effective representation of this.[11] L'Oréal has invested heavily in research activities to understand the ethnic differences in cosmetic usage in different countries. The prevalent investigation technique is that of recruiting volunteers and asking them to repeat daily gestures in the "bathroom-laboratories" set up for the research. From the analysis of the gestures and rituals of the female consumers involved in this research, useful indications for developing the brand in individual markets have emerged. Consider, for example, that a thirty-year-old Japanese woman has the habit of brushing her eyelashes with mascara 80 times after dipping the brush into the tube, while a European woman of the same age does not repeat the same gesture more than 10 times. This means that if a mascara is to be successful in Japan, it must have a less dense formulation than one commercialized in Europe and the United States. Not only this: the cosmetics market feels the influence of numerous factors, cultural and non-cultural. Let's think of the aspects linked to climate: women in Japan prefer more compact foundation cream because of the high humidity of the Japanese climate, which would not allow a more liquid product to stay on. The considerable climatic differences between summer, which is hot and sultry, and winter, which is cold and icy, mean that the Chinese consumer uses cosmetics with different characteristics depending on the season.[12]

Consider Japan again, and the preference the Japanese have for all those miniaturized technological solutions. The requirement for miniaturization in Japan reflects a social custom linked to the fact that houses are very small, and therefore to the fact that space acquires a different value for the Japanese than it does for a Westerner. Again in Japan, rice is considered a basis of the country's food culture, while in the West it is simply a commodity. This is not to mention the cultural associations which characterize pasta in Italy, which can be compared to those of rice in Japan.

The question arises spontaneously of why Starbucks, whose conceptual origin is traceable to Italy, has not yet opened salespoints in the "Bel Paese." The causes can be sought in the aura which envelops the Italian ritual of coffee. In fact, the modalities of enjoying coffee in a bar in Italy are extremely characteristic; people stay in a bar for much shorter periods of time, making them places of quick transit rather than places to remain in for a good while. Moreover, the importance of bars in the Italian eating and drinking model configures a system of supply which cannot be compared to that present in the United States; Starbucks filled a significant gap in supply right from the start. Finally, Italians are proudly convinced that they make the best coffee in the world – they have developed a cultural prejudice of superiority compared with all ways of making coffee which use a different filtering method and a quality of coffee other than Arabica. Premium coffees are thus poorly represented on the Italian coffee market and the average consumer has a low level of knowledge when it comes to alternatives to drinking Arabica coffee.

Because of the high value the French give to gastronomy and the way this has contributed to building their country's identity, French people are culturally against fast food restaurants. It is no coincidence that McDonald's, which modifies its formats to give them greater regional adhesion, characterizes its restaurants in France with an image which is nearer that of a café, proposing espresso coffee and without the pre-formed plastic chairs fixed to the floor.

KFC also understood that it could not simply replicate the United States model in its restaurants in other parts of the world. Therefore, the chain includes "tempura" on its menus in Japan and potato croquettes and onions in Holland, while in China the chicken is spicier.

The food industry is subject to the influence of religion which pro-hibits, in some cases, the consumption of certain foods; Hindus are not allowed to eat beef, for example, while pork is forbidden for Muslims.

The case of Buitoni pasta on the English market is valid for all. Buitoni, an Italian company which has produced pasta for about 180 years, was bought in 1988 by Nestlé, who immediately sought to increase penetra-tion into international markets. From the first analyses it emerged that a low-performance market for the brand was the United Kingdom, where pasta consumption per head was quite modest – about a quarter of that in the United States. The problem was not so much represented by pen-etration of the brand, which held an 18 per cent market share, as by, if anything, penetration of the category. The problem was that Britain had no pasta culture and little was known of the various dishes which can be created with pasta. The first step therefore consisted in strength-ening awareness of the brand in a core of consumers interested in Italian cooking. So, it was understood that promoting an Italian lifestyle was the most effective method of promoting the consumption of pasta and increasing the brand's fame. Therefore, the Club Casa Buitoni project was launched, and a massive communication campaign invited con-sumers to join. Everybody who became a member of the club received a package linked to Italian lifestyle with recipes, vouchers and informa-tion regarding the different Italian regions, each with its own way of cooking the various types of pasta. Membership of the club also came with a freephone number for advice on how to cook, samples of new products and numerous other items.

Buitoni is an effective example of how understanding cultural bar-riers, linked in this specific case to scarce knowledge of modalities of using the category, can make it possible to overcome the obstacles to the development of a branding strategy in some geographic contexts. We could say that Buitoni had the ability to invent a new behavior and create skills which allowed the brand to develop more quickly, thus speeding up its genetic clock. Moreover, Buitoni is an effective example of how a single approach for more than one market is destined to fail when the product presents different forms of symbolic associations from country to country.

To conclude, to be global a brand must confront the local culture and understand the most intimate and profound aspects of it – those most linked with custom and with lifestyle – and, more generally, the cultural paradigms of reference.

Recent research conducted by McKinsey in China confirms what has already been stated, by highlighting how Chinese consumers love brands, but at the same time are full of national pride; many multinationals have lost important opportunities through underestimating this aspect and taking on too "foreign" an identity. Think of Chinese teenagers who, like their Western counterparts, are attracted by innovative products and brands. However, they show a certain force in wanting to preserve their traditional values and cultural traits, still demonstrating a strong nationalistic identity, an aspect which is undoubtedly less relevant in the West. The brands which approach Chinese teenagers thinking that the big youth brands of the West are welcomed as authentic myths and icons to be venerated risk making a big mistake. The big challenge consists in making the symbolic weight of these brands live with the values system of the new Chinese generations, for whom being rebels and politically incorrect is perhaps not so honorable.

Moreover, frontline sales staff in China are able to exert great influence on consumers' decisions, and promotions in points of sale can represent an effective instrument for guiding consumers toward choosing one brand rather than another.

Unlike what happens in more evolved markets, messages focussing on the functional aspects of a brand can be more important in China, where above all many categories are perceived as new. When Procter & Gamble decided to launch Crest toothpaste in China, it came up against not only the complexity of the cultural system, but also the complex Chinese legislative system. Moreover, affirming a premium product like Crest could have met numerous obstacles in a country where the images and promises of Western brands are copied *tout court*, without however guaranteeing the same effectiveness. Crest is a toothpaste which, thanks to its high fluoride content, is particularly effective in cleaning and protecting against decay, while the majority of the toothpastes sold on the Chinese market are not only not very effective but do not contain fluoride. The oral care offer system therefore in some ways reflected the relative lack of oral hygiene culture in China. Research conducted had in fact shown that for the Chinese, teeth were only important for eating and that decay was considered an unavoidable phenomenon, so that prevention was of zero importance. This is surely not surprising in a country in which there was only one dentist for every 24,000 inhabitants and where medical culture is still strongly linked to traditional remedies. Despite this, the Chinese consumer, although considering oral hygiene as a tedious waste of time, has great faith in the dentist, and Crest understood that it had to get approval from the Chinese National Committee of Oral Health (NCOH). Procter saw that this was no simple act of formality but the basis on which to develop its market entry strategy. Together with the D'Arcy agency and the NCOH, a prevention campaign in oral hygiene was promoted which emphasized the importance of fluoride and forced the entire market to raise the quality standards of its offer. The first step of this communication process was that of creating a television campaign in which the NCOH performed a driving role. The impressive campaign was later followed by intense educational activity jointly with the NCOH aimed at schools, which promoted the importance of prevention. Mobile dental surgeries were also created to promote the same concepts in isolated rural zones.

CHAPTER 16

GIVING A BRAND A PASSPORT

When Unilever's advanced washing products, the fruit of considerable investments in research and development, were unsuccessful on the Indian market, the managers of the company racked their brains to understand the cause of failure. The answer was simple and disconcerting: in India, most of the washing is done under running water or in rivers, and therefore neither powders nor liquid detergents represented a real need. Unilever readapted its products to the Indian market by developing a synthetic detergent in a bar, which was just as effective as either powder or liquid detergent but was used differently.[1]

The case just cited confirms that lack of in-depth analysis of local contexts and consequently of effective information inflows from individual markets can often result not only in clamorous failures, but also in subsequent costly adaptations, not to mention losing the ability to seize opportunities at the right moment.

The brands which succeed in growing on an international scale are those able to understand better than others the needs of individual local markets, and to harmonize those needs successfully in a single brand. In fact, they understand better than others the differences which exist between domestic and foreign markets, but, above all, the complexities of the multiple contexts in which the brand must compete and develop simultaneously. For example, the differences between legislative systems (sometimes subtle, sometimes substantial), economic trends, and local ways of carrying out business which exist in different countries, as well as the cultural background and the complexity of different scenarios to be faced every time, represent the real challenge which companies that intend to have a real international vocation must face. The organizations successful in building global consistency for their brands are those which have really understood the differences not only between different modes of consumption, but also between ways of thinking and behaving. This ability has often led them to reappraise the very elements on which the brand was founded by adapting their products to local taste, environmental needs and cultural and religious sensitivity.

A brand, inasmuch as it is a living organism, is by its very nature *dynamic*, and this means that, for its management at international level, new knowledge must be integrated which is different from that held by the executives at headquarters. The real rule for managing a brand on an international scale is precisely the fact that universal rules valid for every brand do not exist.

Some companies have even created specific products for particular countries since they have found unique opportunities in them. Consider, for example, the Coca-Cola group, which launched Georgia Canned Coffee in Japan. This product is a can of coffee which is distributed via vending machines on every street corner, which are able to deliver hot coffee in winter and cold coffee in summer. The positioning of the automatic vending machines in such open-air contexts as streets was possible in a country like Japan where there is an established respect for tidiness and cleanliness in public places. But imagine the same vending machine in a street in New York or Rome – how long would it last without being destroyed by vandals or defaced by writing and other graffiti?

However, despite the presence of strong characterization elements for each country, and therefore important differences, we are witnessing a progressive convergence of the structure of needs on a world scale. This allows companies to gradually make the process of internationalization less expensive, allowing them to realize significant economies of scale by widening their reference markets. The same Nike, Adidas or Nokia product is thus presented in markets which are profoundly different from one other.

The brands which have been able to develop leadership on a global scale are precisely those which have understood when to either adapt their product to specific local needs or homogenize it at a global level. They understand better than others the need to adapt to the requirements of the place rather than develop and maintain the same consistency over time and borders. These are the brands which have been able to affirm new consumption models inspired by principles of cultural and value homogenization, sustaining new categories and consolidating a position of leadership within them. We are talking about companies which, to go back to our model of the genetic clock, have shown they have faster ticks and can set off faster information exchanges, features which made better adaptation to the environment possible, but at the same time allowed the model they conveyed to be better received by that environment.

As already pointed out, having a mental system which includes innovation, social propagation and mobility makes it possible to create dynamic companies whose brands are orientated to the constant creation of value. This principle is even more consolidated when a brand becomes global and the existing mental system is forced to open up in order to cope with a new mosaic of challenges and demands.

When a company decides to globalize its products, it finds itself having to cope with a multiple series of challenges to its organization: consider, for example, the need to have managers who can speak different languages in order to communicate with all the markets the company finds itself operating in.

The greatest challenge is for those brands which have built up strong success at local level and today find themselves having to start almost from zero to build new company infrastructures for each individual country: a process which leads to their questioning and often revising the acquired knowledge which has led to their success and their talent structure. A manager can be talented in one market but not be right for another. So, a new conception of company talent is defined in which the aptitudes and competences of local and expatriate managers are combined.

One of the most critical factors is precisely the need to develop a system of thought and learning on a global scale, not only for the managers involved in the process of developing the brand but also for the entire structure in charge of its management and commercialization. The creation of this system makes it possible for a company to excel compared with its competitors, thanks to greater understanding of local culture and environmental conditions, and to focus more quickly and effectively on the opportunities which emerge. It is in this way that companies are able to establish a presence in different markets and convert it into brand differentiation elements which are rich in meaning over time and borders.

This capacity allows companies to combine speed with effective responses. Being global requires reducing adaptation time and the immediate proposal of valid and relevant offerings. Being quick at both thinking and acting has become imperative for the success of those brands which decides to compete on an international scale.[2]

It is essential to know how to develop a continuous dialogue with customers and consumers in order to monitor attitudes and behaviors in the market, not only so as to make actions relevant but above all to anticipate needs. Consider the famous statement by Ken Olsen, CEO of Digital Corporation, when in 1977 he affirmed that there was no reason why everybody should have a computer at home. The same year, Jobs and Wozniak founded the company which was destined to revolutionize the information technology market: Apple. Olsen's system of thought clearly showed itself to be closed. Steve Jobs's great strength has always been that of anticipating needs by means of deep interrogation–interpretation of the market, monitoring the possible modalities of the mix between new scientific developments and what is utilizable in the present.

A global system of thought also makes the benefit of greater sophistication and understanding possible in the context of processes both of local adaptation and of standardization. The former president of Ford, Jack Nasser, maintained that if one started with a vision of the world as divided into lots of regional markets, with very different characteristics and requirements from each other, it would never be possible to think of a global organization in the right way. Nasser maintained in fact that Ford was not in the business of geography, but in the business of manufacturing products for consumers wherever they were.

Companies which have greater speed and are able to develop a dialogue in depth succeed in anticipating the competitor. The ability to introduce more products into more markets in the shortest time possible is the direct consequence of information exchange processes which are increasingly quicker and more accurate and of an organizational model orientated toward internationalization with effectiveness and efficiency. In order to achieve these objectives, organizations such as Procter, Nokia and L'Oréal have had to revise radically their organizational models so as to improve coordination between the different markets. The US multinational, for example, understood that the excessive autonomy given to individual subsidiaries was in fact the main cause of notable delays in introducing products onto individual markets. It was necessary to create local subsidiaries with structures, policies and practices which were exact replicas of the headquarters; effective information flows and greater coordination capacity in every phase of the product management process, from its initial planning up to its launch, had to be developed between the subsidiaries. Through greater integration of its markets, Procter is today able to develop products which satisfy the needs of consumers in every nation, with increasingly reduced introduction and diffusion times on an international scale.[3]

In fact, while 8 years were needed for Pampers to enter 7 countries, it only took 7 years to insert Pert in 60 countries and only 2 years to insert Vidal Shampoo in 40.

Being able to share knowledge and best practice with extreme speed between the various subsidiaries scattered around the world is another of the elements which characterize a mental predisposition to globalization.[4] The subsidiaries themselves contribute to the creation of a collective cultural heritage, transferring the knowledge acquired in the individual markets and thus generating global sharing of that knowledge. This imposes frequent changes in the reference mindset, making this component of the company the one which undergoes most innovation. The sources knowledge can be acquired from are numerous, and for any company intending to position a brand on a global level it is essential that the subsidiaries learn from a greater number of sources. All this makes it possible to accelerate growth, maintain competitive strength and reduce costs. Leading companies excel precisely in their capacity to code and transfer product and process innovations created by their subsidiaries.

Part of this knowledge is proprietary and is transferred in various forms, for example through training and newsletters. In other cases, think of the advertising company sector, where a large part of knowledge is tacit, often generated by the exposure of categories and brands to the market. McCann-Erickson, one of the most important advertising agencies in the world, has a particularly evolved training programme to help record and share this knowhow. This transfer mechanism makes it possible not only to develop and understand the complexity of the part an advertising agency must play today, but also to share the learning processes which derive from everything in the world which is somehow exposed to the attention of consumers. In order to improve this capacity, employees of the main agencies are often involved in work groups which meet outside the reference market and are made up of people from vastly different backgrounds. The meetings are often held in different countries and employees of different nationalities and cultures are involved. Senior managers themselves gain experience in different countries in order to develop a greater propensity toward understanding cultural difference.

Organizational processes like this make it possible to have better-informed and better-qualified personnel who are able to act extremely quickly because they know how to develop, during short learning times, direct and continuous dialogue with the people in the individual markets, and they also understand the environment in which the brands are called to compete. In this way the company has been able to develop a cultural substratum far from any nationalism and based on a system of increasing global knowledge, which allows quicker and more creative application of its talents and the building of a growing reputation with a recognized ability to create more "robust" brands for its customers.

A further example of adaptation differentiated to individual local contexts comes from Lycra, whose problem was represented by the multiple varieties of its application, each of which requires a specific positioning of the brand. Dupont, the brand's owner, solved the problem by each time delegating responsibility for each of these applications to the manager of a different country, depending on the prevalence in each area of reference of one application rather than another. Therefore, it was up to the manager in Brazil, a country where swimming costumes are used twelve months a year on its famous beaches, to lead the global team concerned with positioning the brand in this category. The manager in France, on the other hand, was responsible for leading the team which defined how to position the brand in the fashion market. The contribution of individual managers thus made it possible to develop a general brand strategy by combining their local experiences and knowledge in the general strategy.[5] In a similar vein, Nestlé headquarters defines the guidelines for strategic planning, but each local business unit is given responsibility for choices regarding marketing, distribution and often the adaptation of a product to the needs of the market by deciding for example how much sauce should be put in a tin of ravioli.[6]

The importance of a brand's intellectual capital implies that companies will be able to maintain their competitive advantage only by developing the capacity to focus on creating and transferring new knowledge rapidly and efficiently. Whoever allows themself to become fossilized on their previously acquired knowledge will risk extinction or, at least, decline, and will never be able to compete at a global level. Worldwide companies systematically discover opportunities for transferring information. P&G, Mars, Coca-Cola and the consultancy group McKinsey excel in transferring and sharing information. McKinsey even shares information via its website which provides those who sign up with research studies and case histories, something which represents a very effective example of how a position of global leadership in action and thought can be acquired.

CHAPTER 17

THE NEW FRONTIERS OF BRANDS IN A CHANGING WORLD: THE CASE OF INDIA

The histories of India and of most of the countries whose economies are growing rapidly show how, following an increase in earnings, consumers tend to spend proportionally less on essential goods and more on discretionary goods. Indian consumers are starting to be able to afford products and services which go beyond the primary needs of eating and clothing.

The extraordinary economic growth and the increase in average income per head are not sufficient however to fully understand the Indian consumer market. It is not really possible to talk about the Indian consumer, but various Indian *consumers,* each of whom modifies their status according to different modalities and speeds. There is a consumer who can be fully compared to one in a developed country, who has a car, televisions and hi-fi systems, and buys holidays, mobiles and designer clothes. This market segment has an extraordinary growth rate of approximately 20 per cent per annum. There is another type of consumer who cannot afford this level of consumption but who strongly aspires to achieving it and, in the Indian market, represents the middle class. This consumer probably does not have three televisions at home, but does have cereals for breakfast and owns a washing-machine. Targeting the offer at this type of "aspirational" consumer can produce important benefits in the future. At the base of this pyramid there is a large part of the population which has nothing to do with the market, hardly able to supply its primary needs.

There are many figures which highlight the extraordinary growth of the middle class in India – consider how the number of cars registered in the five years 2003–8 more than doubled. What characterizes the Indian "aspirational" consumer most is their young age: more than 70 per cent are under 36 and half are under 18. However, this must not trick us into thinking that this consumer has grown up with cultural models from a Western matrix. This is a consumer who, while being attracted to everything that happens outside their country, is deeply rooted in Indian culture and traditions. Their shopping budget is still limited, since they invest half of their income in basic products, but the share allocated to areas of consumption above primary needs is increasing quickly. When their primary needs are satisfied, this consumer feels the need to purchase those products they identify with a better lifestyle, such as a television or the possibility of drinking Coca-Cola rather than the traditional lemon juice.

The Indian television system, with more than 200 channels, has opened up an important window on the world by increasing the consumer's exposure to global brands. While succumbing to the charm, the Indian consumer is not yet willing however to pay a premium price for them, and looks for the best quality product at the lowest price. Moreover, Indians tend to ask for brands which are relevant and which reflect local preferences. MTV India has well understood this fact and has characterized a large part of its scheduling with Indian music and languages. But other big global brands also seem to have understood it and systematically make use of Bollywood actors[1] – who are much more famous in the subcontinent of over a billion potential consumers than any of the vastly higher-paid Hollywood stars.

The axiom "best quality at the lowest price" does not however mean that the Indian consumer is unable to pay a slightly higher price if the product guarantees the right value and relevance. The introduction of details like a torch in the Nokia 1100 phone (particularly appreciated by lorry drivers who find themselves having to stop in the poorer regions where motorways and service stations are not powered) or backup memory in Samsung washing-machines, which avoids the risk of the washing cycle restarting from the beginning (and thus increasing water and electricity consumption, as well as ruining the clothes) as a result of the numerous power cuts and sudden changes in supply voltage, are a valid demonstration of the above principle. They are both examples of how further details which functionally serve the needs of the consumer can be translated into something which is effectively relevant and for which the Indian consumer is *prepared to pay*. Another of the challenges to be faced in India, as in most emerging countries, is not linked to a brand's fame or availability, but to the lack of knowledge regarding what it can do. It is no coincidence that in the early 1990s washing-machine manufacturers promoted their products by explaining the benefits of washing items of clothing inside a machine rather than on the banks of a river.[2]

The fact that an ever growing number of consumers are becoming able to allocate more than half of their spending potential to types of consumption which, unlike food and clothing, are not a primary need, opens up new scenarios for the Indian consumer market. Certainly, it is too early to have a large consumer base able to buy designer clothes, cars or all those types of products whose purchase is widely diffused in more evolved societies, but the change has started and the extraordinary growth rates demonstrate the fact. We are at the gates of an era in which consumption in India too will be guided by choice rather than by need.

We have entered a phase in which, for example, an ever greater number of Indians are starting to visit doctors rather than treat their illnesses with home-made remedies; they are starting to buy jewelry (considered a classic form of saving) or a moped. The passage from aspiring to seeking means that many families have the possibility of being able to buy a mobile phone, or a television, or send their children to private school. Following the sharp increase in earnings, within the next twenty years the proportion of spending on non-primary consumption will be more than 70 per cent. This process is typical of all those economies where in the past low labor costs meant it was profitable to produce, and today higher average earnings have gradually meant it has become profitable to sell. We are talking about countries where the middle class is progressively entering the marketplace and in which radical processes of urbanization are giving life to new and extraordinary urban markets. Rural realities are increasingly giving way to cities which seem to rise overnight and where a growing number of consumers are developing new models of purchase and consumption which are governed less and less by primary needs.

Preferences are progressively changing, and consequently so is the proportion of spending which is destined to the consumption of new categories. What is interesting is that when allotting these growing income shares, high priority is given to those product categories which allow further economic growth – products, goods and services which can lead to improved productivity or facilitate future participation in economic activity. It is therefore not a total coincidence that India has grown particularly in the last few years in the information technology sector. Transport, education and communication are the most important spending categories after those of primary needs and all this guarantees a multiplier effect for future growth.[3]

In the meantime, entertainment and recreation are still extras for a small proportion of consumers compared to the United States or Europe. This is the fruit of a cultural attitude which sees the Indian consumer privilege areas linked to growth (such as education) rather than waste money on something which is of less obvious economic benefit, and this attitude will last for a few years yet. Despite this, in these areas of consumption, spending has doubled in only ten years; it is therefore legitimate to predict that great opportunities will open up in India for all those brands with a global dimension able to understand the change and adapt their offering to a market with deep cultural roots and characterized by exponential growth.

Let's take the example of products for the home. The low penetration of electrical domestic appliances is undoubtedly limited by the shortage of infrastructures, such as, for example, running water and electricity, and by the availability at low cost of substitutes like domestic servants. Moreover, low repair costs considerably extend the useful life of an electrical appliance and this certainly influences the annual share of spending in these categories. In Italy, toward the end of the 1960s, the "useful life" of a washing machine was ten to fifteen years, while today after seven years, if not before, an electrical appliance is ready to be replaced. However, it is predicted that by 2015 the evolution will be extraordinary for this spending category too, changing consumer purchase behavior from the *desired* to the *wanted*.

The entry into the world economy of a vast number of consumers from so-called emerging countries has represented one of the most important opportunities for producers of consumer goods in the last decades. The country which has contributed most to this is undoubtedly China, with 213 million consumers with middle- or upper-class incomes, but neither to be dismissed is the contribution of India, with approximately 123 million consumers possessing the same income characteristics.

In order to come out on top in the battle to secure these new consumers, the big brands find themselves having to undertake two basic strategic choices. The first option consists in offering products and services at a price comparable to that applied in the principal markets, targeting the offer at the higher income bracket and waiting for middle-class growth as a result of increased earnings. There are probably not more than 1.2 million families of consumers able to take up this offer in India, at least as things stand at the present; the figure should rise to 2 million by about 2010.

The other approach is based, instead, on the hypothesis of widening the consumer base by reducing prices and therefore margins, thus succeeding in reaching a potential market of 11 million family units. However, it must be underlined that this market segment is today protected by a considerable number of Indian firms which undoubtedly have deeper knowledge of the cultural, social and consumption dynamics of the country.

The real battlefield on which global and Indian firms will find themselves competing will undoubtedly be that of the urban middle-low classes, whose rate of increase is extraordinary. Indian firms will try to keep these consumers, although they know that they will progressively develop more "aspirational" preferences when faced with the stimuli induced by the big brands. In such a changeable context as this, global enterprises will necessarily have to review their business models. The challenge will center on the capacity to develop new products and services which have relevant appeal to Indian middle classes, characterized by high functionality and performance, and without putting the accent on those features which are not considered useful if they involve an increase in costs and therefore in prices.

The compensation for those who know how to innovate, adapt and develop a deep understanding of the new Indian consumer will undoubtedly be substantial. The Indian consumer market will continue to be an environment in which to operate with the spirit of challenge, and it will not be without opportunities: the challenge will be based mainly on the imagination and ambition of producers and consumers and the capacity of the former to read these dynamics and seize these opportunities.

PART V

LESSONS IN BRANDING: HOW TO LEARN FROM THE BEST

CHAPTER 18

FROM THE REDISCOVERY OF ITS ROOTS TO "SENSE & SIMPLICITY": THE CASE OF PHILIPS[1]

Philips represents an effective example of how brand positioning can be founded on an analysis of the company's past.

Royal Philips Electronics, a Dutch multinational with headquarters in Amsterdam, is one of the most important electronics firms in the world and the biggest in Europe, with activities focussed in the healthcare, lifestyle and technology sectors. With a turnover of €30.4 billion (2005), it has approximately 126,000 employees in more than 60 countries and is world market leader in the sector of diagnostic imaging and patient monitoring services, lighting, personal care, and domestic appliances as well as consumer electronics.

The foundations of the colossus were laid in 1891 when Gerard Philips founded a company in Eindhoven for "the manufacture of incandescent lightbulbs and other electrical products." The story of Philips is that of a company which has always lived on technology and put itself at the leading edge of innovation in this sector. The creation and introduction of revolutionary products has always characterized the company's strategic progress. There are in fact many Philips patented technological innovations which have contributed to changing the world. Consider the introduction of X-ray tubes for medical use in 1918, the invention of the rotating heads on the basis of which the Philishave electric shaver was developed in the 1950s, the introduction of the compact audio cassette in 1963, the manufacture of the first integrated circuit in 1965, and the invention of the compact disc and optical systems of telecommunication in the 1970s.

However, the consumer has not always perceived the brand's avant-garde character because of the company's strategic orientation which privileged the sale of technology to other interlocutors, generating the most considerable part of its earnings by this activity. An important part of the company's profits still comes from the sale of licenses and intellectual property, in the form of direct royalties and exchange of royalties with companies it purchases other technology from. In short, the company's scarce orientation toward consumer marketing has not always permitted it to transform its technology into profits through its own brand.

Although this attitude has constituted an essential feature of the brand, since 1996 we have witnessed a radical change which has seen the company regain control of its brand and try to enhance it more on the consumer front. In fact, until the middle of the 1990s, all advertising and marketing campaigns were conducted locally and linked to individual products. Many campaigns were carried out simultaneously and contextually, without a common thread of communication linked to the brand: Philips's profile was not that of a global company. The first propulsive factor of change was the definition of a brand promise through the slogan "Let's make things better." A global communication campaign followed, traceable to the concept of "One Philips." Through this campaign the company presented itself for the first time with a single claim used for all its products in all the markets Philips was present in.

Until this moment, Philips had operated by allowing each division (up to 400 technology lines) to develop its own brand promise, thus creating great confusion in the perception of the brand's unique character on the part of the end consumer. The global character of the campaign contributed to presenting a single face of Philips to the outside world for the first time, but also to generating a stronger sense of belonging to the brand in all the company's employees.

To consolidate this process, the organization felt the need to confront its origins and rediscover its roots, and this activity of analysis led to a publication through which it aimed at synthesizing its search for its past so as to define directives for future development with greater coherence.

Philips's top management had understood well that the discovery of its genetic matrix was a step which was as complex as it was necessary for undertaking any activity aimed at building an effective and consistent positioning of the brand.

A company which has been present in a market for more than a hundred years must confront its cultural roots: this process contributed decisively to raising, for a second time, the brand's founding "pillars": *pioneering spirit and the capacity to invent and create.* Another element which characterizes the company's history was individuated in its capacity to launch technological innovations on the market at the most opportune moment, never too early and never too late. Finally, an essential feature of Philips's genetic heritage is that the company has always taken on the role of "democratic innovator": think, for example, of the fact that it was the first manufacturer of lightbulbs and that it brought lighting into the houses of half the world. Light is an integral part of Philips's historical identity, not only because of the bulbs it has progressively offered at an ever lower cost, but also because of the technological threads which derive from it, from X-raying to the cathode tube. Precisely because of this democratic character the company's cultural planning is strongly centered on nearness to individuals.

This genetic trait of Philips can also be seen at an organizational level. The company has always been based on consensus, democracy and on the need to improve the lives of both its consumers and its employees. This deep process of gathering and cataloging its roots was the starting point for the process of redefining the brand's positioning in accordance with a more precise identity which allowed potential customers to develop a solid reason for purchase.

Nevertheless, Andrea Ragnetti, who took on the post of chief marketing officer in the company in 2003, immediately felt that Philips was running the risk of limiting its positioning to a simple declaration of the point where the company found itself. Limiting itself to describing itself, affirming what it was, where it was and what it did was not contributing to creating, in the view of the Italian manager, a strong brand identity able to prevail in the competitive arena.

Moreover, the company was coming from a brand promise like "Let's make things happen," which had not fully achieved the objective of positioning it competitively in the markets in which it was present. The campaign had also generated more than a few problems of interpretation linked to the cultural and linguistic implications in the territorial contexts in which it had been launched. Some in fact saw it as an incitement; others, in contrast, viewed it as a promise to make products which worked better than those proposed in the past, sustaining the interpretation of an admission of guilt or, in any case, of weakness. The brand promise proposed had thus a character which was too defensive and neutral, certainly neither aggressive nor conveying a proposal.

However, it must be highlighted that the company's inability to consolidate the image of its brand not only was the direct consequence of a scarce propensity to propose itself to the outside world, but also was dictated by a serious economic crisis which the company was having to face in that moment. Moreover, a large part of its business had derived from the business-to-business areas in which the brand took on less relevance compared with the consumer market.

In 2003, the picture of the company was very different. Following an in-depth restructuring project, the company was financially more solid and streamlined, thanks to the sale of the components division, purely technological, which sold technology at low margins, thus radically influencing company profitability. In 2006, the semiconductor business was also sold, this being a cyclical business with high investment capital, which critically influenced the entire company equity.

The discontinuation of these two divisions further marked the move from highly volatile activities to others such as healthcare, lifestyle and technology, making further consolidation of the company possible.

In this new context, the need was still felt to find a positioning which would act as an umbrella for activities which were profoundly different from each other and which included completely unrelated products, from toasters to magnetic resonance imaging, and thus to avoid excessive dilution of the brand. The real challenge consisted in achieving a different positioning for each area of business while maintaining a common denominator which would make it possible to exploit the strength of a brand which had existed for more than a hundred years and therefore had extraordinary potential.

At this point, the company decided to confront its target. By cataloguing its business, Philips had highlighted the fact that 80 per cent of company profits were generated from a consumer band aged between 35 and 55, with above-average incomes, distributed equally between the sexes and inclined to purchase both more expensive appliances and consumer electronics in general. These are the decision-makers who buy, for example, machinery from the medical systems division or the lighting division.

While the consumer electronics division represents in fact the most significant part of Philips's turnover, the same cannot be said about its contribution to the company's profits. As we have already highlighted, brands live less and less in isolation, and this means that a brand can have different positioning in various sectors, depending on how it changes its frame of reference. The administrator of a hospital who finds themselves having to decide which magnetic resonance imager to purchase is at the same time a person who has a television, a stereo and a computer at home and who therefore also develops associations with a brand as a consumer. The real challenge faced by Philips was precisely that of translating the brand's positioning in the different areas while always keeping it interesting.

Philips had understood well that concentrating on its target imposed a more in-depth analysis of the problems which that target had, and highlighting the most relevant one within that "complexity." Everything contributes to rendering the lives of individuals more complicated and the market, with its multiplication of offerings based less and less on real needs, is no exception, making a simple choice into a complex equation.

Consider, for example, a stroll around the electronics sector, from the analogical to the digital. If, from one point of view, technology has had extraordinary implications, on the market front it has translated into a multiplication of the number of products, brands and suppliers. This is the direct consequence of the process of the dematerialization of technological products, which are increasingly made up of software and less and less of hardware. This process had drastically reduced not only the production costs of high-technology products but also the timescale of their entry onto the market, really beating down the economic barriers to entry.

The digital revolution should have simplified life, but according to research carried out by Philips, exactly the opposite seems to be true. For example, approximately 30 per cent of products for domestic networks are taken back because the purchasers are unable to use them. And 48 per cent of interviewees do not buy videocameras because they think they are too complicated to use.

Philips understood well that users throughout the world, regardless of where they live, want to enjoy the advantages of technology without useless complications. "I don't want to build a car [...] just drive one," commented a participant in one of the surveys carried out by the company. In other words, the world is already complicated enough as it is: what is really needed is *simplicity*.[2] Manufacturers of technology have always shown a certain love for complexity, considering simplicity a synonym of low performance; think of the difficulties Apple had when it introduced the first Mac, whose ease of use could have represented an element of weakness in the information technology sector since it was (wrongly) associated with the concept of low performance. In reality, the technological execution of simplicity represents the most complex thing that can be achieved. The research carried out clearly highlighted an opportunity which was unique in its type represented by the possibility of satisfying the need for simplicity, while at the same time strengthening the brand's prestige with consumers and customers throughout the world.

But what is the solution to complexity? The answer may seem rhetorical: simplicity itself. It is from this principle that Philips's new positioning, "Sense & Simplicity," was born, with the goal of organizing the company's entire technological offer so as to make it easier to use and enjoy, in line with the character of democratic innovator of its cultural matrix. Simplicity is the prime objective of technology and the brand's positioning had to reflect that conviction by acting to simplify and facilitate the choices of individuals and the collective.

Today Philips presents itself as a single company throughout the world which has decided to promise simplicity in a structured way.

There are in fact other companies which are positioned on simplicity (consider Apple again), but none has ever *promised* simplicity. These companies promote simplicity via their products without structural involvement of the entire organization on this theme. It is no coincidence that before launching the "Sense and Simplicity" campaign on a global scale, Philips felt the need to prepare its internal sales on the concept of simplicity. A company can in fact promise something to its consumers only if that something is present within the organization itself. A company cannot sell simplicity if complexity reigns within it.

This requirement was further amplified by the company's need for streamlining and simplification at organizational level following the important restructuring project recently carried out. The imperative was to create a simpler internal environment, where simplicity was the new cultural and operative matrix, putting the company into the condition of materially "delivering" simplicity to the market. The entire organizational model thus needed to be reviewed by transversal internal positioning of simplicity at all levels of the hierarchy. So new figures were created within the company's organization chart, such as "simplicity project manager" and "simplicity program manager," who acted as points of organizational simplification within the company.

Awareness and understanding of the new positioning is monitored periodically at each level of the hierarchy by means of a system of tracking which involves 30,000 internal interviewees. The "Sense & Simplicity" promise therefore concerns not only the products: this approach has been thought out to assure that all the Philips organization adheres totally to the mission and that it involves all the stakeholders, as well as the way of doing business.

After internal sales, the problem was posed of how to translate simplicity and render it feasible at product level. First, the Simplicity Advisory Board was established, made up of five experts in the sectors of healthcare, lifestyle, and technology. The role of this committee was to provide an external view on how the new brand promise of "Sense & Simplicity" could be applied to everything the company did within these sectors. Each member had a different cultural and professional background. Such diversity increased the committee's capacity to understand how people of different cultures perceived simplicity in their lives. The members of the committee, despite being expressions of different experiences and cultures, shared the company's preference for simplicity.[3] The objective was to use the collective experience of the Simplicity Advisory Board to lead the company's creativity and generate further ideas.

At the basis of the executive system of simplicity, three pillars were created: these had to be present simultaneously in every phase connected with the product, from creation to development up to commercialization and after-sales service. Any activity had to be based on the three pillars of "Designed Around You," "Easy to Experience" and "Advanced."

The first pillar, "Designed Around You," implies that everything Philips develops must be the fruit of understanding the ways in which the possible end user runs their life. All of Philips's activities must be guided by consumer insight and in-depth knowledge of the needs, dreams and desires of all the company's stakeholders. Any company uses insights, but they are often those of the owner or product manager, and it is for this reason that the quality of insight in Phillips is periodically verified and certified by outside companies, to make sure that that insight is really that of the end user.

However, many products which start from a valid insight are often not easy to experience. And this is where the second pillar, "Easy to Experience," comes into play. People must always be in the condition to enjoy the benefits of technology without controversies or difficulties. Philips's solutions and products, like its way of running the business, may be very sophisticated, but they must always be simple to use and appreciate compared both with the solutions of the past and with those of the competition.

Finally, as to the third pillar, "Advanced," for Philips a solution is really advanced only when it improves people's lives. The concept of advanced refers not only to the technology but also to the way of thinking and preparing for the future, studying possible future scenarios and guiding innovation toward what is most desirable and sustainable. The term "innovative" was deliberately not chosen, since this refers normally to the latest level of technology which has been reached. Advanced, on the other hand, means the most intelligent choice of technology which makes it possible to resolve the problem in the best way – and this does not necessarily mean that this choice must be the most *recent* one.

Every product and every company process must therefore be founded on these three pillars. A product cannot be simple to realize if it is not based on a real need; it cannot be based on a real need if it is not simple to use; it cannot be simple to use if it does not use the best technology.Any product is based on the existence of a "value proposition," which is built like a house with insight as its foundation. All the key elements of a marketing proposition are built upon market insights such as target, benefit, reason to purchase, competitive environment, and all the elements that differentiate the product in a meaningful way from the competition.

No product is today introduced onto the market if it is not supported by a proposition house which is validated both by insight and by empirical evidence from research. Every phase of a product's life cycle must have a valid proposition house, even that of its creation. Without it, the process of research and development is not begun; all this is to guarantee that the product has an orientation which enables it to deal with the phases of technological change, above all in markets such as those of diagnostic machinery which have rather long development timescales. The existence of a valid proposition house is a key instrument for the success of a product and involves all the stakeholders. Consider, for example, a piece of machinery for medical diagnosis: the subjects interested in this product will be the doctors who have to use it, the CEOs or directors of the health firms who have to authorize its purchase, and (last but not least) the patient who could choose a hospital or a clinic precisely because of the presence of a particular piece of machinery. For every product it is therefore possible to develop different value proposition houses aimed at different publics, thus satisfying their multiple needs.

The launch of the new brand strategy represented a great challenge for the company, and the results already achieved are widely encouraging: greater knowledge on the part of consumers of the wide range of Philips products and a strong association between the brand and the concept of simplicity.

The Philips brand today occupies position number 42 in the Interbrand table which measures the value of the principal global brands (in 2004 it was at 65), showing one of the most significant growths. The new brand positioning will allow Philips to meet the needs of consumers by guaranteeing a distinctive experience which is not limited to the purchase and use of products, but also involves other moments of contact with the company (touchpoints), be they the website, advertising campaigns, product packaging, or, more simply, direct contact with Philips people.

CHAPTER 19

EVOKING SYMBOLIC VALUES AROUND A PRODUCT AND BECOMING A GLOBAL ICON: THE CASE OF STARBUCKS

The history of Starbucks represents a classic demonstration of how an existing business model can be transformed into an extraordinary success story.

Founded in 1971, Starbucks has the fastest growth rate of any company in the history of retailing.[1]

In his autobiography, Howard Schultz, the company's founder and present CEO, recounts how enlightenment came to him one day in 1983 when he was in Milan for a conference. As he was strolling along the Corso Vittorio Emanuele, he noticed the large number of bars there and the role that they had in Italian society not only as places of consumption but also as relational catalysts. It was then that he decided that that model represented the future of coffee in the United States. What makes Schultz's intuition extraordinary is its simplicity: just by seeing what Italians see every day from another perspective, he transformed it into a brand which today is present throughout the world.

After his trip to Milan, Schultz tried to convince the owners of the coffee company he worked for, Starbucks, of his strange idea of building up a chain of coffee bars. They did not understand him: they sold roasted coffee to restaurants and they had no intention of turning into a bar. Schultz walked out, left Starbucks in 1985 and founded his own company called Il Giornale, a name which showed clear traces of the intuition he had had in Italy. Little by little, his bars, which served coffee roasted by Starbucks, became successful: first in the state of Washington and then in others. In 1987, Schultz bought Starbucks for $3,800,000. At the end of that year, he already owned 17 bars; the following year the number rose to 33, then 55, 84, 116, until today's approximately 15,000 in five continents. Let's try and investigate the factors which have determined this success, one which revolves around a product category – that of coffee – which is extremely banal and static, but which Starbucks has managed to give a new cachet to.

Starbucks sells mainly coffee, and even were it the best coffee in the world it would still only be coffee. The question spontaneously arises, therefore: why is Starbucks today a brand to be counted among the elite of mythical brands? What has made the consumer pay a premium price for something they would normally have paid significantly less for? The answer can be found in the fact that Starbucks' marketing approach goes far beyond the tangible component of the product by infusing coffee with new symbolic values.

A high quality of coffee, widespread locations and commercial partnership agreements have undoubtedly contributed to the company's growth, but these elements are not sufficient to make a brand a global myth, an authentic icon of postmodern society.

An exchange from the movie *Duplex* illustrates the bohemian image Starbucks has acquired as a place where writers and other intellectuals are welcomed as part of a specific community. In the film, a young wife, played by Drew Barrymore, turns to her writer husband and says "Well, what if you got out of the house for a little while and went to write at, like a Starbucks or something?" "It would be nice not to have to write at Starbucks with all the other novelists," replies the young man, played by Ben Stiller.

It is precisely this which is the true essence of Starbucks: a place which evokes symbolic values which go beyond coffee and the products sold and which makes a sign a metropolitan legend. It is feeling part of a community like that of the writers looking for success quoted in the film, and many more besides, which makes consumers identify with a place where, when it really comes down to it, what you mostly do is just drink coffee.

The context in which coffee and banana bread are sold, in other words the physical evidence of Starbucks, help to attribute deep values to the brand. The physical evidence is nothing other than all the physical support within which the service is delivered, the environment in which staff and equipment are spatially collocated.

We are talking about an environment characterized by colors, perfumes, procedures, artifacts, materials, shapes, uniforms, where everything contributes to creating physical interaction with the consumer. It is in this context that the organization and processes become

175

transparent, visible and valuable by the consumer, and company values are shared by staff and customers. It is in this context that Starbucks takes on a symbolic value both as a place of consumption and as a place of work: the physical context must reinforce the theme by encouraging active consumer/customer participation, facilitating social interaction both with other consumers and with the person delivering the service. Within the physical context of Starbucks, it is possible to develop social relationships with both the outside and the inside. Thanks to wireless technology, Starbucks is today a wi-fi area where anyone can connect to the web simply by turning on their notebook. Thus, Starbucks has become an elective place where music is shared in MP3 format among the younger age groups of the population, or electronic documents are shared among professionals. It is no coincidence that Starbucks has today decided to develop a partnership with the company which is maybe most similar to it, being also able to propose products which can go beyond their functionality and create the sense of belonging to a community: Apple. The agreement has made it possible for Apple iTunes users to have free access to the wi-fi services in the chain's thousands of coffee bars so as to be able to download music from the online store of Cupertino's company.

It is again in the environment that the product itself finds collocation, that the coffee goes beyond its banality and evokes values and, reciprocally, the values and the culture acquire visibility. The processes of coffee delivery find a collocation within the context, and the front office activity and the definition of standards assume a visual identity.

The scientific definition of the overall process, set down in the service blueprint, makes it possible to meticulously define front office and back office activities. It sets the standards and identifies possible critical points in the whole process, and defines plans for preventing or mitigating failure. Within the context, a symbolic line of visibility is defined; in fact, the consumer has a physical and an emotive journey in the context where some of the things that are going on are visible and others are not. From the moment of ordering a coffee, everything is transparent; what cannot be seen (phases such as purchasing the coffee) is imagined, thanks to the support of visual merchandising material which evokes the coffee and its values. A person who habitually goes into a Starbucks tends to do so not just to drink a cup of coffee but to access a sort of community where they find values, models and behaviors which they tend to recognize themselves in. Starbucks knew how to transform a simple everyday gesture – the morning coffee – into an experience loaded with symbolic contents. While Starbucks continued to enrich its context with new meanings and values, other competitors continued to simply sell coffee, partly decreeing its success.[2] Starbucks's performance demonstrates how, by enhancing the atmosphere and making the place of consumption a space linked to trendsetters and not the minority fringe of the population, by creating a sense of belonging and community, it is possible to achieve success even when satisfying routine needs. Apart from the location, other elements like the style of the building, the sign and the type of entrance contribute to giving users indications of the type of consumption experience they are going to meet. As Volli affirms, Starbucks "is together closed and secret but also open and public, it shows and hides at the same time, it simultaneously exercises modesty and seduction, the secret and the recall."[3]

Individuals really do look for the possibility of developing relations with their neighbors, of feeling part of "something bigger," and in the mind of Schultz coffee represented the catalyzing element for providing this type of experience.

The pervasive widespread nature of Starbucks, in big American cities and in the main capitals of the world, has made this coffee bar an element of urban furnishing, almost a footprint of the process of civilization. Its presence in a place gives a sense of security and if you do not see it, it feels as if something is missing – it is as if its lack were almost a bad omen. You can recognize it immediately: green sign, big windows with a view of the street and, once inside, a pleasant atmosphere make Starbucks not only a bar but a square or a meeting place, rather a clever idea, but at the same time one so banal that it is hard to think that nobody before 1987 had had it. A Starbucks in the historical and prestigious streets of a city center acquires strength from the positive connotations of the place, and contributes to the charm and appeal of the big capitals.[4]

Starbucks has generated a profound social paradox: it is hated by many, especially by those intellectuals and New York bohemians who deplore the homogenizing – what they call the "midtownization" – of the modern city, which makes every block identical to the next. But it is precisely in its proposing a contemporary way of being bohemian that one of the main reasons for Starbucks's success can be found.[5]

Starbucks also introduced a new vision of a working environment. For its founder, Starbucks represents the "third place," a sort of extension of both home and workplace. The staff in Starbucks perform a role of particular strategic importance. Above all, the frontline workers are not called "employees" but "partners," and personalized professional growth paths are designed for each partner, based on individual potential. The company supports and encourages diversity, not least in the sense of multi-ethnic representation, even in deciding personalized training paths; what is more, diversity has become a transversal value at every level of the hierarchy – from line staff to the "high" rooms of the board of directors. Starbucks also believes that job rotation is essential, and uses it as an element of professional development; career planning is carried out in great detail, up to defining development paths and succession processes for the top 200 company posts by evaluating the availability of internal candidates, the socalled "benchers," destined in the future to occupy higher positions. The involvement of every single employee, from the "barista" (Italian for bartender) to the member of the board, is inborn in the company culture, and the majority of training activities are strongly orientated to modalities of group work.

It is precisely this involvement which makes members of the organization important, able to determine the course of company decisions and actions and exercise some form of control over their own organization, not merely subject to its destiny but contributing, if anything, to building it. The staff play a strategic role since, with their attitude, they must strengthen the existence of a culture and reference horizons and so make it possible for consumers to experience them. The staff are encouraged to be spontaneous, since spontaneity is innate in the company's values: it is precisely because it cannot be programed that spontaneity renders credible in the eyes of the customer the formal and pre-codified part of the process of communication set up by the front- line personnel and the physical context. The very fact that most employees are college or university students contributes in some way to reinforcing the bohemian image of the brand. Schultz has affirmed a new style of leadership by dedicating a large part of his time to listening and to inserting people into the right places, involving them in the process of creating new ideas.

We can definitely affirm that at Starbucks work ceases to be experienced as only a chore, and becomes an extraordinary opportunity for personal innovation and interior growth. In Starbucks, however, the importance of the products sold and the cultural matrix of coffee is not underestimated. Every barista, in fact, undergoes intense training about coffee. Coffee is the basis of the entire narrative path in Starbucks, the heart of the experiences which develop around it, through the brand.

Starbucks has in fact contributed to the development of coffee culture and this has generated a new consumer approach toward this category. What some people have defined as the "Starbucks effect" has shown itself not only in the offer with a considerable increase in premium segments, but also in demand by generating masses of consumers who are increasingly demanding and qualified when it comes to both choosing and consuming coffee.[6] A barista must therefore be able to answer questions of every type about the different modalities of use and the different types of coffee. It was essential to build a strong goods culture for a product for which the company wanted to evoke symbolic values.[7]

These are the elements which have decreed the success of Starbucks, and the ever more widespread opening of points of sale, the launch of new products and the activation of new commercial partnerships, while contributing to the growth process, have been only a direct consequence. Through partnership agreements with Alberton's, the third United States retailer operator, Starbucks has opened coffee bars throughout the chain: The most significant agreement made by Starbucks, however, has been that made with the famous bookshop chain of Barnes & Noble, which has led to the opening of coffee bars in all the group's points of sale, thus contributing to strengthening the brand's distinctive character. The increase in market share has undoubtedly benefited greatly from a development policy centered on choice of location: a Starbucks at every corner. As far as communication is concerned, the budget invested in advertising is rather limited, since a strategic role is performed by the widespread distribution, word of mouth and the symbolic value the sign has taken on. In this sphere, too, Starbucks has known how to invent a new way of communicating, strongly centered on the communicative processes among members of its brand community and between its members and the outside world.

Today, Schultz is beginning to understand that the "halo effect" of the extraordinary growth process is gradually dissolving and, as he has himself admitted, the brand is progressively becoming more banal. The great challenge Starbucks now finds itself having to deal with, as more and more new points of sale are being opened and the chain enters new countries, is how to identify a way to reconcile such quantitative growth with the preservation of the values which are its original cultural matrix and the principal determinant of its success. Schultz, as he admits in a memo sent to top management which was leaked to the press, is realizing that the economic rationalization processes which are necessary to improve the company's efficiency and satisfy the demands of investors are in fact penalizing the level of experience delivered in his points of sale, turning it into something which is less and less exciting.

The competitive scenario has also evolved; new direct competitors, who have imitated the model, have entered, while others – indirect competitors – have started to offer similar products and atmosphere: think of the introduction of premium coffee in McDonald's restaurants.

The greater standardization of the "structures" has slowly made them lose the bohemian charm which the first points of sale had, and that aroma of coffee which represented the heart of the symbolic offering in Starbucks has progressively weakened. The sensory connotation which immediately hits you when you enter a Starbucks and which creates around it a relaxing atmosphere similar to that felt in a club of people who share the passion for coffee, is gradually getting weaker. But the problem is not limited to reduced olfactory involvement; if anything, it involves the fact that the chain is losing its soul of the past, becoming more and more like a conventional chain and losing that atmosphere which was so dear to its founder of a small neighborhood shop, whose emotive warmth can generate particularly intense experiences. We could say that this is one of the risks which companies which have been able to build real communities around their brands find themselves having to face. When the brand becomes as developed as Starbucks, its audience widens and new consumers, with characters different from those of the community's original members, take possession, thus reducing the initial followers' feeling of belonging. In fact, belonging to a community satisfies the desire of individuals to share common aspects with other individuals and in that way express their distinctiveness from other social groups. When those very people they are trying to distinguish themselves from try to become part of the community, it is necessary to know how to manage this process by trying to preserve the symbolic consistency of the brand rather than adapting it to the new context. This is a natural process: the company does not live so as to remain in the ghetto of the niche; it is in development and growth that we find the preservation of its vital functions, but the process must be handled with extreme care, avoiding compromising the good and (in the case of Starbucks) the unique that has been built.[8]

The challenge has begun: Schultz has been able to understand that this process could not be ignored and has looked for the cultural roots of the experience in the company's origins. We will soon see if Starbucks's genetic clock will be able to carry on ticking at the same speed.

CHAPTER 20

BUILDING A CREED BY PROMOTING A LIFESTYLE: THE CASE OF WHOLE FOODS

In a country like the United States, where the system of food offerings is characterized by such an extraordinary abundance as to make obesity the national illness, Whole Foods teaches us that to attract the attention of the middle/high classes, it is necessary to go beyond the sale of the product in itself, and attribute important and deep meanings to it by promoting a lifestyle and the affirmation of a creed.

Founded in 1980, when on 20 September, John Mackey opened his first point of sale in Austin, Texas, Whole Foods Market has achieved its present position of leadership in the natural supermarkets segment with a coherent policy, centered on three pillars: Whole Food, Whole People, Whole Planet.

– Whole Food: an assortment dedicated, above all, to fresh natural or organic foods of high quality;
– Whole People: transparent, committed, and enthusiastic;
– Whole Planet: a commitment to reducing negative effects on the environment.

After the buyout of its rival, Wild Oats Market, the chain has 300 points of sale spread throughout the United States, Canada and Great Britain, and employs 43,000 people. The offer is strongly centered on perishable goods, which account for approximately two-thirds of sales. In 2004, Whole Foods Market entered the British market when it bought seven Fresh & Wild outlets in the capital.

All the products sold by Whole Foods have ethical and environmental credentials. The majority of perishable goods are grown without the use of chemicals and using natural fertilizers.

The evolution of the organic products market has been character- ized by extreme discontinuity and alternating purchase motivations with connotations which have differed profoundly in their temporal evolution. The pioneers of organic product consumption discovered "organic" in the mid-1970s. It was a consumption of the elite, characterized by stable purchases of a wide range of merchandise by consumers looking primarily for physical wellbeing. Toward the 1980s, as a reaction to various natural disasters and the increased level of concern for the health of our planet, organic consumption took on a strongly ecological connotation. The people who bought organic products in those years showed a preference for consuming products which were not dependent on chemicals; this demonstrated greater attention toward the health of the body and the ecosystem, and the healthiness of food developed. But it was with the arrival in the 1990s of the "New Age" as a consumer phenomenon that we began to see consumption attitudes ranging from a generic search for quality of life to more complex philosophical interpretations. The consumer sought to reduce the anxiety and emotional load of existence with various practices, one of them the search for healthier food. Food scandals such as "mad cow disease" (bovine spongiform encephalopathy, BSE) have drawn large groups of new consumers closer to organic products, as health worries regarding the consumption of some foods have increased beyond measure.

In the early days, the consumption of organic products, while having its political–ideological roots, was seen as an elitist consumption, often as difficult to understand as to manage, and with a market dominated by small-sized firms. The communicational sphere was rather weak, limited and ineffectual. When John Mackey opened the first Whole Foods, organic products were thought of as characterizing a minority lifestyle, often associated with the image of radical or hippie. It is no coincidence that Mackey was a hippie in the past: the founder of Whole Foods spent a few years in a commune and developed a conception of the environment characterized by a strong ideological content.

The first outlet in the chain was presented as a possible alternative to traditional supermarkets where the needs of the "one-stop shop" could be satisfied in different ways.[1] Over the years the interest in organic products has progressively increased, becoming a fundamental point on the political and social agenda, and Mackey has certainly played an important role in making organic products a priority on the American consumer's agenda. He has achieved this not just by drawing attention to the health motives behind such a priority, but also by enriching it with multiple symbolic content, such as a "romantic" image which links it to a vision of a more authentic world; in so doing he has created new reasons for purchasing organic products.

Precisely because it is free from the logic of economics, the organic sector presents itself with an elitist air. Producing an organic product is currently more expensive and does not allow those economies of scale which can be achieved with the use of intensive cultivation methods – pesticides, chemicals, antibiotics, hormones. The concept of organic at Whole Foods is therefore associated with that of a better world and evokes ideas such as social justice, localism, health, and affirming a new reason for consuming organic products: the environment.

Mackey has challenged his consumer, inviting them to make a choice, however difficult it may be: simply buy, or buy in order to change the world, thus adhering to his belief and his vision. He has pulled organic consumption out of the ghetto of ideology as well as that of prevention and the romantic retrieval of the past.[2] All this and much more besides is present at Whole Foods: Mackey has not only contributed to promoting organic food, but has also affirmed its multiple cultural matrices by means of a process of democratization of a category the consumption of which has today taken on a slightly less elitist dimension.

The chain has been able to affirm a new way of shopping, bound less and less by the needs of supplying food, by satisfying others linked to affirming status, the need for fun and escape. With Whole Foods the supermarket has changed shape, becoming something more complex and lasting, attributing new symbolic aspects to food which are less and less connected with alimentation. Buying organic products is no longer a choice of fashion, conscience or ethics, but represents something to aspire to in order to incorporate new value models into one's own lifestyle.

The experience in Whole Foods produces a positive effect on both individual and collective wellbeing – emotional, physical and mental. This is perhaps the most important form of "wholeness" and "integrity" associated with the brand. The consumer who goes into one of the chain's points of sale can decide whether to do the shopping personally or leave a list of food to buy with an employee who will take care of it while the customer relaxes with a massage in the area specifically dedicated to customer wellness.

Commerce must be able to supply effective responses for the consumer who has less time available to shop, above all considering that people will tend more and more to do the shopping while they are out, rather than go out to do the shopping. There is in fact a tendency toward more daily purchasing and meeting the needs of the moment rather than of the big weekly shop.

Whole Foods has understood this need well by giving particular prominence to perishable goods, encouraging the customer to consume fresh products by emphasizing the nutritional and taste benefits, thus stimulating more frequent visits. More than 70 per cent of the 20,000 items present in the assortment of Whole Foods' points of sale is represented by products which have a rather short shelf life.

The biggest revolution to hit the United States retail industry in the last ten years is that called "Solution Selling." Social changes, above all the fact that women have taken on more "active" roles, have forced United States retailers to build a new offer identity which is centered less and less on the sale of products and more and more on the sale of solutions.

Retailers realized in fact that growing proportions of food consumption were moving gradually toward catering or toward nearer points of sale, often being open 24 hours a day, as in the case of the minimarts linked to gas stations. As we have already noted, the share of the food market supplied by United States retailers became smaller and smaller, while that supplied by the most diverse forms of catering, particularly fast food or takeaways, grew. We have therefore witnessed the advent of convenience foods, products which are ready to use immediately (as in the case of pre-sliced and pre-washed vegetables), semifinished products for use in "assembly cooking" (that is, products which have to be put together and mixed with others before being consumed, like pizza bases and pasta sauces) and, finally, ready meals like lasagne, risottos and pizzas.

Whole Foods has thus introduced not only a wide variety of convenience foods into its points of sale, but also real fast food, supplying it from restaurants of a type very different from that of traditional fast food chains. The consumer can make up their own meal by choosing from about fifty different dishes such as, for example, couscous, tempeh cooked on a hot plate, grilled tofu, samosas, rice dishes and sushi, and paying by weight at a price of about $6.50. Whoever said that fast food could not be healthy? Not Whole Foods for sure: with its restaurants it has changed the habits of many consumers who have given up the classic hamburger for a more healthy and informed choice of food. We could say that Whole Foods has revolutionized the very concept of fast food: IT IS no longer fast food, but good, healthy food which consumers can eat quickly.

The chain recently opened a new flagship store in the Warner Center in Columbus Circle, Manhattan, a "shop" with 42 checkouts and 390 employees, a vast array of fruit and vegetables, high ceilings, wide aisles, a sushi bar with 11 employees, a pizza bar which prepares 14 types of pizza, a salad bar with 40 types of salads and Indian, Asian and European snack bars.

Nevertheless, every outlet satisfies the five principles of the 1985 "Declaration of Independence" which promulgated the company's mission, not least of these principles being that of satisfying and delighting the consumer, something which has become the real heart of the brand experience. Shopping at Whole Foods is in fact freed of its compulsory dimension and takes on a new one able to make this activity less and less a duty and more and more fun and interactive. Every point of sale has a strong connotation of escape and entertainment while performing an educational function through which it aims to inform and increase both intellectual and physical knowledge. Whole Foods effectively represents that concept of the training shop which we developed in a previous book:[3] a shop which teaches people how to use what they purchase or, at least, diffuses the culture, style and way of being part of the "worlds" which the products displayed represent only to some extent. In this context, emphasis is placed not on what is sold, but on its use and the values connected with it, and the shop thus carries out a training role and makes purchasing seem less serious and more fun.

Whole Foods' goal is to improve the quality of products offered to the consumer, and inform them of this so as to make the offering more educative, interesting and exciting. Through its outlets it has affirmed a new lifestyle which synthesizes need, health and pleasure.

Whole Foods has also become more than just a place where goods are sold. Consider how in the Seattle outlet evenings are organized for single people one Friday a month. The company provides wine and food tastings on these occasions, but the rest is left to the initiative of the individual customers, who can decide to wear a red or a blue bow depending on whether they are looking for a male or a female partner. This is also a way of communicating and tightening the links with its most loyal customers, creating communities which ideally can increase sales, setting up an effective process of "conversation." All this contributes to making Whole Foods a gratifying experience, from the "dessert island," where you can dip a strawberry into a fountain of chocolate, through the "Fifth Fish Avenue," where you can get one of the 150 different fish products available cooked on the spot, to the

Whole Body, the area dedicated to massages. It is no coincidence therefore that many people have defined Whole Foods as a food amusement park or the Disneyland of food.

Every outlet in the chain has its own assortment mix deriving from the possibility of purchasing directly from local producers, as long as these satisfy Whole Foods's ethical and quality principles. The very design of the points of sale reflect, in some way, the taste of the community it is located in. So the shop in Albuquerque in New Mexico has a slightly Hispanic "flavor." Purchasing from local producers, thus creating an extremely important market outlet, makes it possible to satisfy one of the main objectives which characterize the brand's mission, thus generating a considerable impact from both an economic and a social point of view. The producers who succeed in introducing their products onto the shelves of the chain do not simply find market outlet, important as it is, but also qualify their product further, giving it credentials no certifying body is able to award with such certainty.

Probably reflecting the vegetarian choices of its founder, Whole Foods has always been committed to looking for more humane and natural ways of rearing and butchering animals and has carried out numerous activities aimed at this specific area. Whole Foods introduced a new system of meat labeling developed with the Compassion in World Farming organization. The program envisages subdividing meat products into five categories according to the treatment the animal received during rearing. The aim is to award farms where animals are allowed to live as naturally as possible, with the hope that their example will be followed. The company has also proclaimed that it will sell only "selected raw or frozen cooked lobsters," killed "with pressurized water" – a technique which ensures immediate death – from fisheries whose "humane" methods of killing the company guarantees.

The company no longer buys foie gras from one particular high-quality producer, since the product is the result of highly artificial methods of forced fattening which the geese are subjected to. New suppliers are thus required to ensure that the geese are free to move about and to swim in suitable areas and are comfortably transported, without being too squashed or hitting their heads. Even more unusual are the requests made to pork suppliers. Piglets cannot be taken away from their mothers before they are 28 days old and they must remain with their companions from birth to slaughter. The introduction of the Animal Compassionate Standard project imposes verification, with nothing being left to chance, that the animals' conditions, from birth to slaughter, take account of their physical, "emotional" and "behavioral" needs. Suppliers who want to get into Whole Foods must respect these rigid regulations.

Under this profile, the company performs a fundamental filtering action for their consumers. By selecting suppliers on the basis of these rigorous criteria for safeguarding a "natural" existence for animals destined to be slaughtered, Whole Foods delivers its own experience to its consumers, and diffuses and fortifies its belief.

Whole Foods has always faced up to the question of energy, trying to develop management models which allow not only growing ecocompatibility but above all a progressive saving of energy produced from conventional sources and an increasing quota of energy produced from new ones. Whole Foods produces energy from renewable sources: in every supermarket there is a screen which informs consumers in real time about the energy produced, usually via a photovoltaic system on the roof of the shop. Inside the outlets there are collection points for glass, tin, paper and plastic, and consumers are invited to collaborate with the company in this activity, which is so important for protecting the environment.

But it IS precisely in one of the elements which most greatly characterizes the chain's commercial proposition that the most concrete form of reducing the business's impact on the environment can be individuated. The fact that the majority of the products sold by the chain are purchased from local producers drastically reduces the pollution which is the inevitable consequence of transporting a product from one end of the United States to the other. Whole Foods has in fact highlighted one of the contradictions which most greatly characterizes the organic market: how ecofriendly can a product, for example a tomato, be considered, when to transport it from California to New York not only reduces some of its nutritional properties but also costs $0.56 in aviation fuel? It appears evident that the chain's environmental credentials are extremely well established.

The organizational model in Whole Foods is absolutely democratic and encourages transparency. Being taken on by Whole Foods involves a particular procedure: every employee is signed up provisionally only. After four weeks however they are subject to the vote of the other team members, and to be approved must get two-thirds of the votes. The vote is fundamental, and therefore reasoned, because at the end of the year only the team which has achieved its objectives will get a financial bonus or benefit such as health assistance. And that is not all.

Every shop has a volume in its office where every worker's pay-packet is registered. The register can be accessed by everybody so that anyone can compare, in a completely transparent way, their salary with that of their colleagues (a regime described as "no-secrets management").

Mackey has also set up a fund to help employees cope with some emergencies connected with health, family and personal problems. Moreover, 73 per cent of the stock option is aimed at line personnel and only 25 per cent at top management, thus inverting the proportion which characterizes the majority of quoted companies.

What has been highlighted so far clearly demonstrates that the success of Whole Foods is not limited to the consumption of food but is rather a real cultural phenomenon, which leverages both the new generations of mounting consumer concerns about food safety and the need to satisfy the "desire for health" of aging baby boomers.

Whole Foods has not limited itself to creating a culture based on organic foods; it has itself become a culture, rising to the status of a real cultural icon, succeeding in communicating the multiple meanings of a postmodern world. It is in this postmodern vision of contemporaneity that the chain's customers seek, through purchasing, the soul of the values of a past they want to retrieve for their lifestyles. For a long time a return to origins has been happening, a return to the primary matrix of commerce which stakes everything on the consumer: the customer seems to have gone back to liking an intimate, confidential, "personal" relationship with the shop, and Whole Foods understood this long before most other retailers did. Whole Foods has known how to enhance the old mercantile vocation of the shop which does not derive from mere income of position but is aimed at taking on a very important role in the economy and in society. All this is accomplished by enhancing niches of products, relationships and entrepreneurial models which would have had difficulty finding a place on the shelves of conventional retailers. It is no coincidence that the experience of Whole Foods seems to be the iconographic representation of what a neighborhood shop should be like. The chain has succeed in creating an environment around its products able to tell a real and attractive story about origins, a story of food and foodstuffs which goes well beyond their functional dimension.

Shopping is tending to become an activity which responds increasingly to cultural models, values systems and lifestyles, going beyond its connotation of the simple "act of purchasing" to take on a new one, that of the *experience of purchasing*. It is precisely in shopping that the consumer, like a modern Indiana Jones, looks for the "Lost Ark," a "space" almost equally impossible to find in a society they identify with less and less – which represents less and less of their "essence." From this stems the difficult search on the part of the consumer for "origins," traditions, the pleasure of play, of being a child again. It is in this new context that the experience proposed by Whole Foods finds a precise economic collocation, in which the consumer finds something real through the rediscovery of the "ethical" dimension, of the exchange relationship and the human relationship with the place of purchase, the product and the person wanting to sell it. Moreover, the experience of purchasing takes on a strong functional connotation when it is linked to learning and the need for information.

Whole Foods does not limit itself to creating spaces in which products are sold according to the old rules of mass consumption, or where you meet people who have the same style of life and consumption, but it creates a temple in which the rites of the past are enacted and this contributes to strengthening the brand creed, and therefore also the mechanism of promulgation toward the outside. The philosophy of the shops is spread by means of the culture, and John Mackey promotes an ambitious model: as he himself has often declared, he believes that the affirmation of his model can change the world. In a recent conference held at the Berkeley School of Journalism, he in fact declared: "The world is going in our direction and change is increasingly following in its lines of development the principles of authenticity and quality."[4] Whole Foods has not limited itself to promoting a product category and a style of consumption: it has built a real creed and, through knowledge of the product, it has been able to carry out a real process of evangelization.

When the wholefood industry was concentrating most of its communication efforts on the safety and culture of food, Whole Foods in fact understood that the problems linked to healthy food are not driven exclusively by the need to eat in a healthy way. The reasons which can lead to making more cautious informed food choices are many, dictated not least by the need to feel a responsible person rather than simply a good mother. Whole Foods has succeeded in grasping the elements at the basis of these motivations, not limiting itself to seeing only those on the surface. It has been able to understand how a woman, when buying products, rediscovers food culture as a symbolic representation of her ancient role of mother, which saw her busy looking for the best that was available for her children and not only the most convenient the market can offer to reconcile the multiple needs which derive from taking on new roles. The Whole Baby project was in fact developed to help future mothers purchase and consume healthy products and follow a diet suitable for pregnancy. The project is part of what is defined as the chain's "tradition" in supplying its consumers with special services in order to improve their lives.

It is precisely the strong cultural connotation the brand has acquired which has made its business model difficult to replicate. Whole Foods has been able to build an entity of values, lifestyles and symbols which cannot be reproduced simply by producing slogans alone, which however stimulating probably nobody would believe.

Other competitors have gathered or are gathering the fruits of Whole Foods's commitment in promoting organic consumption. New organic chains have established themselves, such as Trader Joe's, and even conventional supermarkets are investing heavily in offering organic products. But despite all this, the cultural matrix of their choice will always find its basis in the history of the pioneer, condemning them eternally to the role of imitator unless they are able to turn themselves into prophets of a new cultural paradigm.

The competitors of Whole Foods, both direct and indirect, are in fact positioning their organic offer system on its "tangible advantages," particularly low price, but as long as the Whole Foods chain is able to render its offer of "intangible advantages" unique, there will be no real competition. However, the risk could show itself if Whole Foods, squeezed by the price war and conditioned by pressure from investors, should become conventional, thus making its creed lose consistency.

In conclusion, we would like to cite a further case which makes it really possible to understand the mystical character that this chain of supermarkets has been able to attribute to its brand. As part of a campaign aimed at sensitizing people to recycling plastic, Whole Foods announced that canvas bags would be launched in its points of sale, designed by the famous British accessories designer Anya Hindmarch and with the phrase "I'm not a Plastic Bag" printed on them. The number of bags on sale would be limited: 3000 for the biggest shops and 600 for the smaller ones. The fact that Whole Foods was launching a bag with limited availability generated such expectations that at 6.30 a.m., two and a half hours before opening time, the queues of consumers outside the shop in Union Square, New York, longing to get hold of the precious "reliquary" (nothing other than a simple canvas bag) extended for more than two blocks, and some consumers had even been camping out from the night before. The 3000 bags in stock were sold in only two hours.

CHAPTER 21

PROMOTING A BRAND THROUGH NATIONAL IDENTITY AND A CULTURE OF CONSUMPTION: THE CASE OF S. PELLEGRINO[1]

S. Pellegrino mineral water has its source in the municipality of San Pellegrino Terme in Val Brembana in the Italian Alps. It naturally springs from the earth after a long journey, rising from a depth of 1,000 meters, during which nature filters, purifies and enriches it with mineral salts. It is aerated with a carbonate which comes from a natural source, and boasts 14 minerals, including calcium and magnesium. Its properties have been famous since the fifteenth century: it is documented that even Leonardo da Vinci visited the Bremban town and on that occasion called the water of San Pellegrino "miraculous."

San Pellegrino owes its great development, which happened in the second half of the nineteenth century and the beginning of the twentieth, to the birth of the thermal baths and the consequent influx of visitors. In 1899 the Società Anonima delle Terme di San Pellegrino was founded and industrial production of S. Pellegrino water began: in the first year 35,343 bottles of sparkling water were produced, of which 5000 were destined for overseas. In 1932 the product was joined by orangeade made using S. Pellegrino water. In 1957 S. Pellegrino bought Acqua Panna, which produces still water; until a few years ago, S. Pellegrino also made another non-fizzy water, Limpia, which also comes from a spring in the municipality of San Pellegrino Terme.

In 1970 the company took on its present name of Sanpellegrino SpA; in the following decade the company was the main soft-drinks producer in Italy. Besides water and orangeade, numerous other fizzy drinks were produced, the most famous of which is Bitter Sanpellegrino (Sanbitter), a red aperitif.

Currently, S. Pellegrino water has a prime role in the international panorama: in New York restaurants alone more than 60,000 bottles are consumed daily. In October 2006, the goal of selling 500,000,000 bottles of water in a year in 110 countries throughout the world was achieved.

Right from the start, the positioning of the brand has been based on the common denominator of its international vocation and its presence on the tables of restaurants in all the world. Via this positioning, the brand has been able to develop its consistency in time and beyond national borders. Since 1908, bottles of S. Pellegrino water were reaching all five continents: as well as the main European cities, S. Pellegrino water was also sold in Cairo, Tangiers and Shanghai, in the USA, Brazil, Peru and Australia. Since the 1990s, S. Pellegrino has achieved a substantial overturn in the percentage between the national market and the overseas one, until today it has arrived at having more than 80 per cent of volume achieved in international markets.

The brand audit research studies carried out by the company have highlighted the fact that there are three main brands in the international water market, each with a specific positioning:

– Evian, in the still-water category, represents *the water* by definition, suitable for every usage and perfectly multichannel.
– Perrier, in the very-sparkling-water category, has, owing to both its level of fizziness and its formats, taken on the characteristic of a natural sparkling soft drink, almost a kind of healthier alternative to the traditional soft drink Coca-Cola.
– S. Pellegrino, in the slightly sparkling water category, is the water traditionally dedicated to restaurants.

The S. Pellegrino brand has therefore always been strongly positioned toward restaurants. In the beginning, this positioning found its justification in the functional aspects of the product. Its organoleptic characteristics, its rich content of minerals, such as magnesium and calcium which facilitate the digestive process, and the addition of a natural carbonate which goes well with these minerals and creates a balance within the product made it impossible to equal the product in terms of its function. Today the choice to strengthen this positioning represents a clear and convinced strategic orientation for the company. What has contributed most to strengthening the international image of S. Pellegrino as a restaurant water was the extraordinary success which

Italian restaurants had in the world toward the end of the 1980s. The company knew how to effectively ride the emotional wave which had been created around "Made in Italy" gastronomy, and also became an important ambassador of it.

Today, S. Pellegrino is a habitual presence in 100 countries on five continents. In the best restaurants and on the great occasions, it has become one of the protagonists of the global dinner table, accompanying tagliatelle, sushi, clam chowder and goulash, on cruise ships and on boats taking part in regattas, at weddings and inaugurations. There are millions of consumers living very different lives, but they have in common a certain respect for things done well and a passion for well-cooked food. The millions of S. Pellegrino consumers, even if they have never read Dante or Pirandello, love living the Italian way.[2]

Italian lifestyle, even with its multiple contradictions, is seen abroad as one of the best ways of living, a style which makes it possible to achieve that difficult balance between *doing things well while living well*. Italians are sometimes lazy, sometimes indolent, but they are a talented people who do things well yet still know how to enjoy themselves. It is no coincidence that the company's last worldwide campaign had the claim "Live Italian" and was strongly focussed on this concept.

The international research study *The Restaurant Scenario out of Home in the Five Continents*, carried out by the Osservatorio S. Pellegrino e Acqua Panna, has highlighted that in recent years Italy has further marked its distinctive traits, orientated toward traditional, social and postmaterialist values. The cultural capital of Italians must be considered a qualifying element in the demand for S. Pellegrino and a driving force for planning and innovation as regards the company's offer, and it is precisely on that offer that S. Pellegrino continues to strengthen its identity. S. Pellegrino, a water in the Italian tradition, has thus become an ambassador of the values of Italianness, a symbol of culture and elegance, to such a point as to represent, in the enogastronomic world, one of the winning elements in the entire offer system.

Building a positioning such as that of S. Pellegrino necessarily requires time and long-term strategies, based on the promotion of a style of life, a way of being and of feeling which is linked closely to a specific social model: the Italian model. However, it must be underlined that today fine dining is increasingly becoming unconnected with the concept of country of origin and is taking on a more transnational identity. What today makes the case of this brand extraordinary is how it has been able precisely to affirm such a powerful brand image for a product which represents the quintessence of the process of brands becoming commodities and the consumption of which responds to satisfying a primary need.

This positioning has in fact required the widening of the brand's vision well beyond the confines of the single relevant market, forcing it to develop the sensitivity which is necessary to understand the changes in food culture, the habits of individuals and the evolution in the gastronomic art, and thus confront a series of multiple elements which are often extremely divergent.

The modern consumer spends more time out of the home, with greater gratification and greater brand infidelity. Eating out is allowing oneself a luxury, especially if the choice falls on an expensive, chic and exotic restaurant. But restaurant scenarios are changing: tradition is chasing experimentation, territorial cooking is having to confront an enogastronomic one born from the fusion of different cultures. For S. Pellegrino, competing in the water market means having to understand this type of change and be one of the promoters.

In this respect, we can strongly affirm that the brand is already in the future of restaurants, thanks to some farsighted initiatives among which the culture of good drinking and good eating represents the common thread for all the activities connected with the brand.

The company understood that it was indispensable to work with the great chefs who have increasingly become the trendsetters in the restaurant sector, so much so that they have themselves become brands. Those chefs, and the tables of their restaurants, are the principal medium through which to communicate the brand. The chef, as recent research conducted by S. Pellegrino has highlighted, is no longer simply the director of the kitchen but is increasingly becoming the attraction of the restaurant and of many other stages. Think, for example, of Gordon Ramsay, less and less a protagonist in the kitchen and more and more a protagonist of show business, with more than 14 restaurants scattered throughout the world, 2 pubs, 16 publications and numerous lines of gastronomic products, Ramsay, with his rough and hot-tempered character, is the protagonist of the reality show *Hell's Kitchen*, the winner of which receives as a prize a restaurant in Las Vegas. But, contrary to widespread perceptions, it is exactly the great chefs who have "democratized" cooking through the creation of quick and less expensive restaurant formulas which have made *haute cuisine* accessible to an ever wider number of consumers. Think also of the case of Ferran Adrià in Spain who, with the Fast Good chain, has created a quick, excellent menu anyone can afford.[3]

The birth of this new kind of chef has made it possible to widen the audience for *haute cuisine*, with big benefits for those brands, among them S. Pellegrino, which are able to build strong associations with it to the point of becoming one of the elements of its offer.

There are many events organized in individual markets which see S. Pellegrino as one of the most important partners: think of the James Beard Award, a sort of Oscar of the culinary industry in the United States, or the Almost Famous Chef, a sort of *Fame* in gastronomic key, which sees the principal cookery schools in the country compete among themselves, the final being held in November in Napa Valley, California, at the Culinary Institute of America.

Still in the area of fine dining, S. Pellegrino has recently developed the "map of the stars," a new page on its website (www.sanpellegrino.com) which reviews the best restaurants in the world based on the evaluations of the most prestigious international food and wine guides.

To be a winner, a restaurant will have increasingly to offer excellent but simple cooking and it will be appreciated if it knows how to keep prices low without eroding quality. The most sought-after will have a water list and a sommelier at the client's disposal. The new sommelier will be responsible for indicating the most suitable type of water to harmonize and enhance the structural characteristics of the wine which goes with the cuisine; but they will also have to be familiar with the soft drinks, beers, liqueurs, teas and sakes which increasingly find themselves "sharing" the same table in the now globalized food and beverage market. All this will require of the sommelier a rigorous and constant professional upgrading as well as an updating of their knowhow as regards drinks other than wine, including, of course, water.

To this end, S. Pellegrino has elaborated an in-depth study into the art of water-tasting and its harmonization with wine, food and other drinks, through the publication of three "water codices," carried out in collaboration with the Associazione Sommelier Internazionale (ASI). The indications supplied by each "codex" have been the object of intensive training of the company's sales team so as to guarantee that this knowledge is divulged to its clients – the restaurant owners throughout the world.

The need to renew gestures and modalities of consumption and to define new sensorial experiences, as well as completing the rituals of presenting mineral water, harmonizing it with the environment in which it is tasted, has, for example, been the object of a partnership with the company Guzzini, one of the leading Italian companies in design. Accessories have been designed which are able to express and enhance water in high-quality restaurants, in the domestic environment and also outdoors. Design as a functional and aesthetic search becomes therefore a means of promoting water in its best form and of exalting the experience of drinking it, serving it and keeping it.

Many producers, as noted already, have understood that attention had to be moved from the contents of the bottle to the packaging. In recent years, many brands have become successful in the mineral water category precisely because of the high design content of their bottles (think of Voss and Ty Nant), affirming the increasingly cultural aspect of this consumption. The image of fine dining water that the brand has been able to build is also reflected paradoxically in the purchase motivations of the part of the turnover which has been developed in the modern trade. The consumer who chooses S. Pellegrino in a supermarket, in fact, wants to recreate the experience of a restaurant at home.

Individuals are increasingly going to a restaurant in order to be with friends, and they attribute an important role as a relational catalyst to the specific physical context. Recreating the restaurant experience at home thus reinforces the socializing character of sitting together round a table. So, in trade too, S. Pellegrino is not presented as a water for everyday drinking; it leaves the other competitors to fight that battle with no holds barred, contenting itself with being perceived almost as an artifact through which to recreate a specific experience.

Opposite these multiple initiatives, there is however a more traditional marketing plan, which in using the various media available tends to privilege the press and serves to work on the awareness of the brand. The presence of advertising pages in all the main gastronomic guides in the world should be seen in this light.

The product placement in the marketing mix is one of the most important aspects, so much so that the company usually considers the exposition of the bottle in front of the ideal typical client – often a Hollywood star – very important. Unlike many products on the table (think of pasta) and which are not easy to identify, the recognizability of the label and packaging of a bottle of S. Pellegrino is extraordinary – at least this is what the research studies carried out by the company conclude. The mix of green glass, blue label and red star, as well as the blue lettering, render the bottle easily recognizable. The label is almost as well known as a banknote. The presence of the minerals gives it a certain classicality, without the water being seen as medicinal. The brand and the label are a sort of evergreen, which adapts itself well to contemporaneity while still maintaining a certain nostalgic charm. One of the first jobs done with the setting-up of the business unit in 1999, following the buyout of the group by Nestlé, was precisely that of reducing autonomy to the level of the single market, providing for homogenization of the image on a global scale. Each market worked with great autonomy, so that the German label referred to "the Lombard Alps," the American to "the Italian Alps." The big "cleaning-up" task which was done was aimed precisely at returning to an original standard label, because of the conviction that the product should be experienced as an evergreen. The objective was that of not losing the basic identity of a product which represents the history of water in the restaurant sector from 1899 to the present day. Moreover, enlivening activities are carried out, such as a special edition to celebrate the 500,000,000 million bottles sold, aimed at big restaurants. These activities, however, always respect the brand's tradition.

NOTES

Chapter 1 The Brand as a Social Phenomenon and Cultural Icon

1. N. Klein, *No Logo* (London: Flamingo; Milan: Baldini Castoldi Dalai, 2002). The author's desire to be openly militant and the nature of the approach result in a biased text. The information presented is selective and the data analyzed subjectively; arguments are dealt with in a way which dramatizes certain aspects while others, which would cast doubt on or limit the argument proposed, are ignored. All in all, however, *No Logo* is an intellectually honest and well-documented book, which justifies particularly well its charge against the universe of brands and the companies which steer them. See also A. Semprini, *Marche e mondi possibili: Un approccio semiotico al marketing della marca* (Milan: Franco Angeli, 2004), particularly p. 20.

2. See the draft essay by R. Ollé and D. Riu, *The New Brand Management: Lessons From Brand Indifferentiation.* http://www.globalbrands.org/academic/working/Brand_Indifferentiation. pdf, p. 37.

3. A. Semprini, op. cit., p. 37.

4. "For some reason, people like to share their experiences with one another – the restaurant where they ate lunch, the movie they saw over the weekend, the computer they just bought – and when those experiences are favorable, the recommendation can snowball, resulting in runaway success." (R. Dye, "The Buzz on Buzz," *Harvard Business Review* 78(6), 2002, 139–46.)

5. S. Hilton, "The Social Values of Brands," in R. Clifton and J. Simmons (eds) *Brands and Branding* (New York: Bloomberg, 2003), pp. 47–64.

6. D. B. Holt, *How Brands Become Icons. The Principles of Cultural Branding* (Boston, MA: Harvard Business School Press, 2004), p. 36.

7. See, for example, Michele Fioroni, *Lo shopping dell'esperienza* (Perugia: Morlacchi, 2004), pp. 53 –9.

8. Fioroni, op. cit., pp. 16–26.

9. For a discussion of this, and in particular the immaterial and spiritual value of brands, see M. Sawhney, "Create Value From Values," *CIO Magazine* (15 November 2002). www.cio.com/article/31517/

10. The subject of contemporary consumers' needs is dealt with in D. Lewis and D. Bridger, *The Soul of The New Consumer: Authenticity – What We Buy and Why in the New Economy* (London: Brealey, 2000), pp. 45–68.

11. A. M. Tybout and G. S. Carpenter, "Meeting the Challenge of the Post-modern Consumer," in *Mastering Marketing: The Complete MBA Companion in Marketing* (London: Financial Times, 1999), particularly p. 103.

12. Of particular interest regarding this argument is R. Clifton, "The Future of Brands," in Clifton and Simmons (eds), op. cit., particularly p. 227.

13. Ibid.
14. K. Nordstrom and J. Ridderstrale, *Karaoke Capitalism* (London: FT/Prentice Hall, 2004), p. 13. This book, which has been translated in many countries, is now widely considered a classic.
15. "Pressure, says the National Coalition for the Protection of Children & Families. The Cincinnati-based organization boasted this week that Abercrombie took the step after it started campaigning for a boycott of the retailer because of its 'Christmas Field Guide.' The group alleges that the chain uses the catalog as a pretext to sell sexual ideology to teens." (P. Bhatnagar, *Abercrombie: What's The Naked Truth? Advocacy Group Says Retailer Pulled Racy Mag Over Protest: A & F Says It's Making Space for Perfume*, http://money.cnn.com/2003/12/02/news/companies/abercrombie_catalog/.the)
16. Nordstrom and Ridderstrale, op. cit., pp. 13–19.

Chapter 2   Brand Religion

1. In the last five years, the topic has been actively dealt with in scientific marketing literature. See, for example, M. Lindstrom, *Brand Sense: Build Powerful Brands Through Touch, Taste, Smell, Sight, and Sound* (New York: Free Press, 2005), p. 165.
2. Fioroni, op. cit., particularly p. 100.
3. This topic is more widely discussed by Fioroni (op. cit., p. 5).
4. On the "functional/emotional" dialectics of product performance and brands, see D. H. Pink, *A Whole New Mind. Moving from the Information Age to the Conceptual Age* (New York: River Head, 2005).
5. Lindstrom, op. cit., p. 165.
6. B. Cova, *Il marketing tribale: Legame, comunità, autenticità come valori del marketing mediterraneo* (Milan: Il Sole 24 Ore, 2003), particularly p. 21.
7. The topic is widely discussed in Tybout and Carpenter, op. cit.
8. Cova, op. cit., pp. 35–9.
9. Holt, op. cit., p. 8.
10. "I could never operate in a system like ours: corruption, clientelism ... are words that I don't know. When I watch television and I see a scene which is bad, wrong, unjust, I turn over. It's stronger than I am ... Left or Right isn't important. I choose whoever builds. Whoever thinks about the future. And why not think that one day even a Marela suit could be a statement, despite the fact that it has nothing to do with the 'formal,' the establishment, the classic? There is the mass and there is classic luxury, what is missing is the modern what in big American stores are the contemporary floors ... In my early days it also happened to me to go into big hotels and be thrown out ... Not any more ... I even went to the Quirinal in denim." Interview with Renzo Rosso, *Corriere della Sera Magazine*, no. 23 (2007).
11. The topics of wishes and rebellion and how these are expressed in the so-called Generation Y's purchasing and consumption preferences are extensively discussed not only with reference to the Italian market in Fioroni, op. cit., particularly ch. 1, pp. 35–46.

12. Ibid.
13. Cova, op. cit.
14. Most recently regarding this argument, see H. Hartman, *Five Steps to Building a Cultural Brand.* http://www.marketingpower.com/content21255.php
15. Cova, op. cit.

Chapter 3   Between Past and Present: Nostalgia Branding

1. L. Mizzau, "Nostalgia, nostalgia canaglia ...," *Ticonzero*, no. 69. Also available at http://www.ticonzero.info/articolo.asp?art_id=2265.
2. Ibid.
3. www.dixancenereattiva.it
4. Particularly appropriate is the analysis by K. Naughton and B. Vlasic, "The Nostalgia Boom. Why The Old Is New Again." http://www.businessweek.com/1998/12/b3570001.htm
5. Ibid.
6. S. Brown, *Marketing – The Retro Revolution* (London: Sage, 2001), pp. 39–54.
7. Again see Mizzau, op. cit.

Chapter 4   The Human Nature of Brands

1. Think of the fireplace as a physical representation of the spirit of the family.
2. J. L. Aaker, "Dimensions of Brand Personality," *Journal of Marketing Research*, 34(3), 1997, 347–56.
3. S. Fournier, "Consumers and Their Brands: Developing Relationship Theory in Consumer Research," in D. Miller (ed.), *Consumption: Critical Concepts in the Social Sciences* (London: Routledge, 2001), pp. 57–119.
4. See A. M. Tybout and B. Sternthal, "Brand Positioning," in A. Tybout (ed.), *Kellogg on Branding: The Marketing Faculty of The Kellogg School of Management* (Hoboken, NJ: Wiley, 2005), pp. 11–26.
5. See the now classic text, J. Seguela, *Hollywood lava più bianco* (Milan: Lupetti, 1996), p. 19.
6. Aaker, op. cit.
7. Ibid.
8. An appropriate analysis is that by A. B. Thompson, "Brand Positioning and Brand Creation," in Clifton and Simmons (eds), op. cit., p. 83.
9. Semprini, op. cit., pp. 79–83.
10. Ibid.
11. T. Allen and J. Simmons, "Visual and Verbal Identity," in R. Clifton and J. Simmons (eds), op. cit., pp. 113–26.
12. Ibid.
13. The problem is widely discussed in H. Edwards and D. Day, *Creating Passion Brands – Getting to the Heart of Branding* (London: Kogan Page, 2005), p. 41.

Chapter 5   The Brand's Genetic Clock

1. We are grateful to Prof. Luciano Binaglia, Professor in Chemistry and Biochemical Propaedeutics at the University of Perugia for his assistance in drafting this chapter.
2. This book is now rightly considered a classic: A. de Geus, *The Living Company: Growth Learning and Longevity in Business* (London: Brealey, 1997), particularly the chapters "Ecology" (pp. 131–70) and "Evolution" (pp. 171–98).
3. Among others, see G. Fabris and L. Minestroni, *Valore e valori della marca: Come costruire e gestire una marca di successo* (Milan: Franco Angeli, 2004), p. 394.
4. Ibid., pp. 393–417.
5. "As in every family tree, a brand also has a progenitor: the person who originated the species, the original ancestor. We are talking about the subject who generated the 'breed' by a simple phenomenon of reproduction and multiplication […] He/she is the initiator of the stock. For this reason, his value is endowed with a depth and a perspective which only history can give us." (Ibid., p. 418.)
6. In 2006 *The Times* (London) noted that "Crocs might be the ugliest footwear ever created, but the cumbersome clogs are about to get the fashion industry's seal of approval."

Chapter 6   Genetic Familiarity: The Brand in Search of its Roots

1. D. Stiff, "So You Think You Know Your Brand?", MIT *Sloan Management Review*, 47(4), 2006, 95–6.
2. "The meaning of a brand is no longer the result of a dialogue between buyer and seller, but a multilogue. A company that wishes to extend its brand must therefore negotiate that transition among all the various parties involved." P. Berthon, M. B. Holbrook and J. M. Hulbert, "Understanding and Managing the Brand Space," *MIT Sloan Management Review*, 44(2), 2003, 49–54.
3. "Has a surplus of similar companies, employing similar people, with similar educational backgrounds, working similar jobs, coming up with similar ideas, producing similar things, with similar prices and similar quality." K. Nordstrom and J. Ridderstrale, *Funky Business: Talent Makes Capital Dance* (London: Pearson, 2000 [Stockholm: Jan Lapidoth–Book House Publishing]), pp. 79–96, 141–51.
4. "Companies have defined so much 'best practice', that they are now more or less identical." J. Kunde, *Unique Now ... Or Never: The Brand is the Company Driver in the New Value Economy* (Upper Saddle River, NJ: Pearson-Prentice Hall, 2002), p. 13.
5. Pink, op. cit. The second part of this book, "The Six Senses," is fundamental to our argument here and in the following chapters.
6. L. L. Bryan, C. I. Joyce and L. M. Weiss, *Making a Market in Talent*. http://www.mckinseyquarterly.com
7. "In this sense, it is mission that is closer to belief, but you wouldn't know it from the flaccid, formula-speak mission statements of companies around the world. Most seem to be some kind of permutation of the usual business buzzwords:

excellence, highest standards, superior quality, partnership, performance, people, choice, achievement, potential, value, leadership, commitment, admired, world class and customers. Brand Belief should be just that: a genuine belief. The biggest difference between belief and mission is that belief doesn't end with the statement, to be forgotten in the day-to-day cut and thrust of business life." (Edwards and Day, op. cit., p. 44.)

8. Ibid.
9. Pink, op. cit.
10. "Today, we celebrate the first glorious anniversary of the Information Purification Directives. We have created, for the first time in all history, a garden of pure ideology. Where each worker may bloom secure from the pests of contradictory and confusing truths. Our Unification of Thoughts is more powerful a weapon than any fleet or army on earth. We are one people, with one will, one resolve, one cause. Our enemies shall talk themselves to death and we will bury them with their own confusion. We shall prevail!" (Script of the Macintosh ad filmed by Ridley Scott in 1984. It was aired on prime time during the interval of the Super Bowl final, the most followed sports event in America.)
11. Particularly important are the analyses of J. McFarland, "Branding From The Inside Out," *Harvard Management Update*, 7(2), 2002, 1–4.
12. "To differentiate the company and garner competitive advantage, there must be a transition from mere brand consciousness, to consistent brand articulation, and brand behavior, both inside the company and 'on the street.'" (Stiff, op. cit.)

Chapter 7 Brand Name: "The Importance of Being Earnest"

1. The "classic" treatment of this argument is in M Botton, J. J. Cegarra and B. Ferrari, *Il nome della marca: Creazione e strategia* (Milan: Guerini, 1992), particularly p. 41.
2. D. N. Bristow, K. C. Schneider and D. K Schuler, "The Brand Dependence Scale: Measuring Consumers' Use of Brand Name to Differentiate Among Product Alternatives", *Journal of Product & Brand Management*, 11(6), 2002, 343–56.
3. A. Belén del Río, R. Vázquez and V. Iglesias, "The Role of the Brand Name in Obtaining Differential Advantages", *Journal of Product & Brand Management*, 10(7), 2001, 452–65.
4. Ibid.
5. S. S. Srinivasan and B. D. Till, "Evaluation of Search, Experience and Credence Attributes: Role of Brand Name and Product Trial, *Journal of Product & Brand Management*, 11(7), 2002, 417–31.
6. L. Minestroni, *L'alchimia della marca. Fenomenologia di un moltiplicatore di valore* (Milan: Franco Angeli, 2002), pp. 131–7.
7. The arguments are amply discussed in the important work by D. A. Aaker, *Managing Brand Equity. Capitalizing on the Value of a Brand Name* (New York: Free Press, 1991).
8. Minestroni, op. cit., pp. 131–7.
9. C. L. Bernick, "Finding the Right Brand Name," in A. Tybout (ed.), op. cit., pp. 289–96.

10. *2005 Tipping Sprung Survey of Top Brand Names, Summary Report*, 1 September 2005.
11. Ibid.
12. Bernick, op. cit.
13. "Ernesto" is the Italian translation of the name "Ernest," but it does not sound at all like the Italian word for "earnest," namely "*probo.*"
14. Fabris and Minestroni, op. cit., p. 217.
15. T. Blackett, "Choosing a Powerful Brand Name." www.brandchannel.com, 10 October 2005 issue.

Chapter 8   Brand Sex: A Confused Identity Heading Towards Androgyny

1. There are feminine brands – which are, therefore, stereotypically sweeter, kinder, more seductive, more caring, but also more fragile – and masculine brands – which according to the stereotype will be stronger and more energetic, overbearing but also rigorous and reliable. At the source of this, the two ideal types of parental figures which psychoanalysis has described to us can be traced: the generous and giving mother who nourishes and cares, is disinterested and affectionate and asks for nothing (or little) in return, and the severe, castrating father, a sort of inflexible super-ego who imposes, prohibits and must be obeyed, who is respected but not loved – a worrying figure for brands, often impersonated by public and monopolistic brands. But perceiving the brand as a woman can also excite fear and ambivalence: in some cases – again in terms of deep psychology – the archetype of the "dentate vagina" is always there, behind the door, as it were. See Fabris and Minestroni, op. cit., p. 387.
2. The car was a thing for men: think of the stereotypical image of women hardly able to drive or the susceptibility of husbands to comments by their wives about how they drove. In short, when it came to gender and the ability to be a driver no complaints were allowed.
3. G. Fabris, *Il nuovo consumatore: verso il postmoderno* (Milan: Franco Angeli, 2004) p. 261.
4. Fioroni, op. cit., pp. 26–35.
5. See the analyses by A. Fels, "Do Women Lack Ambition?", *Harvard Business Review*, 82(4), 2004, 50–60.
6. R. Burgelman and L. Dened, "Nike's Global Women's Fitness Business: Driving Strategic Integration," *Stanford Graduate School of Business*, Case SM-152, 23/04/07.
7. "When we started the women's footwear division, every single shoe was made based on a woman's biomechanics. They had Shox for her and the air bags were engineered with the right pounds per square inch, based on female rather than male weight. This was the point in time when all of this became non-negotiable in our women's products." (Ibid.)
8. Fels, op. cit.
9. D. A. Thomas and R. J. Ely, "Making Differences Matter: A New Paradigm for Managing Diversity," *Harvard Business Review*, 74(5), 1996, 79–90.

10. Edwards and Day, op. cit., p. 79.
11. D. De Masi's discussion of the "Alessi case" is interesting: *Alessi neo-pop.* http://www.nextonline.it/archivio/04/12.htm

Chapter 9   The Brand Between Emotions and Experiences

1. The initial pages, particularly p. 4, of Fioroni, op. cit., are useful regarding this topic.
2. L. L. Berry, L. P. Carbone and S. H. Haeckel, "Managing the Total Customer Experience," *MIT Sloan Management Review*, 34(3), 2002, 85–9.
3. B. Cova, *Il marketing tribale, legame comunità, autenticità come valori del marketing mediterraneo* (Milan: Il Sole 24 Ore, 2003), p. 103.
4. Ibid.
5. B. H. Schmitt and M. Ferraresi, *Marketing esperienziale: Come sviluppare l'esperienza di consumo* (Milan: Franco Angeli, 2006), p. 41.
6. Fioroni, op. cit., pp. 80–1.
7. E. Arnould, L. Price and G. Zinkhan, *Consumers* (New York: McGraw-Hill, 2002).
8. A fundamental work concerning these problems is J. B. Pine and J. H. Gilmore, *The Experience Economy, Work Is Theatre and Every Business Is a Stage* (Boston, MA: Harvard Business School Press, 1999), pp. 31–8.
9. Pine and Gilmore, op. cit., pp. 27–33.
10. Ibid., p. 30.
11. Fioroni, op. cit., p. 82.
12. F. Gallucci, *Marketing emozionale* (Milan: EGEA, 2006), p. 11.
13. Ibid., p. 19.
14. F. Furedi, *Il nuovo conformismo* (Milan: Feltrinelli, 2005).
15. Fioroni, op. cit., p. 16.
16. Gallucci, op. cit., pp. 13–34.
17. Fioroni, op. cit., p. 85.
18. Fabris, op. cit., pp. 267–71.
19. Ibid.
20. "The case of Times Square in New York is particularly significant of how, by means of effective privatization of public space which had been left to the worst urban decay, it was possible to create an open air commercial area ... Times Square created its identity based on experience and every commercial activity, receptive or recreational, can be thought of as a part of a bigger stage, that of Times Square, where every minute a show is put on in which the consumer is the protagonist." (Fioroni, op. cit., pp. 109–10.)
21. Fabris, op. cit., pp. 267–71.
22. Gallucci, op. cit., pp. 123–32.

Chapter 10   Brand Senses: The Challenge of Polysensualism

1. Fabris, op. cit., pp. 199–203.
2. "Our several senses, which feel so personal and ... far beyond us. They're an extension of the genetic chain that connects us to everyone who has ever

lived; they bind us to other people and to animals, across time, country and happenstance." (D. Ackerman, *A Natural History of the Senses* (New York: Vintage, 1995), p. 308.)

3. http://www.profumo.it/marketing/marketing.htm
4. Still valid are the analyses in E. R. Spangenberg, A. E. Crowley and P. W. Henderson, "Improving the Store Environment: Do Olfactory Cues Affect Evaluations and Behaviours?", *Journal of Marketing*, 60(2), 1996, 67–80.
5. C. Childress, "Supermarkets Coming to Their Senses, All Five of Them," *Progressive Grocer: Equipment & Design*, June 2004; now available at http://envirosell.com/index.php?option=com_content&task=view&id=94&Itemid=101
6. Gallucci, op. cit., p. 243.
7. Lindstrom, op. cit., pp. 18–31.
8. Ibid.
9. Gallucci, op. cit., p. 237.
10. Fioroni, op. cit., p. 96.
11. Lindstrom, op. cit., p. 38.
12. C. Fischler, *L'onnivoro: Il piacere di mangiare nella storia della scienza* (Milan: Mondadori, 1992), p. 70.
13. Ibid.
14. www.elbulli.com
15. Fabris, op. cit., p. 221.
16. M. Del Duca, *Manager dei processi ristorativi* (Perugia: Morlacchi, 2004), p. 128.
17. Ibid.
18. Gallucci, op. cit., p. 244.
19. A. Greimas, *Del senso* (Milan: Bompiani, 1985).
20. www.gillette.it
21. www.motorola.it
22. Gallucci, op. cit., pp. 244–6.

Chapter 11   Building a Frame of Reference Between Advantages and Parity

1. Tybout and Sternthal, loc. cit.
2. M. Shapiro, "Marketing Leverage in the Frame of Reference," in Tybout (ed.), op. cit., p. 283.
3. A general overview of the problem can be found in K. L. Keller, *Strategic Brand Management*: *Building, Measuring, and Managing Brand Equity* (Upper Saddle River, NJ: Prentice Hall, 2007), chapter 3.
4. K. L. Keller, B. Sternthal and A. Tybout, "Three Questions You Need To Ask About Your Brand," *Harvard Business Review*, 80(9), 2002, pp. 3–8.
5. Keller, op. cit. [2007].
6. J. Birchall, "Marchi costruiti in rete," *Il Sole 24 Ore*, 3 Maggio 2007.
7. Rome, 5 March 2007: presentation of Adidas campaign.
8. K. L. Keller, "The Brand Report Card," *Harvard Business Review*, 78(1), 2000, 147–57.

9. R. Ollé and D. Riu, op. cit.
10. D. A. Aaker, "The Power of the Branded Differentiator," *MIT Sloan Management Review*, 44(1), 2003), 83–87.
11. Tybout and Sternthal, op. cit., p. 17.
12. R. Reeves, *Reality in Advertising* (Macgibbon & Kee, 1961); a classic.

Chapter 12   Performance Anxiety and the Illusion of Quality

1. P. Barwise and S. Meehan, "Don't Be Unique, Be Better," *MIT Sloan Management Review*, 45(4), 2004, 23–27.
2. P. Berthon, M. B. Holbrook and J. M. Hulbert, op. cit.
3. A. Ries and L. Ries, *The 22 Immutable Laws of Branding:. How to Build a Product or Service into a World-Class Brand* (New York: HarperCollins, 1998), pp. 57–65.

Chapter 13   Brand and Category: A Complex Relationship

1. www.ferrero.it
2. This is a digital magnetic–optic medium for recording and playing back audio information, contained in a rigid plastic case (7cm × 7cm), which can hold approximately 145MB of digital information.
3. The main advantage of the MiniDisk compared with previous digital media was represented by the fact that, connected to the playback system, it was totally rewritable. This made the MiniDisk extremely versatile and it was thought that this was the last frontier when it came to portable music devices – until the arrival of MP3 players.
4. A. Diamantopoulos, G. Smith and I. Grime, "The Impact of Brand Extension on Brand Personality: Experimental Evidence," *European Journal of Marketing*, 39(1–2), 2005, 129–49.
5. D. A. Aaker, "Should You Take Your Brand to Where the Action Is?", *Harvard Business Review*, 65(5), 1997, 135–43.
6. The concept is dealt with in A. Ries and L. Ries, op. cit., pp. 65–73.
7. For a general framework of this problem, see G. Lugli and G. Cristini, *Category management: Come creare sintonia tra il marketing industriale e commerciale* (Milan: Il Sole 24 Ore, 2001). See also M. Fioroni, *Le nuove frontiere del marketing distributivo* (Perugia: Morlacchi, 2001).

Chapter 14   Brand Perception and the Power of the Subconscious

1. G. Zaltman, K. Braun, N. Puccinelli and F. Mast, "Implicit Predictors of Consumer Behavior," Harvard Business School 9-502-043,October 2001.
2. In 2004 the brand was bought by the Wrigley Company of Chicago for $1.48bn.
3. In reality new consumption segments were to appear in the category, for example, of probiotic yoghurts.
4. The original Italian claim, "*Fate l'amore con il sapore*" (Make love with the flavor) is particularly effective because of its rhyme.

5. R. F. Bornstein, D. R. Leone and D. J. Gally, "The Generalizability of Sub-liminal Mere Exposure Effects: Influence of Stimuli Perceived without Aware-ness on Social Behaviour," *Journal of Experimental and Social Psychology*, 53, 1987, 1070–9.
6. F. Lange and M. Dahle'n, "Let's Be Strange: Brand Familiarity in Original Famil-iarity and Ad-Brand Incongruency," *Journal of Product & Brand Management*, 12(7), 2002, 449–61.

Chapter 15   Developing a Brand in Different Cultural Contexts

1. G. M. Eckhard and M. Houston, "Cultural Paradoxes Reflected in Brand Mean-ing; McDonald's in Shanghai, China," *Journal of International Marketing*, 10(2), 2002, 68–82.
2. D. A. Aaker and E. Joachimsthaler, "The Lure of Global Branding," *Harvard Business Review*, 77(6), 1999, 137–44.
3. N. Negroponte, *Being Digital* (New York: Vintage, 1996).
4. D. B. Holt, J. A. Quelch and E. L. Taylor, "How Global Brands Compete," *Harvard Business Review*, 82(9), 2004, 68–75.
5. J. W. Jun and H. S. Lee, "Cultural Differences in Brand Designs and Tagline Appeals," *International Marketing Review*, 24(4), 2007, 474–91.
6. N. Kinra, "The Effect of Country-of-Origin on Foreign Brand Names in the Indian Market," *Marketing Intelligence & Planning*, 24(1), 2006, 15–30.
7. Holt *et al.*, op. cit.
8. J. L. Aaker, V. Benet-Martinez and J. Garolera, "Passion and Peacefulness: A Study of Japanese and Spanish Brand Personality Constructs', Stanford GSB Research Paper 1622, March 2000.
9. Ibid.
10. G. Hofstede, *Culture's Consequences: Comparing Values, Behaviors, Institutions and Organizations across Nations* (Thousand Oaks, CA: Sage, 2001).
11. Z. Tao and L. Dongya, *L'Oréal: Expansion in China* (University of Hong Kong, 2006).
12. F. Porciani, "Fondotinta alla giapponese e smalto alla brasiliana," *Corriere della Sera*, 16 September 2007.

Chapter 16   Giving a Brand a Passport

1. C. Macrae and M. D. Uncles, "Rethinking Brand Management: The Role of 'Brand Chartering'," *Journal of Product & Brand Management*, 6(1), 1997, 64–77.
2. V. Govindarajan and A. K. Gupta, *The Quest for Global Dominance: Trans-forming Global Presence into Global Competitive Advantage* (San Francisco: Jossey-Bass, 2001), particularly chapter 2, "Building Global Presence," pp. 22–50.
3. C. A. Barlett, "P&G Japan: The SK-II Globalization Project," Harvard Business School 9-303-003, March 2003.
4. C. Macrae and M.D. Uncles, op. cit.

5. D.A. Aaker and E. Joachimsthaler, op. cit.
6. A. J. Parsons, "Nestlé: The Vision of Local Managers". www. mckinsey quarterly.com

Chapter 17   The New Frontiers of Brands in a Changing World: The Case of India

1. http://en.wikipedia.org/wiki/Bollywood
2. V. T. Bharadwaj and L. Vittal, "Winning the Indian Consumer." http://www. mckinseyquarterly.com
3. "The economic, social, and cultural diversity of Indian consumers forces marketers and retailers to view the mass of consumers not as one single market but as a mass of niches." K. Bijani, "The Promised Land for Retailers", *Images Retail*, 6(4), 2007, 37.

Chapter 18   From the Rediscovery of its Roots to "Sense & Simplicity": The Case of Philips

1. We would like to thank Andrea Ragnetti, Executive Vice-President and Chief Executive Officer, Philips Consumer Lifestyle.
2. www.philips.com
3. www.philips.com

Chapter 19   Evoking Symbolic Values Arounds a Product and Becoming a Global Icon: The Case of Starbucks

1. B. George and L. Pierce, "Howard Schultz: Building Starbucks Community (B)," Harvard Business School 9-407-127, June 2007, pp. 1–8.
2. Shu-pei Tsai, "Integrated Marketing as Management of Holistic Consumer Experience," *Business Horizons*, 48(5), 2005, 431–41.
3. U. Volli, *Block modes: Il linguaggio del corpo e della moda* (Milan: Lupetti, 1998), p. 65.
4. H. Schultz and D. J. Yang, *Put Your Heart Into It: How Starbucks Built a Company One Cup at a Time* (New York: Hyperion, 1997), p. 183.
5. A. Mei, "Mr Starbucks da Milan al successo mondiale," *Il Giornale*, 8 June 2006.
6. V. Vishwanath and D. Harding, "The Starbucks Effect," *Harvard Business Review*, 78(2), 2000, 1–3.
7. M. M. Crossan and A. Kachra, "Starbucks (Case 12)," in M. M. Crossan, N. Fry, J. P. Killing and R. E. White, *Strategic Management: A Casebook*, 6th edn (Toronto, ON: Prentice Hall, 2002), pp. 189–211.
8. J. Berger, *From Cool to Passé: Identity Signaling and Product Domains*. www.wharton.upenn.edu

Chapter 20   Building a Creed by Promoting a Lifestyle: The Case of Whole Foods

1. N. F. Koehn and K. Miller, "John Mackey and Whole Foods Market," Harvard Business School 9-807-111, May 2007, pp. 1–36.
2. J. R. Wells and Travis Haglock, "Whole Foods Market, Inc.," Harvard Business School 9-705-476, June 2005, pp. 1–26.
3. Fioroni, op. cit., particularly p. 83.
4. Koehn and K. Miller, op. cit.

Chapter 21   Promoting a Brand Through National Identity and a Culture of Consumption: The Case of S. Pellegrino

1. We would like to thank Paolo Sangiorgi, Director, Nestle Waters UK Ltd.
2. www.sanpellegrino.it
3. The average price is €15.

BIBLIOGRAPHY

D. A. Aaker and E. Joachimsthaler, "The Lure of Global Branding," *Harvard Business Review*, 77(6), 1999, 137–44.

D. A. Aaker, "Should You Take Your Brand to Where the Action Is?," *Harvard Business Review*, 65(5), 1997, 135–43.

D. A. Aaker, "The Power of the Branded Differentiator," *MIT Sloan Management Review*, 44(1), 2003, 83–7.

D.A. Aaker, *Managing Brand Equity: Capitalizing on the Value of a Brand Name* (New York: Free Press, 1991).

J. L. Aaker, V. Benet-Martinez and J. Garolera, "Passion and Peacefulness: A Study of Japanese and Spanish Brand Personality Constructs," Stanford GSB Research Paper 1622, March 2000.

J. L. Aaker, "Dimensions of Brand Personality," *Journal of Marketing Research*, 34(3), 1997, 347–56.

D. Ackerman, *A Natural History of the Senses* (New York: Vintage, 1995).

T. Allen and J. Simmons, "Visual and Verbal Identity," in R. Clifton and J. Simmons (eds) *Brands and Branding* (New York: Bloomberg, 2003), pp. 113–26.

E. Arnould, L. Price and G. Zinkhan, *Consumers* (New York: McGraw-Hill, 2002).

A. Bahr Thompson, "Brand Positioning and Brand Creation," in R. Clifton and J. Simmons (eds) *Brands and Branding* (New York: Bloomberg, 2003), pp. 79–95.

C. A. Barlett, "P&G Japan: The SK-II Globalization Project," Harvard Business School Case 9-303-003, March 2003.

P. Barwise and S. Meehan, "Don't Be Unique, Be Better," *MIT Sloan Management Review*, 45(4), 2004, 23–7.

A. Belén del Río, R. Vázquez and V. Iglesias, "The Role of the Brand Name in Obtaining Differential Advantages," *Journal of Product & Brand Management*, 10(7), 2001, 452–65.

J. Berger, *From Cool to Passé: Identity Signaling and Product Domains.* www.wharton.upenn.edu

C. L. Bernick, "Finding the Right Brand Name," in A. Tybout (ed.), *Kellogg on Branding: The Marketing Faculty of The Kellogg School of Management* (Hoboken, NJ: Wiley, 2005), pp. 289–96.

L. L Berry, L. P. Carbone and S. H. Haeckel, "Managing the Total Customer Experience," *MIT Sloan Management Review*, 34(3), 2002, 85–9.

P. Berthon, M. B. Holbrook and J. M. Hulbert, "Understanding and Managing the Brand Space," *MIT Sloan Management Review*, 44(2), 2003, 49–54.

V. T. Bharadwaj and I. Vittal., "Winning the Indian Consumer." http://www. mckinseyquarterly.com

P. Bhatnagar, "Abercrombie: What's The Naked Truth? Advocacy Group Says Retailer Pulled Racy Mag Over Protest: A & F Says It's Making Space for Perfume." http://money.cnn.com/2003/12/02/news/companies/abercrombie_catalog/.the

K. Bijani, "The Promised Land for Retailers," *Images Retail*, 6(4), 2007, 37.

J. Birchall, "Marchi costruiti in rete," *Il Sole 24 Ore*, 3 Maggio 2007.

T. Blackett, "Choosing a Powerful Brand Name." www.brandchannel.com, 10 October 2005.

R. F. Bornstein, D. R. Leone and D. J. Gally, "The Generalizability of Subliminal Mere Exposure Effects: Influence of Stimuli Perceived without Awareness on Social Behaviour," *Journal of Experimental and Social Psychology*, 53, 1987, 1070–9.

M. Botton, J. J. Cegarra and B. Ferrari, *Il nome della marca. Creazione e strategia* (Milan: Guerini, 1992).

D. N. Bristow, K. C. Schneider and U. K. Schuler, "The Brand Dependence Scale: Measuring Consumers' Use of Brand Name to Differentiate Among Product Alternatives," *Journal of Product & Brand Management*, 11(6), 2002, 343–56.

S. Brown, *Marketing – The Retro Revolution* (London: Sage, 2001).

L. L. Bryan, C. I. Joyce and L. M. Weiss, *Making a Market in Talent*. http://www.mckinseyquarterly.com

R. Burgelman and L. Dened, "Nike's Global Women's Fitness Business: Driving Strategic Integration," Stanford Graduate School of Business, Case SM-152, 23 April 2007.

C. Childress, "Supermarkets Coming to Their Senses, All Five of Them," *Progressive Grocer: Equipment & Design*, June 2004. Now available at http://envirosell.com/index.php?option=com_content&task=view&id=94&Itemid=101

R. Clifton, "The Future of Brands," in R. Clifton and J. Simmons (eds) *Brands And Branding* (New York: Bloomberg, 2003), 227–40.

B. Cova, *Il marketing tribale: Legame, comunità, autenticità come valori del marketing mediterraneo* (Milan: Il Sole 24 Ore, 2003).

M. M. Crossan. and A. Kachra, "Starbucks (Case 12)," in M. M. Crossan, N. Fry, J. P. Killing and R. E. White, *Strategic Management: A Casebook*, 6th edn (Toronto, ON: Prentice Hall, 2002), pp. 189–211.

A. de Geus, *The Living Company: Growth Learning and Longevity in Business* (London: Brealey, 1997).

D. De Masi, *Alessi neo-pop*. http://www.nextonline.it/archivio/04/12.htm

M. Del Duca, *Manager dei processi ristorativi* (Perugia: Morlacchi, 2004).

A. Diamantopoulos, G. Smith and I. Grime, "The Impact of Brand Extension on Brand Personality: Experimental Evidence," *European Journal of Marketing*, 39(1–2), 2005, 129–49.

R. Dye, "The Buzz on Buzz," *Harvard Business Review* 78(6), 2002, 139–46.

G. M. Eckhard and M. J. Houston, "Cultural Paradoxes Reflected in Brand Meaning: McDonald's in Shanghai, China," *Journal of International Marketing*, 10(2), 2002, 68–82.

H. Edwards and D. Day, *Creating Passion Brands: Getting to the Heart of Branding* (London: Kogan Page, 2005).

G. Fabris, *Il nuovo consumatore: Verso il postmoderno* (Milan: Franco Angeli, 2004).

G. Fabris and L. Minestroni, *Valore e valori della marca: Come costruire e gestire una marca di successo* (Milan: Franco Angeli, 2004).

A. Fels, "Do Women Lack Ambition?," *Harvard Business Review*, 82(4), 2004, 50–60.

M. Fioroni, *Le nuove frontiere del marketing distributivo* (Perugia: Morlacchi, 2001).

M. Fioroni, *Lo shopping dell'esperienza* (Perugia: Morlacchi, 2004).

C. Fischler, *L'onnivoro: Il piacere di mangiare nella storia della scienza* (Milan: Mondadori, 1992).

S. Fournier, "Consumers and their Brands: Developing Relationship Theory in Consumer Research," in D. Miller (ed.), *Consumption: Critical Concepts in the Social Sciences* (London: Routledge, 2001), pp. 57–119.

F. Furedi, *Il nuovo conformismo* (Milan: Feltrinelli, 2005).

F. Gallucci, *Marketing emozionale* (Milan: EGEA, 2006).

B. George and L. Pierce, "Howard Schultz: Building Starbucks Community (B)," Harvard Business School Case 9-407-127, June 2007, pp. 1–8.

V. Govindarajan and A. K. Gupta, *The Quest for Global Dominance: Transforming Global Presence into Global Competitive Advantage* (San Francisco: Jossey-Bass, 2001).

A. Greimas, *Del senso* (Milan: Bompiani, 1985).

K.H. Hammonds, *The Starbucks Effect*, http://www.fastcompany.com/magazine/106/next-essay.html

H. Hartman, *Five Steps To Building a Cultural Brand*. http://www.marketingpower.com/content21255.php

S. Hilton, "The Social Values of Brands," in R. Clifton and J. Simmons (eds) *Brands and Branding* (New York: Bloomberg, 2003), pp. 47–64.

G. Hofstede, *Culture's Consequences: Comparing Values, Behaviors, Institutions and Organizations across Nations* (Thousand Oaks, CA: Sage, 2001).

D. B. Holt, *How Brands Become Icons: The Principles of Cultural Branding* (Boston, MA: Harvard Business School Press, 2004).

D. B. Holt, J. A. Quelch and E. L. Taylor, "How Global Brands Compete," *Harvard Business Review*, 82(9), 2004, 68–75.

J. W. Jun and H. S. Lee, "Cultural Differences in Brand, Designs and Tagline Appeals," *International Marketing Review*, 24(4), 2007, 474–91.

K. L. Keller, "The Brand Report Card," *Harvard Business Review*, 78(1) 2000, 147–57.

K. L. Keller, *Strategic Brand Management: Building, Measuring, and Managing Brand Equity* (Upper Saddle River, NJ: Prentice Hall 2007).

K. L. Keller, B. Sternthal and A. Tybout, "Three Questions You Need to Ask about Your Brand," *Harvard Business Review*, 80(9), 2002, pp. 3–8.

N. Kinra, "The Effect of Country-of-Origin on Foreign Brand Names in the Indian Market," *Marketing Intelligence & Planning*, 24(1), 2006, pp. 15–30.

N. Klein, *No Logo* (London: Flamingo; Milan: Baldini Castoldi Dalai, 2002).

N. F. Koehn and K. Miller, "John Mackey and Whole Foods Market," Harvard Business School 9-807-111, May 2007, pp. 1–36.

J. Kunde, *Unique Now . . . Or Never: The Brand Is the Company Driver in the New Value Economy* (Upper Saddle River, NJ: Pearson-Prentice Hall, 2002).

F. Lange and M. Dahle'n, "Let's Be Strange: Brand Familiarity, in Original Familiarity and Ad-Brand Incongruency," *Journal of Product & Brand Management*, 12(7), 2002, 449–61.

D. Lewis and D. Bridger, *The Soul of The New Consumer: Authenticity: What We Buy and Why in the New Economy* (London: Brealey, 2000).

M. Lindstrom, *Brand Sense: Build Powerful Brands Through Touch, Taste, Smell, Sight, and Sound* (New York: Free Press, 2005).

G. Lugli and G. Cristini, *Category management: Come creare sintonia tra il marketing industriale e commerciale* (Milan: Il Sole 24 Ore, 2001).

C. Macrae and M. D. Uncles, "Rethinking Brand Management: The Role of 'Brand Chartering'," *Journal of Product & Brand Management*, 6(1), 1997, 64–77.

J. McFarland, "Branding From The Inside Out," *Harvard Management Update*, 7(2), 2002, 1–4.

L. Minestroni, *L'alchimia della marca. Fenomenologia di un moltiplicatore di valore* (Milan: Franco Angeli, 2002).

L. Mizzau, "Nostalgia, nostalgia canaglia ...," *Ticonzero*, no. 69. http://www.ticonzero.info/articolo.asp?art_id=2265.

K. Naughton and B. Vlasic, "The Nostalgia Boom. Why The Old Is New Again," http://www.businessweek.com/1998/12/b3570001.htm

N. Negroponte, *Being Digital* (New York: Vintage, 1996).

K. Nordstrom and J. Ridderstrale, *Funky Business: Talent Makes Capital Dance* (London: Pearson, 2000) [Stockholm: Jan Lapidoth–Book House Publishing].

K. Nordstrom and J. Ridderstrale, *Karaoke Capitalism* (London: FT Prentice Hall, 2004).

R. Ollé and D. Riu, *The New Brand Management: Lessons From Brand Indifferentiation*. http://www.globalbrands.org/academic/working/Brand_Indifferentiation.pdf

A. J. Parsons, "Nestlé: The Vision of Local Managers." www.mckinseyquarterly.com

J. B. Pine and J. H. Gilmore, *The Experience Economy: Work is Theatre and Every Business is a Stage* (Boston: Harvard Business School Press, 1999).

D.H. Pink, *A Whole New Mind. Moving from the Information Age to the Conceptual Age* (New York: River Head, 2005).

R. Reeves, *Reality in Advertising* (London: Macgibbon & Kee, 1961).

A. Ries and L. Ries, *The 22 Immutable Laws of Branding: How to Build a Product or Service into a World-Class Brand* (New York: HarperCollins, 1998).

M. Sawhney, "Create Value From Values," *CIO Magazine*, 15 November 2002. ww.cio.com/article/31517/

B. H. Schmitt and M. Ferraresi, *Marketing esperienziale: Come sviluppare l'esperienza di consumo* (Milan: Franco Angeli, 2006).

H. Schultz and D. J. Yang, *Put Your Heart Into It: How Starbucks Built a Company One Cup at a Time* (New York: Hyperion, 1997).

J. Seguela, *Hollywood lava più bianco* (Milan: Lupetti, 1996).

A. Semprini, *Marche e mondi possibili: Un approccio semiotico al marketing della marca* (Milan: Franco Angeli, 2004).

M. Shapiro, "Marketing Leverage in the Frame of Reference," in A. Tybout (ed.), *Kellogg on Branding: The Marketing Faculty of The Kellogg School of Management* (Hoboken, NJ: Wiley, 2005), pp. 283–6.

E. R. Spangenberg, A. E. Crowley and P. W. Henderson, "Improving the Store Environment: Do Olfactory Cues Affect Evaluations and Behaviours?," *Journal of Marketing*, 60(2), 1996, 67–80.

S. S. Srinivasan and B. D. Till, "Evaluation of Search, Experience and Credence Attributes: Role of Brand Name and Product Trial," *Journal of Product & Brand Management*, 11(7), 2002, 417–31.

D. Stiff, "So You Think You Know Your Brand?," *MIT Sloan Management Review*, 47(4), 2006, 95–6.

Z. Tao and L. Dongya, *L'Oréal: Expansion in China* (University of Hong Kong, 2006).

D. A. Thomas and R. J. Ely, "Making Differences Matter: A New Paradigm for Managing Diversity," *Harvard Business Review*, 74(5), 1996, 79–90.

Tipping Sprung LLC, *2005 Tipping Sprung Survey of Top Brand Names, Summary Report*, 1 September 2005. tippingsprung.com

S-P. Tsai, "Integrated Marketing as Management of Holistic Consumer Experience," *Business Horizons*, 48(5), 2005, 431–41.

A. M. Tybout and B. Sternthal, "Brand Positioning," in A. Tybout (ed.), *Kellogg on Branding: The Marketing Faculty of The Kellogg School of Management* (Hoboken, NJ: Wiley, 2005), pp. 11–26.

A. M. Tybout and G. S. Carpenter, "Meeting the Challenge of the Postmodern Consumer," in T. Dickson and N. Hawcock (eds), *Mastering Marketing: The Complete MBA Companion in Marketing* (London: Financial Times, 1999), pp. 103–7.

V. Vishwanath and D. Harding, "The Starbucks Effect," *Harvard Business Review*, 78(2), 2000, 1–3.

U. Volli, *Block modes: Il linguaggio del corpo e della moda* (Milan: Lupetti, 1998).

J. R. Wells and T. Haglock, "Whole Foods Market, Inc.," Harvard Business School Case 9-705-476, June 2005, pp. 1–26.

G. Zaltman, K. Braun, N. Puccinelli and F. Mast, "Implicit Predictors of Consumer Behavior," Harvard Business School Case 9-502-043, October 2001.

INDEX